TONY ADAMS was a commanding figure on the football field, a true leader for Arsenal and England. He won league titles in three separate decades, and after the club moved to their new stadium at the Emirates, it was fitting that a statue of him was erected outside to celebrate his extraordinary career. But, for much of that time, he was also drinking heavily and eventually he admitted in his book *Addicted* that he was an alcoholic.

Now, in that book's stunning successor *Sober*, Adams reveals what happened next. He discusses the impact that Arsène Wenger had when he arrived at Arsenal in 1996, and how the manager's new methods helped extend his career and brought new success to the club. Always a great thinker on the game, Adams moved into coaching and management on retirement, playing a key role in Portsmouth's famous FA Cup triumph in 2008, and taking on new challenges in the Netherlands, Azerbaijan, China and now Spain to broaden his perspective.

He movingly explains the struggles he's faced to stay sober for 20 years and why he set up Sporting Chance, the charity that provides treatment and support for sports stars suffering from addictions. He gives his incisive thoughts on England's continued failings in major tournaments and assesses why Arsenal have struggled to repeat the title-winning formula of his own time there. *Sober* is a truly inspirational memoir from someone who has battled with his demons, but has continued to take things on, one day at a time.

SOBER

SOBER

FOOTBALL. MY STORY. MY LIFE.

TONY ADAMS

WITH IAN RIDLEY

**SIMON &
SCHUSTER**

London · New York · Sydney · Toronto · New Delhi

A CBS COMPANY

First published in Great Britain by Simon & Schuster UK Ltd, 2017
A CBS COMPANY

1 3 5 7 9 10 8 6 4 2

Simon & Schuster UK Ltd
1st Floor
222 Gray's Inn Road
London WC1X 8HB

www.simonandschuster.co.uk
www.simonandschuster.com.au
www.simonandschuster.co.in

Simon & Schuster Australia, Sydney
Simon & Schuster India, New Delhi

A CIP catalogue record for this book
is available from the British Library

ISBN: 978-1-4711-5674-8
Trade paperback ISBN: 978-1-4711-6643-3
Ebook ISBN: 978-1-4711-5676-2

Typeset in Bembo by M Rules
Printed and bound by CPI Group (UK) Ltd, Croydon, CR0 4YY

CONTENTS

1

What we used to be like . . .

We rise by lifting others.

ROBERT INGERSOLL,
American lawyer and politician

Part of the process for many alcoholics once they stop drinking and then get into recovery from the illness of addiction is to give their testimony to their fellows at an Alcoholics Anonymous meeting when they feel they are ready. It is what is called in AA 'a chair'. The talk takes in their experience, strength and hope, telling of – as it says in the 'Big Book' of AA, the definitive guide for an alcoholic to getting and staying sober – 'what we used to be like, what happened and what we are like now'.

The audience will comprise men and women of all age groups, backgrounds, colours and creeds, some of whom may only have just stopped drinking, up to those, like Tony Adams, with many years of sobriety. In Tony's case, that is more than 20 years after his acknowledgement of his alcoholism in August 1996, following a seven-week drinking spree amid the disappointment of Euro 96 when the England team he had captained lost on penalties to Germany in the semi-finals.

Tony speaks regularly at local AA meetings, or indeed wherever in the world he is asked to speak, even in prisons. The following was delivered in March 2015 to four sportspeople newly arrived at the Sporting Chance treatment centre that Tony founded in 2000 . . .

'Hi. My name is Tony and I am an alcoholic. It's a privilege to be speaking to you. I am a grateful recovering alcoholic today but I have been in the same place you are right now – which is maybe full of shame about life with alcohol and fear of life without it. We all have our own experience and this is mine. The only thing I ask is that you listen for the similarities, not the differences. Sometimes I talk more about my recovery, sometimes about my drinking. I'll talk about both, but you might want to hear what my drinking was like, as you're new to this like I was once, so that you can get some identification.

My last drink was on the back of a four-day bender. It is very patchy and I had blackouts, so some of it I can't remember. I do know I went out on a Tuesday but that is a blank. On the Wednesday, I went to a restaurant and nightclub in Chelsea called Barbarella's and got smashed. I can't remember where I stayed. I do remember pissing and shitting in my pants and peeling them off and going out again.

I remember bits about the Thursday. I went to a strip club off Piccadilly I used to go to. I would get girls there. You could take them off somewhere and pay them. I was drinking with twin girls. It sounds glamorous, all sex and drugs and rock and roll, but it wasn't. It was all shit and passing out. I took one of the girls off to a hotel in Kensington.

I was off the planet. I passed out at two, three or four in the morning. I don't know when. I woke up Friday morning seeing the minibar empty and bottles all over the room. I'd smashed it. I had sex with this girl and it was nothing and I think she could see the pain in my face. I was completely lost. The alcohol wasn't working for me any more and nor was the sex. Nothing was. I was lost. It was four days of chaos and mayhem.

I got a cab back to a mate's pub in the East End, then went on to my local in Essex for lunch. It wasn't really lunch. I got smashed again. The more I was drinking, the less drunk I was getting.

At 5pm that Friday, I am sitting there with a pint of Guinness. I used to put brandy in it. I couldn't drink spirits straight. Same as Scotch – I would spew it straight up. But the spirits worked quicker. Jack the barman came up to me and said: 'You all right, Tone?' I said: 'No, I'm not, Jack,' and started to cry.

It felt like my moment of clarity. Something inside me said, 'You are fucked. You are beat.' It was my moment of surrender. Big men don't cry, do they? But I was in floods and floods of tears. Jack said: 'Have another one, Tone.' I said: 'I can't drink any more.' Enough was enough.

And then my journey began.

How did I get to that place? It was the 16th of August, 1996. I was 29. I had plenty of issues that had made me pick up the drink and go to the pub in the first place. I had to go back and look at the Twelve Steps of Alcoholics Anonymous and go through a hell of a lot of therapy to find out what made me tick. And I have done.

I can place it back in my childhood. I was a shy, insecure little boy frightened of everything. Football was my first love, my first escape, my first addiction. That was the thing that I ran to if I had a problem.

I had the worst attendance at my school. I am not proud of that. I just couldn't handle a classroom. There was too much fear. I used to get panic attacks. I remember once when the book was going round and you had to read. I was 13 or 14. I thought, 'Oh fucking hell, it's coming to me,' and I am shitting myself. When I read it, because I was in such a state, I said 'wheally' instead of 'really'. After that, I was known as 'the wheally kid' and everybody was taking the piss out of me in the playground.

I just put on a brave face and said, 'I'll go and play football.' I was so self-conscious and sensitive to these comments. It went to the bone. It really did hurt. I put the mask on as Tony the footballer.

My old English teacher, Mr Beech, used to say: 'Oh, Adams is here. It must be a football day.' I would only go in when it was football. My parents were confused, and pulling their hair out, looking back, at this young man who just wanted to play football, making out he was ill some mornings, then getting up at 10 or 11 and going over the park.

This boy was very scared. I had to take my O levels and I had lived in fear through my teenage years of having to take these exams in my last year at school. It absolutely terrified me since the age of 11. I ran away. Luckily – or maybe it might not have been luckily if I had been able to face these things and grow, but I didn't know anything about it at that age – I had been picked for England Under-16 and there was a tour to Hungary at the same time as the exams. There was no choice. I was gone.

Mr Dury, my headmaster, was a West Ham fan and he was pulling his hair out as well. He didn't know what was going on. Funny, I met another old teacher of mine not long ago, Mr Allington, the head of year. We used to laugh about him being a West Ham fan and me signing for Arsenal.

One more illustration of how uncomfortable I was at that age – girls. I had this phantom girlfriend in my head. It was a lot safer. I didn't have to talk to them. I called her Juicy Lucy. One day, I was trying to do a hundred headers in a row outside my house and two girls walked past. One of them said: 'Katharine wants to go out with you.'

Oh shit. I put the ball down and I walked round the block

with Katharine. She kissed me and then said she didn't want to go out with me any more. Oh no, what have I done? Did I do something wrong? I got the ball, put it on my head and did the hundred and I escaped back into football. I didn't have to face that any more.

That was the pattern throughout my life. I got lucky with football. I became successful and it was enough. I joined Arsenal at 16. I had my first experience with alcohol at 17. I broke my fifth metatarsal and drank when I was out injured. It healed and I got playing again and, from then on, my football career and my alcohol career went hand in hand.

I was first getting smashed Saturdays after games, then Saturdays and Sunday lunchtimes. I would find little pubs and working men's clubs that would open on Sunday afternoons. Then it became a nightclub in Islington on a Sunday night.

For six or seven years, I was really struggling to maintain midweek games. I could make it on Saturdays, but then to go again a few days later was becoming difficult. In all the summers when I didn't have football, I was smashed. Ibiza one year, Majorca the next. Canary Islands, Torremolinos. I was off the planet. There were blackouts, fears, paranoia, things coming out of cupboards. A lot of pissing myself. Women. Sometimes I would gamble – horses, greyhounds, anything.

Gradually this illness was taking me over. And it is a progressive illness. It always gets worse, never better, if you continue to drink. It was taking my football career away. From 1994 and '95 to reaching my rock bottom in '96, it was becoming very difficult to play football to a high level. I had a certain amount of talent and I could disguise it and thought I was doing OK, but there were periods where I couldn't control it, where I missed the timing. I remember three games I played pissed.

One was against Swindon Town and the manager pulled me off and we made out I was ill. One at Everton I hadn't timed it right. I thought, 'Let's have another drink' and I had one the day of the game but I came off knowing I hadn't done well. I wasn't well. The other one at Sheffield United was hard work physically. It really was.

Still, at that time I could justify it as we were still winning, and comfortably against Swindon. Against Sheffield United, I was man of the match and got awarded some cutlery. That was confusing to me.

These were tough days. The game that I loved and which gave me everything was no longer my first thought. I was spending a lot of time in pubs and clubs, so what did I do? I married a barmaid.

I met her during a blackout and was told I went back the week after and saw her again. I couldn't remember the previous week. I had sex with her the week after. I brought two children into the world with her. Her drug of choice was coke, but I didn't know that at the time. Using addicts attract other addicts. I was too busy getting smashed anyway to worry too much about her problem at the start.

The arrangement worked for both of us. It propped me up. Then when I did come to realise her addiction, I could say, 'You're the druggie. I'll never be a druggie like you. At least I'm not a cokehead.' It justified my drinking behaviour. She went on from coke to crack so I sent her to a treatment centre because she needed help. I drove her down one Saturday morning to Clouds in Wiltshire and basically threw her in there.

Two counsellors then sat down with me, not with her there, and said, 'How are *you*, Mr Adams?' They asked me about my behaviour in the relationship. I went, 'Hold on. I don't get this.' One part of me was scared and wanting to cry and the ego side of me was, 'Hang on. I am Arsenal and England captain. Why are you fucking questioning me?' I really wanted to say, 'Help . . .'

I got back in the car and ran for home. That was January '96 and it coincided with my cartilage coming out. I couldn't get my football and I couldn't blame my wife any more. My life circumstances changed and, for the first time in 11 and a half years of drinking and using it to suppress my feelings, I didn't want to drink and I was still getting pissed. It frightened the life out of me.

I didn't want to do this but I had no tools to do anything different. I was sitting in the hospital after a knee operation and my situation and my fears hit me hard. So I had a drink. It was a private hospital and I ordered two bottles of Chablis. I'd also had a pethidine shot up my arse and I was on the roof.

But everything that goes up has to come down.

My wife was away in treatment and I thought, 'I can't do this any more.' I passed out one day at home, with the kids there. I had a stepdaughter aged 11, a son aged four and a little girl aged 18 months. The stepdaughter had the presence of mind to phone my mother-in-law and she came round. She called me a drunken bastard. She took the kids and part of me said, 'Hallelujah. Party time.' Another part said, 'Shit. What's happened?'

I had pissed on my sofas, my beds. The house was a complete khazi. I didn't want to drink but I was still getting drunk. I managed to stop for a few days here and there in the February and March. Four days, five days. I got to three weeks on will-power. Then I got pissed again. I thought I was Superman but I couldn't beat this. I had no mental defence against a drink. That progression of the illness again.

April came and my knee was OK. I had used football to sup-press feelings and deal with things and so I threw myself into it. England had a big tournament, Euro 96, and I concentrated on getting fit.

Before the tournament, we went to Hong Kong and we were in a hotel. The lads went on the piss to a bar and there was that incident with the dentist's chair. The pictures went round the world. I knew if I went with them I would be on the piss and gone. The tournament would be gone for me.

That night, I locked myself in my room and couldn't wait for training the next day. I was shaking with the fear of whether I would take a drink. It was a massive hotel. I was there on tour with Arsenal the previous year, and I went out to bars with a couple of the lads and got involved in an incident that involved the police, some of the locals and all sorts of shit.

Some of the boys were wondering, 'Where's Tony? He's the lad ...' I said to two guys, Robbie Fowler and Steve McManaman, 'When we win the tournament, I'll go out and get pissed again, I'll be the first to the bar, but I am going to focus in for now.' It was my excuse to get them out of the way. I wanted to play the games.

Soon as that last game against Germany was over, I had no mental defence against a drink again. Nothing to keep me sober. After Gareth Southgate's penalty miss, I went down the tunnel and had a drink in the dressing room. It felt fantastic, I have to admit. In the next seven weeks, I did everything – pissed myself, shit myself, hallucinating, things coming out of the cupboards. I was up and down and sideways.

All the 12 years of drinking came out in those seven weeks. I slept with people I didn't want to sleep with. It was just shit. During those 12 years, I had gone to prison for drink-driving, had 29 stitches in my head after falling down steps drunk, been in intensive care. That's where alcohol took me.

That Friday in August in my local in Essex at 5pm was my rock bottom. That's when it all started. I threw in the towel. I was beaten. I gave in and asked for help. I got some fish and chips, ate them in bed and stayed there over that weekend, detoxing. It wasn't really a safe one. I was shaking badly. I got up on the Monday and got a cab into work at the Arsenal training ground at London Colney.

I went in to see if I still had a job. Paul Merson was there and I had ignored him before. He was clean and sober for 18 months and wasn't part of the groovy gang. Now he's well and it was weird. He looked at me and I looked at him with like, 'Help', in my eyes. He said some funny things about getting sober then said there was an AA meeting in St Albans the next week.

I went to one before that, at Dawes Road in Fulham. We had a guy in the club who was in Gamblers Anonymous and was helping Paul. He told me about this meeting in Dawes Road. I was sitting outside in my car and shitting myself, wondering whether to go in or not. I was frozen. I wanted something and didn't know how to stay sober.

I went through the door and it was a meeting about Step Nine of the AA programme, about making amends to people. I heard stuff that made sense to me. I heard me. I heard somebody share about football, about the old phrase 'win or lose, on the booze'. Still, I wasn't sure if this whole thing was for me or not and I needed more meetings to find out.

But I felt all right that night and I didn't have an alternative. I didn't know where else to go. The next week, I went to a lunchtime meeting in St Albans with Paul after training and loved it. I opened my mouth and just said my first name and a few sentences about my drinking and why I was there. I had made a start. Then I got to another meeting soon after and loved it and just got on with it.

Therapy was also important to me and I had been going to see a man called James West on a recommendation. I thought at first I was going to see him about my wife's problems, not about me. To understand her. It was those one-to-one sessions that took me into the AA rooms. And those one-to-one sessions are still a part of my life today. At first, I went to see James on a Monday and was pissed by the weekend. I said maybe I needed to see him on the Thursday as well. James said: 'I think I'd better move in with you.'

I'll never forget what I told him, and he reminds me of it to this day: 'I know how to get drunk and how to play football but I don't know who I am.'

I kept going to AA meetings and kept going. They suggest 90 in 90 days when you start out and I probably went to more. My knee had suffered during the European Championships and needed a clear-out and I had another op, so I had time off work to throw myself into AA and into therapy. Into changing. Because I knew that if I didn't get some tools, something was going to take Tony down the pub again. I needed something to deal with all this stuff.

The AA rooms and the therapy and the books about recovery and the friends I made gave me the tools I needed to stay off drink. That and all the things I heard, like 'stick with the winners', those people who had proved how to stay sober. I jumped in and changed. I dropped pals that I had only drink in common with.

My wife had gone by now. She came out of treatment earlier in the year when I was still drinking and said, 'I don't want to be with you any more. You are a drunk. Get out.' The rejection fuelled my drinking at the time. I can see now why she didn't want me but, at the time, my pride ate at me. How dare she?

Self-loathing was getting to me: 'You don't deserve this woman,' it told me. But there was also my ego – she's mine. My life was built then on competition. Win, lose. So I tried to win her back. I wrote letters but it never felt good.

I moved home and was sober three weeks, going to meetings and working the AA programme, and then she told me she had met someone else. That went to my heart. At the time, I couldn't play football and now I can't get drunk either. Drink doesn't work any more. I thought, 'I've just got to deal with this,' but it was dark, it was winter now. Sometimes I would be over the house we had lived in and see the curtain closing and thinking, 'He's up there with her.'

Listen, guys, I know I didn't want her back but it killed me. The green-eyed monster of jealousy took me over. Along with the red mist. I wanted to go in and punch him. I drove over Putney Bridge and went to an AA meeting in Wimbledon where I shared it.

I was told to pray for them. What, pray for my wife who's rejected me and the bloke who was sleeping with her? In a house that I was paying for? But I did and I got through that day without a drink. And I grew another day. Gradually the feelings passed.

That's been my story. Any situation that's arisen since, today I don't have to drink. That's fucking amazing. What happened in my life with alcohol makes me feel sad but also grateful that I found a way out of it. I have so many tools for coping today.

I've had both parents die since I've been in recovery and not had a drink. I've got married again. I've had three more children with a beautiful new wife and I can do a job now. I've had highs and lows in and out of football, given up playing and gone into coaching and management. Not had a drink through any of it. My self-esteem has come back and I am all right.

For years and years I used to think I was a piece of shit and not worthy of good things. Fear affirmed everything. Now I know that fear stands for 'face everything and recover', but not then. I thought I had AIDS. I thought I was going to die. I thought about suicide but I was too scared to kill myself. I was too afraid of dying. I was in that no-man's land.

I still go to AA meetings and I am in therapy. The simple slogans still work for me: one day at a time, first things first, live and let live, keep it simple, easy does it. Having a good share-up like today with fellow addicts and alcoholics helps keep me sober. Hearing back about their stories and getting their wisdom and insight. There's a saying: mad, sad or glad – share it.

I can forget as time goes on and think, 'Was it really that bad?' Yes, it was. 'Did I really do that, piss myself, behave like that?' Yes, I did. But there is a way out and you guys are in the right place. We can forge new lives. I have such a fantastic life today. Today is a wonderful day. Thank you for listening.'

2

A New Player

If we are painstaking about this phase of our development, we will be amazed before we are halfway through. We are going to know a new freedom and a new happiness.

ALCOHOLICS ANONYMOUS, *page 83*

Distance lends enchantment to the view, they say. As I look back now on my playing career, from the vantage point of 20 years of not having taken one drink of alcohol one day at a time over that period, it clearly falls into two categories for me: the drinking years and the sober years.

I will always be proud of what I and Arsenal – and to a sadly lesser extent England – achieved during the period from making my debut at Highbury less than a month after my 17th birthday in November 1983 through to my retirement in 2002. The bare statistics tell of leading the club to 10 trophies, 13 if the Community Shield is included, with four league titles across three decades, making 669 appearances and scoring 48 goals. On top came 66 international caps, with five goals.

I am less proud, however, of some of the scrapes I got into and the way I treated some people during that time, not least myself, when I look back. And I never want to forget them. Part of the reason I keep going to AA meetings these days is to remind myself of what it was like and so avoid complacency.

But if the past is a foreign country, as LP Hartley said, to me it now seems one on the other side of the world. Crashing my car and serving 58 days of a four-month sentence in Chelmsford Prison over Christmas and New Year 1990/91 for drink-driving, for example, now seems such a minute period of my life. I have long since dealt with all the pain and shame of the old days and ways, and no longer live like that. After my retirement came coaching and management at home and abroad, and I believe I am a very different being to the snarling defender of my early days, though retaining the drive and determination.

The times were as they were. Back in the 1980s, and even through the early years of the Premier League in the 1990s, drinking was part of the culture of the game. I drank and I played football. It may be hard to picture now, with the intensity of the modern game, but I was not alone and it made it easier to hide, and justify, my behaviour. Most players could stop, or it didn't affect their lives. I crossed a line and couldn't get back.

In 1987, after winning my first trophy with Arsenal, the Littlewoods Cup, I went on a bender and lost my club jacket. In 1989, after winning the First Division with that amazing 2-0 victory over Liverpool at Anfield, I went on a bender and lost my dignity. That night, I stayed at my colleague Paul Merson's house and wet the bed. It might have been acceptable if it was just the once, but it happened too often.

With England too. The death of Graham Taylor in January 2017 reminded me of the time in the early nineties when, as England manager, he urged me to sort myself out after I had knocked down a bedroom door in my drunken state, at the team hotel at Burnham Beeches in Buckinghamshire. I wasn't ready for his advice at the time, though I would remember it.

Graham was a lovely, intelligent man, a gentleman, and he gave me a lot of confidence by saying that he was going to make me his number one choice as centre half after Euro 92, for which he had not picked me. We had something in common too: sections of the media branded me a donkey in my early playing career and some fans threw carrots at me during games. Graham was portrayed as a turnip in the *Sun*. Who would have thought that root vegetables could hurt so much?

To top all those episodes, my jail sentence came when Arsenal won the title again, in 1990/91, but could perhaps have gone unbeaten. We lost one match, however, at Chelsea, when I was inside and we ended up with David Hillier alongside Andy Linighan in defence. Who knows what might have been? What I do know is that when Arsenal's team of 2003/04 did become the Invincibles, they had their captain Patrick Vieira with them all season.

The FA and League Cup double of 1992/93 was another cause for celebration, naturally, but while others went home to their families after any parties, mine would just go on. And on ... I was drunk after winning the European Cup Winners' Cup by beating Parma in Copenhagen in 1994, drunk after losing to Real Zaragoza in the final in Paris the following year. It was the drabness of life that followed the highs that got me. The booze calmed and changed me. It dulled any pain I was feeling in my private life, gave me respite. If I could have bottled that feeling, I would have been OK. But I couldn't.

Some of the incidents off the field were frightening, looking back, like crashing the car into the front wall of a house in the Southend suburbs and going to jail, or falling down the concrete steps of a nightclub and needing 29 stitches in my brow. Some of them were funny, but only really because I survived them. A club tour to Hong Kong in 1995 embraced both the laughable and the dangerous.

One night, I was out with all the guys and, playing the big shot when I'd had a few, I went behind the bar and took over the DJ's role for a while. Then, when I left, I jumped into a taxi – except there was already a young woman in there. It terrified the poor girl. After getting out, I somehow found my way back to the hotel – and it is amazing how drunks have a homing-pigeon instinct for returning to base – where I passed out in my room. In the morning, Ray Parlour knocked on my door. When he came in, he wondered if I'd felt hungry during the night, and I suddenly noticed a trolley-load of untouched sandwiches that I must have ordered in blackout.

Dear Ray. He has made a living out of telling drinking stories about me and him, so I have little hesitation in telling one that has him at the centre. It's not the one about us being drunk in a pizza restaurant – and our old manager George Graham disciplining him but not me as I was more of a first-team fixture at the time. Nor is it a tale about Ray writing off a car owned by the Arsenal scout Steve Rowley when he was just 16, that after having persuaded Steve to buy it off his brother, who was a car dealer. No, it comes from another night out on that same tour of Hong Kong.

As I left a bar in the notorious Wan Chai district with Ray, I noticed a row occurring on the other side of the street. I could see it involved our striker Chris Kiwomya. Chris had apparently got talking to a girl and it all kicked off, with her boyfriend taking offence. I went over to try to sort it out, as Ray walked on. As it calmed down, I turned to look back across the street where a local was coming at Ray and I could see the guy was carrying a machete. Undeterred, Ray decked the bloke, who was a taxi driver who had taken exception to Ray apparently lobbing prawn crackers into his cab. I dragged Ray away and we began to hurry off, only for the police to appear at the end of the road. I turned into a side street but Ray got picked up, as did Chris, who had begun fighting again with the girl's boyfriend.

Drunk again, but beginning to realise the seriousness of the situation after I got back to the hotel, I went and knocked on the Arsenal chairman Peter Hill-Wood's door. He stood there in his dressing gown and slippers. He was smoking a big cigar. I told him about the trouble and that Ray and Chris had been arrested.

'Don't worry, Tony,' he said. 'I know a good barrister out here. He'll sort it out.'

And it was sorted out. Chris got off and although Ray was fined HK$4,000 (around £300 at the time), he was lucky to avoid a jail sentence, the barrister apologising to the people of Hong Kong on Ray's behalf. Arsenal were not about to let Ray escape that easily, however, and he was presented with a bill for the lawyer, which came to £12,000. He was on £600 a week back then and it took him several seasons to pay it off. I remember that Stewart Houston was the caretaker manager at the time and it was probably one reason why he didn't get the job full time.

That all happened the year before I got sober and the year before I returned to Hong Kong with England ahead of Euro 96. The memory played a big part in me shutting myself in my 15th-floor hotel room and declining the chance to take part in all that dentist's chair stuff with Paul Gascoigne, Teddy Sheringham and the rest, as I knew if I did, I might well jeopardise being able to play in the tournament.

As it was, I gritted my teeth – white-knuckling it, they call it in AA – and stayed off the drink during that tournament, playing some of my best football, as Terry Venables' captain. That came between more of the injuries I was sustaining, as we reached the semi-finals only to go out on penalties to Germany. Cue that seven-week bender. Guinness was always my favourite, about four pints an hour when in flow, but anything would do; lager, even the spirits I hated but which worked fast. I would pour them into the beer to dilute the taste.

When I did hit my rock bottom in my local in Essex that day in August 1996, it had all become too hard, overwhelming in fact, physically and emotionally. The more money I earned, the quicker my drinking and the illness of alcoholism had accelerated. And football had become irrelevant to me. For a man who loved the game, felt free on the pitch, that was desperately sad.

I guess for a footballer being destroyed by alcohol, I wasn't that bad a player. I did have some talent and also a great squad around me. 'Your mother and father made you a fighter,' George Graham's successor, Arsène Wenger – the two of them huge figures in my life and career – said to me early on, after he took over in October 1996.

It was true. I had some great assets that I could use in my recovery from my addiction. For a long time, I thought it was the booze that was making me durable, keeping me strong. But in the end it was tearing me apart. What I thought was my medicine became my poison.

I've heard it said that many creative people and celebrities believe that if they give up drink and drugs, or whatever their flavour of addiction or damaging behaviour, they will lose their mojo, what makes them what they are. In football, the example always cited was my dear old friend Gazza. Try to change Paul Gascoigne, the argument went, and he wouldn't be the player he was. I've never subscribed to that line of thinking and my encounters with celebrated, creative people show that their work – not to mention their lives – gets better and takes on a new level of quality when they get sober.

I can only really speak for myself, though, and say that when

I quit drinking, I became a better footballer for the six years of my career that it would prove I had left in me. I was calmer, smarter, and even more successful. I felt free, played free, as Arsenal's captain and Arsène Wenger's field marshal.

I never really worried about not being as good as before. I knew I had the ability, and I knew I had not done full justice to that ability previously. It had been exhausting trying to combine top-level football for club and country while an active alcoholic and keeping up a chaotic lifestyle.

It was Neil Ruddock, the Liverpool and England centre back, who has had his own struggles with drink, who said to me: 'Tony, you were a good player when you were drinking. When you gave up, you were a great player.'

The comedian Jack Whitehall would also sum it up when I appeared years later with him on the Sky panel show, *A League of Their Own*: 'You are,' he said, 'the donkey who became a champion racehorse.' Not that I personally thought I was a donkey, of course.

What I did lose was that need in me to laugh and joke and entertain everybody. In the old days, I had been the social secretary, the old leader of the Tuesday Club for the drinkers in the team, but I no longer felt I had to be that person who needed people to like him all the time. We all want to be liked but now I felt more that I preferred to be respected.

I guess the Tuesday Club disbanded with the arrival of Arsène. If it did continue, I certainly wasn't invited and wouldn't have wanted to be. Over the coming years, although I would always feel close to them on the pitch, I would slip away from many of my colleagues who still liked a drink – and that was fine; they lived their lives whichever way they chose. I think some of the guys were probably relieved that the Tuesday Club did end, actually. I dragged Ray Parlour round all sorts of drinking places and it probably contributed to his expensive divorce.

My team-mates were always respectful towards me and never took the mickey out of me or, to my knowledge, told jokes about me. I appreciated that. My closer friendship with Lee Dixon in my last years was evidence that you see people in different lights and are drawn to different people when you get sober. Lee is a thoughtful man with an open mind, interested in people and behaviours – interested in life.

Others? I travelled to the odd away game with Dennis Bergkamp on the train because we shared a fear of flying but never really got close to him. Towards the end of my time, the game would change – as I did – with more and more overseas players coming into the Arsenal squad, and they tended to stick together by nationality: Dennis and Marc Overmars, Patrick Vieira and Thierry Henry. It was understandable. I guess it's the same with Brits abroad.

There was also the age thing, with the younger ones obviously not sharing the same conversation topics and interests as a back four who were well into their thirties. Plus the language barrier. The Brazilian Edu was a good player and a lovely guy, but his English wasn't great and my Portuguese non-existent. It is true that you don't have to be close to your team-mates as long as you respect them and appreciate them on the pitch.

Acceptance of a changing dynamic within the group, both on their part and mine, probably stemmed from the day when I sat them down in the dressing room after training soon after quitting drinking and acknowledged my alcoholism to them. They all heard me out in silence, broken at the end by Ian Wright apparently saying: 'You've got some bottle, Tone.' I say apparently because it was reported and I can't say I remember it, so bound up in my own zone was I at that moment. Ian would later say that the group was grateful to have back the captain they had been lacking for a while, and I too would soon feel like I was back.

This respect and new way of life was open to Gazza too, another alcoholic who had this desire to please people, and to his own detriment. I may have been a defender and him a more creative player, but it still boiled down to realising potential and making the best of your God-given talent. I look back and remain convinced that Gazza would have gone on to even greater things, made better decisions in his life and career, if only he could have stayed stopped after one of those many times when he quit drinking for a while. But it was not to be. His path was not my path.

I did have ups and downs as I learned to deal with my emotions – getting sent off twice, at Derby and Newcastle – and I was still finding my way off the field as I learned to settle down in my new life. I had found out that life is unmanageable with drink. Now I was discovering that, without it, it can take a while still for it to be manageable.

Less than a year after getting sober, for example, I decided to take the kids to St Lucia on holiday. I probably felt guilty at having not been a proper dad during the last days of my drinking and thought I should take them on a grand, expensive trip. Due to an electrical storm, the plane was diverted to Antigua, however, and we had to wait in the airport there for seven hours. I was not a great flyer and my anxiety levels rose.

Even with a nanny along to help me – by now I was separated from my then wife, Jane, who had decided she didn't want to be with me any more and was then in her own early recovery from cocaine addiction – I was going spare looking after my three children, Clare, Oliver and Amber, who were then 12, five and two. They were active kids and other passengers were getting annoyed. I glugged Coca-Cola from a machine. The only place open was a bar – and so I went over there and bought a packet of cigarettes. I had never smoked before, nor would I after, but I had that addict's desire to change the way I felt when anxious that seems so intense in early recovery, although I was desperate too not to give up my hard-won sobriety by drinking alcohol.

I smoked four of the cigarettes before deciding I'd had enough. I then took the kids out on to a patch of tarmac in the pouring rain and did something I knew how to do: played football with them – using an empty can of Coke. They got tired, the episode passed and I learned more about staying off drink during stressful moments. And about being practical. The following year I took them to Portugal – along with my mum and dad for help. Such common sense didn't mean, however, that I couldn't still behave insanely even without the stuff.

At that time, I had two cars, including a nice new Jaguar that had caught my eye, three homes and a boat. There was the old family home in Essex and a new one I bought in Putney, south-west London, to be near to Clare, Ollie and Amber, who were all living in Fulham with Jane. Then there was a flat in Hampstead, which I rented to look cool, thinking it might even impress Jane enough to come back to me. It cost me £27,000 for six months and I never spent one night there.

On top of that was the boat, a speedboat, which I'd noticed in a showroom in Finchley, north London, one day when I decided to drive home from our London Colney training ground through the city rather than round the M25. I thought that it might be fun for the kids, for when we went to stay at my caravan on Mersea Island in Essex.

I picked it up on a trailer one day and decided to take it down to the Thames at Putney Bridge, where I had seen people launching boats by the slipway of a rowing club. I backed the Jag and the trailer on to the slipway and uncoupled it, jumping on as it began to float into the river. As I did so, people asked me if I needed any help.

AA had taught me to ask for help but in those early days my pride was still prevailing. 'No, I'm fine,' I lied.

Pretty soon, as I looked back towards the bank, I realised I had left the front door of the car open. It was too late. The current was now taking me upstream. I vainly tried to start the engine. I knew nothing about boats. All I got was a puff of smoke. I had never taken the trouble to find out that an engine needed to be run in before the boat went into the water.

Soon I was being carried past Fulham Football Club, rowers now asking me if I was OK. Of course I was. I daren't tell them I was getting a bit worried. Fortunately, some reeds in the shallows near Kew intervened and the boat came to rest. There I waited for four hours until the tide turned. There was one paddle in the boat and, with the tide in my favour, I finally managed to get the boat back to Putney Bridge in another couple of hours.

The good news was that the Jag was still there, despite me having left a door open. The bad news was that the water had risen from the river and flooded the car. Finally, lesson learned, I was forced to ask for help and some people kindly helped me load the boat back on to the trailer and get it and the car somewhere out of the way.

It didn't quite end there. I still needed to learn a further lesson or two. Trying to be the doting dad, I took the kids down to Mersea with the boat and slowly drove car and trailer carrying the thing on to a beach there, with Clare, Oliver and Amber all excited sitting in the boat. The idea was that I would push it gently off the trailer into the sea. The reality was that the car stuck in the sand and I couldn't budge it. Thankfully, all this was observed by a local farmer and I started waving to him for help. He brought down his tractor and dragged the car out of the soft sand. He was pretty angry with me, as well.

'What the bloody hell were you thinking?' he asked. 'You should be using a slipway. And haven't you seen the weather forecast? There's hailstones and high waves coming in. You might have killed yourself out there.' In fact, it was a good job I hadn't used the slipway and instead got stuck in the sand. If I had gone to sea, I might have endangered the kids.

There is a passage in the Big Book of AA that says something about God doing for us what we could not do for ourselves . . .

Gradually, I decluttered my life, getting rid of the Hampstead flat and selling the old Essex house. Along with the boat and a second car. And as life became simpler, so football became easier. Sobriety also quickly gave me back the competitive edge that was in danger of dissipating in drink. I was so glad and grateful. I desperately wanted to make up for lost time and win things. And I did.

It helped that Arsène was creating a new approach at the club that was right for a new me. 'Just go and play,' was his instruction. He was fortunate that he had inherited George Graham's back four – Lee Dixon, myself, Steve Bould (with Martin Keown as back-up at centre back) and Nigel Winterburn – just as George Graham had been lucky to inherit a clutch of players from the youth team, such as me, Paul Merson and David Rocastle, who would go on to be full internationals. Meanwhile, we were fortunate that Arsène helped prolong our careers. It was a good deal all round, with Arsenal the winner.

We were, admittedly, sceptical at first of this professorial figure we nicknamed Windows on account of the spectacles he wore, but we soon bought into his then innovative methods as we recognised that they could extend our playing days.

Much has been made of his dietary regime, but we were already eating well and I recall our midfield player Paul Davis bringing in a book on nutrition back in 1986. What Arsène did introduce was the 'layering' of food – eating the chicken first then the pasta, in the belief that protein followed by carbohydrate, as opposed to being consumed together, released energy more slowly and therefore was better for a player's constitution.

One thing he couldn't change, though, was my treat of fish and chips on a Friday night. It held comforting memories for me of eating the good old English dish the night I quit drinking . . .

Arsène was also big on ensuring that players' bodies were in good condition externally too, and he brought in a man called Philippe Boixel, an osteopath with amazing healing hands who would massage feet, legs and backs. He even realigned my jaw as he thought it was affecting my posture and causing ankle injuries.

Philippe also had a unique method of dealing with some back pain I was suffering. On telling him that my tailbone hurt, he put on some rubber gloves, inserted a finger up my anus and promptly massaged my prostate. I was in agony – the lads outside the room having a good laugh at my expense – but when I left that room I was pain free.

Then there was nutritionist Dr Yann Rougier, who would oversee supplements such as creatine and vitamin B12 and whom Glenn Hoddle, having taken over as England manager from Terry Venables after Euro 96, would also use before the 1998 World Cup in France. Arsène's other little trick was to provide us with sugar lumps and caffeine tablets as energy boosts at half-time in matches. The sugar was even coated in alcohol, though naturally I had mine without. Otherwise, Arsène was not in favour of the peaks and troughs that sugar could bring and did not want players to use it.

Arsène was certainly the best physiologist I have ever encountered and was a man open to ideas and dialogue with you. All of that, combined with the talent of the existing players and ones he recruited, made Arsenal a renewed force over the rest of my career.

That first full season after I got sober, in 1997/98 – which was also Arsène's first full campaign – brought another celebrated Arsenal league and cup double, the FA Cup secured with a comfortable 2–0 win over Newcastle United in the final. We had a very fine blend of players, from the solidity of that defence, through a midfield that now had Manu Petit arriving to partner Patrick Vieira, and Nicolas Anelka and Dennis Bergkamp magnificent up front. Chistopher Wreh also weighed in with some important goals and performances.

I got over an ankle injury to lead the side in the final home league match, a goal of mine when I half-volleyed home from Steve Bould's through-ball against Everton to seal a 4–0 win being a memorable personal highlight. My final pose of arms outstretched in a moment of pleasure and serenity would form the image used when the club decided to put up a statue of me outside the Emirates Stadium nearly 14 years later.

It's a goal and moment I'm still asked about . . .

When I was a young player at Arsenal, Kenny Sansom would often make a run from left back and demand the ball with a shout of, 'Stick me in. I'm gone.' I always had it in my mind that I would like to do that one day. The time arrived at last. 'Stick me in. I'm gone,' I shouted to Steve Bould. He did and I was.

The moment was all the more magical because it came via my weaker left foot, on which I had worked hard since the age of 10 or 11. That aftermath of the goal embraced bliss and a oneness with myself that verged on the spiritual.

'That sums it up,' the Sky commentator Martin Tyler said in his commentary on the day, and indeed it did.

Afterwards, I had to be a little careful not to get too close to the champagne celebrations, as would happen more times over the next few years. I did get sprayed a little but while I was a bit uncomfortable, I wasn't going to let it bother me. Nor did I want others not to enjoy the moment. I've always wondered about Formula One drivers spraying the bubbly about after a Grand Prix and ask myself what message that sends out about drink-driving.

The euphoria of that title-winning day was up there with that moment not long after quitting drinking, and the physical obsession to drink had been taken from me, when I came to believe that there was a Higher Power in my life – some people choose to call it God – as outlined in the AA programme. It felt like a force looking out for me and which could help me enjoy a sober life. It meant I need never feel alone and while on bad days I may not have been able to recognise it, it was always there. On my good days, its presence is obvious to me.

I am sure it was watching over me that day when I was stressed with my kids in the Caribbean, even if I was preoccupied and anxious. And it would mean in the future that I could tap into it in tough times. Thinking it through, too, why would I take again the very drug that had been destroying my life? Why, if you've been burned by fireworks, would you go near them again?

Mostly, my life was a series of enjoyable moments in early recovery. I can remember, for example, feeling an overwhelming sense of gratitude and peace in the October of 1997 when in Rome with England. It came the day before the game when I was at the team hotel reading M. Scott Peck's self-help book *The Road Less Traveled* and just had this sense that all was, and would be, well. I went on to have one of my better games for my country as we drew 0-0 with Italy in that backs-to-the-wall game where Paul Ince finished with his bloodied head bandaged.

The result meant that I finally went to a World Cup with England – and we could and should have gone beyond that France 98 last-16 match against Argentina when we drew 2-2 but lost on penalties. We had a young and exciting Michael Owen coming through – though the defender in me always thought the Argentine defender allowed himself to get a bit square on as Michael raced past him to score that wonderful goal, running from almost the halfway line.

David Beckham's red card for the lightest of retaliations towards Diego Simeone was a turning-point moment, but he was unfortunate and did not deserve the vilification that came his way. It showed the immense character that he has that he went on to achieve so much in the game. That day, as I consoled him in the dressing room afterwards, I knew he would be a big part of England's future.

Perhaps things would have been different had we had a fit and firing Paul Gascoigne, as he had been at Euro 96, but before the tournament came that notorious episode at the Spanish training camp in La Manga when Glenn left Gazza out of the squad.

I, along with Paul Merson, who was then also not drinking, had tried to get Paul sober enough – by talking to him, filling him with coffee, getting him in the swimming pool – to enable Glenn to pick him, but we were powerless and in retrospect I feel that both England and I, in my last World Cup, were cheated. France would go on to win the tournament they hosted, with Zinedine Zidane pulling the strings for them. Gazza could have been our Zidane. I personally may have been sober but the reach of alcoholism was still besetting English football.

Was I angry with Gazza? More sad for him, really, knowing all about the addiction we share. He has always been a dilemma – how much do you help him, how much do you let him go? Too many have kept him stuck in his illness by enabling his drinking and behaviour, but the anxiety is always what might happen to him if you let his illness play itself out. In the end, you are powerless until somebody decides they truly want help.

The next year – 1998/99 – Arsenal should, in my opinion, have gone on to do a treble, such was the quality of the squad we had then. That group was almost as good as my favourite one of all, that '91 team of just one league defeat.

In fact, I remember saying to Sir Alex Ferguson in 1999 that it should have been us, rather than his Manchester United, winning the league (in which we were runners-up to them by a point), the FA Cup (in which we lost to them in an epic semi-final) and the Champions League, in which we somehow managed to finish behind Dynamo Kiev and Lens in our group.

Sir Alex's response? 'Aye, well,' he said. 'We should have done the double in '98.'

He once, incidentally, called me a Manchester United player in an Arsenal shirt. My response: Sir Alex was an Arsenal manager in charge of Manchester United. Twice he tried to sign me, and both times I considered it but turned him down because I was Arsenal through and through.

The first was in '91 after we had won the title. It was at an England get-together and Bryan Robson, then United's captain, spoke to me about it, perhaps having been asked by Sir Alex to have a quiet word in my ear. Tapping up? Yes, of course, and anyone who doesn't think it goes on in the game informally all the time is being naive. George Graham even once got me to have a quiet word with David Seaman, then at Queens Park Rangers, at an England get-together and David ended up joining us.

At the time, the wages weren't going to be much better, as they were pretty much on a par at all the big clubs in that era, just before the Premier League started. And, anyway, I was stuck in my drinking and the London life with my mates and family around me. I wouldn't have had the tools to cope up in Manchester on my own.

The second United approach came in '96, in the autumn just five weeks after I had stopped drinking and in that period of uncertainty when Arsène was taking over from the sacked Bruce Rioch. I did entertain the idea, I have to admit, given my reservations about a new manager, a Frenchman as well, who knew nothing about English football. I had lost the boss I so respected, George Graham, a year earlier. I was questioning the club's ambition. We hadn't won the league since 1991 after all.

I guess Sir Alex might also have wanted me because, as well as feeling he might be strengthening United, he might be weakening Arsenal. The two clubs would become great rivals over the next few years, but then we had many other rivalries – including, of course, our north London neighbours Tottenham, and they were always the ones we wanted to beat. In the 1980s, it was Liverpool, with George Graham forever saying that we were the club that would go up North and take them on. Those were the days when we were so much closer to the fans, in touch with the community, than players are now and so felt it more. We also had big London rivalries, which made it more difficult to win league titles with so many derbies to contend with.

There were personal rivalries as well, such as Roy Keane and Patrick Vieira, though I thought that was more a product of the modern-day media. Paul Davis and Bryan Robson had their battles too, in an earlier era, and some of the confrontations at Old Trafford in the 1980s and early 1990s were much fiercer than in latter days. Whenever we met up for England, we were all fine, even if the United lads always sat together. I particularly got on well with David Beckham.

After the second Old Trafford approach, I met with the ever dignified Ken Friar, the club secretary, and Danny Fiszman, one of the club directors of the old school. Danny was a wonderful man who loved the club with a passion and would sadly die prematurely, from throat cancer, at the age of 66 in 2011. He was a diamond merchant who was generously putting money into the club at the time – around £50 million, I believe. They offered me a contract that more than tripled my wages, from £300,000 a year to £1 million, and it convinced me that Arsenal were going to be ambitious and competitive.

Their assertion that the club was going to invest in high-quality players to support and blend with Dennis Bergkamp was equally important in stopping me going to United and, besides, at this time I needed some stability in my professional career, with a lot of change going on in my personal life. Naturally, the pull of Arsenal was also always overwhelming.

They were such fine margins that spring of '99. That FA Cup semi saw Peter Schmeichel's penalty save from Dennis in the last minute that would have won us the game, before Ryan Giggs' wonderful solo winning goal, me desperately trying to cover and make the final tackle. Then, on the penultimate weekend in the league, having just before won 3-1 at Tottenham, we went to Leeds and lost to Jimmy Floyd Hasselbaink's late goal. Nelson Vivas made a rare appearance late on as a substitute and made a costly error. Arsène would not have Nelson after that. He hardly played, would go out on loan, and his contract ran down.

That season was also notable for something significant that happened in my private life: my four-month relationship with the model Caprice Bourret.

My old team-mate and friend Ian Wright had retired and had an ITV show late on a Friday night. He invited me on. It was live and I was worried about doing it, but I agreed as I thought it might be interesting – and good for me, having always been so uncomfortable about speaking in public in the past. AA is, after all, a programme of change. And so I did it, and it was good for me. I felt calm and relaxed and able to open up about my former life with drink and new life without it.

I was on the show with Ulrika Jonsson, who slipped her phone number on a piece of paper into my pocket. Given that I had never been much of a ladies' man, since my early history with girls had been a bit rubbish, I was flattered but I had no desire to follow up her interest. I was more interested in Caprice, who was Ian's sidekick on the show and who made it plain she was attracted to me. I don't think it was purely physical – and there were plenty who would say I was punching above my weight. I was aware of that, but I think I was then a more attractive person than I had been, more at ease with myself and open to new experiences.

The next day, Caprice's people phoned my people. Her PA phoned the agent who had arranged the interview for me, Stuart Peters, to pass on Caprice's number to me as an invitation to ring her. I did and we arranged to have dinner. Not wishing it to become a paparazzi circus, we dined at my house one night, then at hers, then with friends.

I liked her very much. She was an honest and sincere woman. It was all very romantic early on, especially our first kiss, which happened down the Mall, where I'd stopped my Jaguar, in sight of Buckingham Palace. And, I have to say, I felt like a king in the company of this beautiful woman.

When I got home and thought about it, I could not believe this was happening. How does this drunk go from sleeping with prostitutes and cheating on his wife – due to such a lack of self-esteem generated by the illness of addiction – to being with one of the most attractive women on the planet? It came through more than two years of sobriety, of self-awareness and self-confidence. I was discovering myself, reinventing myself.

It was all a lot of fun. I was a single guy, the divorce from my first wife Jane having gone through two years earlier. Naturally, the relationship with Caprice became public knowledge soon after and the tabloids were all over it. And naturally the boys in the dressing room wanted to know all the details. They didn't get them.

It got a bit more serious after a couple of months and we had one or two weekends away. I got to see a different, human side to her from the public persona of top model and serious businesswoman. We are all human beings and we all get scared, and she was no different. We put attractive people on pedestals because of their looks but they, too, can be insecure and shy.

Those instances of her opening up were rare, however, and as the relationship continued, I didn't get the feedback from her that I hoped for. I would often make myself vulnerable, in sharing my thoughts and feelings, but did not get that back in return. Too often I would get the showbiz mask – and the showbiz game.

I remember once we went out to the cinema in the West End, then an Indian restaurant in Curzon Street. The photographers were all outside the restaurant waiting for us when we came out. It was not pleasant, though I knew it went with the territory of us both being in the public eye.

I rang up a press guy I knew and he made some enquiries. He suspected that one of Caprice's people was ringing up the snappers telling them where we would be. They wanted the publicity for her, whether she wanted it or not. That wasn't my world, even if I wasn't naive enough to believe that certain celebrities didn't like all the attention that was also good for their business. I felt used, yes, but put up with a certain amount of it because being with her was worth it for a while.

In the end, though, I knew I would have to end the relationship due to the lack of emotional connection. It felt like an act, that she was playing a game before and after she met me. The honesty and sincerity I saw initially got lost behind the facade. She was successful as a businesswoman at that time and had so much more substance to her, but I never got that when we were dating. I got much more of the show and the face.

All the while, I was going to AA meetings four or five times a week and conversing intimately with like-minded women without being intimate physically with them. I was learning that there was a difference between emotional and physical connection. I wasn't getting the same connection with Caprice, wasn't feeling it. I spoke to my therapist James, after which I knew I had to voice my feelings to her face to face and finish things.

And so I went round to her place just off the New King's Road in Chelsea. It was scary for me. This was how grown-ups do things: with respect and dignity and in person. I had had short relationships in recovery before and had tried to end one this way previously, only for the girl to tell me to 'go fuck myself'. That was fair enough. I wasn't responsible for her reaction and I had been clean about it. Then, so immature and uncertain was I at the time, I contacted her three months later to say I thought I had made a mistake. She told me I must be joking.

Memories of all that meant I was nervous when I went to see Caprice, but I had grown up a bit since then. I have to say she looked stunning and I was tempted to say nothing and stay the night, but I knew I had to go through with it.

'Look, Cap,' I said. 'I can't go on with this. It's fucking my head up. I'm not getting anything back from you. I need to put my recovery first. It's more important than any relationship.'

Her reaction surprised me and she suddenly got emotional, saying that she had strong feelings and thought this relationship was the real thing.

It left me confused; it was probably the first time we had been really intimate in the months we had known each other. If she had been like this before, we may have got through it.

Underneath all the confidence she showed as a model and businesswoman, Caprice had a fragility. Warmth too. I did have second thoughts, and there is always regret when a relationship ends, but I knew it was right to move on. Sex can be such a drug, and could have kept me in the relationship, but part of my recovery was to be the master of that and look beyond the physical to the spiritual and emotional as well. This from a bloke who once dumped a girl because the underwear she wore was, to his eyes, too big.

Not that I felt I could explain any of that to team-mates or anyone outside of an AA room. I'm sure it would have made me sound weird – a charge that I came to know would be levelled at me through my recovery down the years. The lads all wanted to know about why I had ended the relationship, such are dressing rooms, but what could I say? That I thought Freddie Ljungberg, next to whom I had the honour of getting changed, had a better arse than Caprice?

I had relaxed, become less earnest and more light-hearted with my team-mates after the seriousness of the first year or two of recovery, but this deeper way of trying to be was important to me. The one person I could talk to freely about all this was Lee Dixon, to whom I got really close. He got it and would share back as well. I couldn't imagine that happening with, say, Ray Parlour, my old drinking buddy.

I remember one Arsenal game against Spurs around that time, and naturally there was plenty of winding-up going on. Tim Sherwood was next to me and Lee Dixon and said to Dicko – Tim incredulous and shaking his head – 'Caprice? Him – Caprice?'

Dicko answered Tim back and I could only smile. 'Yes,' he said. 'And he bombed her out.'

A few years later, I was asked if I would be interested – for £50,000 – in going on *Celebrity Big Brother*. I then read in the papers that Caprice was going on the show and rang her up, as we were still civil towards each other. We both agreed that the producers were probably looking for fireworks between us in the 'house', and I told her that it was not for me. I was by then making better decisions, and not based on money.

After the break-up, I got back to playing football, ever my haven, though I had it more in perspective these days, as I also had a life that involved going to the theatre, eating out, even going to jazz clubs. And coming home from nights out, and waking up from them, sober.

As an indication of how much my life had changed, in the

summer of 1999 this ex-jailbird and drunk was awarded an MBE, and was delighted to go to Buckingham Palace with his mum and dad to receive the medal from the Queen. She asked me if I was managing to get a long enough rest that summer, after the World Cup the previous year. I was impressed with her absorbing the information with which she had been briefed, what with more than a hundred people receiving awards that day.

I did have an enforced rest due to a double hernia operation and the team also underwent a bit of surgery. Steve Bould departed to join Sunderland for his swansong, but we still had the traditional back four of Lee, Martin Keown, myself and Nigel Winterburn, with David Seaman behind us. Then the dream midfield duo of Manu Petit and Patrick Vieira, one who held and one who drove, flanked by the industry of Ray Parlour on the right and the pace of Marc Overmars on the left. Up front was Dennis, with a new partner following the departure of Nicolas Anelka to Real Madrid. In return, we got Davor Suker from them, as well as a younger player who hadn't quite clicked at Juventus. A lad by the name of Thierry Henry.

It was one of those meant-to-be events. Arsène had desperately tried to hang on to Nicolas, who was a sweet young boy but had his head turned by people supposedly advising him and who frustrated Arsène. Had Nicolas stayed, we might not have got Thierry.

I first came across Thierry in '98, just before the World Cup, when England played a warm-up tournament in Morocco and he was appearing for France. He was playing wide on the left in the match I watched and looked to me like he didn't know how to get on the ball often enough. He was quick but raw; nothing special, I thought then. Even though he played a part in France's World Cup win that year, I don't think even Arsène knew quite how good Thierry would turn out to be. Signings are often made up of 50 per cent the manager's knowledge combined with the talent of the player, then 50 per cent luck.

While he was lightning quick – and he could run faster with the ball than I could without it – there were no early indications that Thierry would become an Arsenal great, go on to be the club's leading goalscorer, surpassing Ian Wright, and be deserving of his own statue. Indeed, 1999/2000 would be a season of transition for us. Alex Manninger began to get more appearances in goal in place of David Seaman. The Brazilian left back Sylvinho and Ukrainian right back Oleg Luzhny also arrived, as Arsène began the process of replacing the ageing back five.

We were never in the title race and would end up 18 points behind Manchester United in 2000, our second place coming as a result of eight wins late in the season. I played 21 league matches, as I nursed my declining body through games, and another 11 in Europe.

Our Champions League campaign started badly and finished sadly. Playing our home games at Wembley, while Highbury was being brought up to standard for that level (and with the Emirates still seven years away from construction), did not really help and we limped in third in our group behind Barcelona and Fiorentina, despite a good 1-1 draw in the Nou Camp that I enjoyed and in which Pep Guardiola played. The Barcelona game at Wembley was notable for one Jose Mourinho, then Bobby Robson's assistant at Barca, coming into our dressing room and asking for my shirt from our laundry basket as a souvenir, I was told by one of our kit men. Nobody really knew much about him at the time.

Wembley just didn't feel like home. Highbury was a tight venue, one of the smallest playing surfaces in English football – and I often joked that I signed for Arsenal as I would have less ground to cover. Wembley was open and expansive. I'm sure it was good financially for the club, with crowds of 73,000 doubling the normal home capacity, but there were a lot of neutrals watching and it simply wasn't the same.

Third place in the group meant that we were put into the UEFA Cup, now the Europa League, and we embarked on a good run, beating Nantes, Deportivo La Coruna, Werder Bremen and Lens to reach the final against Galatasaray in Copenhagen, scene of our European Cup Winners' Cup final victory over Parma back in 1994, when Alan Smith's goal won it for us. That was a great defensive display by a team with a lot of injuries and organised well by George Graham.

This one wasn't an especially memorable game, except for the Turkish side's talisman, the Romanian Gheorghe Hagi, getting sent off, and we lost 4-1 on penalties after a goalless draw. Thierry missed one – and, in fact, he would never score in the final of a competition, be it World Cup, Euros, Champions League, FA Cup or UEFA Cup. I know it came to bug him. Why exactly did they put up a statue of him at the Emirates? All ribbing aside, I suppose that record 228 goals, two league titles and three FA Cups might have had something to do with it.

It had been a poor period with club and it wasn't going to get any better with country. On top of that would come an event in my private life that would test my sobriety and my newfound faith to their limits.

3

LOSS

Grief is in two parts.
The first is loss.
The second is remaking of life.

ANNE ROIPHE

If not physically, then certainly emotionally, success in football gives you energy, while losing drains you. And so after the UEFA Cup final defeat against Galatasaray, I didn't feel in the greatest shape. In fact, I felt like I was limping into Euro 2000 in Belgium and Holland with England.

We had struggled in the qualifying group, finishing nine points behind Sweden, with a defeat in Stockholm meaning that Glenn Hoddle had few backing him when he made some remarks about the disabled, suggesting that they might be paying for the sins of a past life, which cost him his job. His sacking was only a matter of time when Prime Minister Tony Blair condemned what he said.

It was a shame, as Glenn had a lot of promise as a coach. A devotee of Arsène and his methods, his 3-5-2 formation was at least an attempt to carry on Terry Venables' work and make us a more modern side by being more fluid of movement, not playing in straight lines. It was not long after Glenn had found a God of his understanding and I remember having the odd conversation with him about it. He was in that phase of being excited, wanting to share his beliefs, but you have to be careful about these things, as I was with who I talked to about AA. People can wonder what the hell you are on about.

The England job probably came too early for Glenn, who was 38 when appointed, as a more experienced manager might not have ignored a golden rule: stick to footballing matters. As we say in AA, we may have our own opinions on outside issues, but we don't express them publicly. 'AA is not allied with any sect, denomination, politics, organisation or institution; does not wish to engage in any controversy; neither endorses nor opposes any causes,' our credo says. That works for me if I'm a football coach and going to be asked about anything other than football.

After Kevin Keegan took over, we just squeaked through to the play-offs on goal difference over Poland, but he would prove not to be a long-term solution, despite having a good crop of players at the time.

I played in both play-off games against Scotland, a 2–0 win at Hampden Park when the excellent Paul Scholes – quality and loyalty in one package – scored twice to establish him as a great number 10 in the Peter Beardsley/Teddy Sheringham mould, and the 1–0 defeat at Wembley when Don Hutchison scored for the Scots. I recall little about that game. I tend to blank such defeats from my memory.

I also scored the last goal by an Englishman at the old stadium before it was rebuilt, in the 2–0 win over Ukraine in a warm-up game in May 2000. It was my fifth for England and meant I held a national record for the longest period between international goals. It had been almost 12 years since my fourth, against Saudi Arabia in Riyadh.

Come the tournament, I played only the opening game, against Portugal, which we lost 3-2 from being 2-0 up, before a back injury forced me to watch the rest from the stands. It was a poor campaign, with a 1-0 win over one of the weakest ever Germany sides papering over the cracks under Kevin's management and then a 2-1 defeat by Romania sending us home early.

The whole thing was a mess from my point of view, right from arriving at the hotel to find the Racing Channel being piped in – Kevin being a horse racing fan – and a group of players too intent on gambling. The day before the Portugal game, I knew we were going to get turned over when, in training, Kieron Dyer was asked to play a floating role against the first-choice defence to replicate Luis Figo's for Portugal and Kieron destroyed us. As a result of that chastening exercise, I asked Kevin and the coaching staff what we were going to do about it in response, to plug the leak that Kieron had exposed, and never got an answer. We never did sort it. It duly came to pass that Figo also took us apart on the day.

It was a relief not to be associated with it all after that, I have to say. It was everything that was wrong with English football, all gung-ho and little technical or tactical expertise. I prolonged my international career after that tournament mainly because Alan Shearer was retiring and I wanted to be captain again, which happened in a 1-1 friendly draw against France, Euro 2000 winners, in Paris in the September. The next month, though, after the 1-0 defeat in a World Cup qualifier in the teeming rain at Wembley against Germany, who were learning lessons of the summer while we weren't, I knew my time was up, my tally of caps ending at 66. What with Euro 96 and Arsenal playing Champions League there, I held the record for Wembley appearances, having made 59.

It was ironic that my last international game was against the Germans because I would find out some years later that I had Teutonic ancestry. Yes, this archetypal Englishman, who had been through losing on penalties to the Germans in '96, had a German great-grandmother. It was discovered by a cousin researching our family tree. It turned out that my mother's side were Scottish and my father's grandparents had come to England from Freiburg in the early 1900s and been bakers in London. There they had children, including my grandmother, Dad's mum, who gave birth to Dad in 1933.

Anyway, I wasn't going to announce any retirement that night of the Germany loss, especially when I got overtaken by events. Kevin decided he was going to resign there and then, and he was not going to be talked out of it by either me or David Davies, the FA chief executive, when we took him into the toilets next to the dressing room for a private conversation. We told him to think about things overnight, not to do anything impulsive, but Kevin was an impulsive man.

For all his tactical deficiencies, he was well liked by the players and probably the best Englishman around for the job at the time due to his transformation of Newcastle United. He fostered a good spirit by and large and the players were all behind him. He was adamant, however, that he had gone as far as he could.

To me, Kevin's problem was that he didn't surround himself with the best. In fact, it has been a problem with the England team for a long while. And whereas the German FA and the Bundesliga got together after Euro 2000 to work on a plan to solve their problems, we never did. The rivalries and power struggles between our FA and the Premier League have always been detrimental to the game as a whole, in my opinion. They were then and continue to be now.

Kevin had great motivational qualities and ran entertaining training sessions, but he never had expertise around him in the way, say, Terry Venables had at Euro 96, with the late Don Howe – a wonderful man and coach I also worked with as a kid at Arsenal – and Bryan Robson. Kevin had Derek Fazackerley and Arthur Cox, good footballing figures but without the experience of World Cup and European football. Alan Shearer was captain and had never played in Europe as extensively as I had. Our game was about playing to the strengths of an old-fashioned centre-forward and we were exposed as outdated. Our movement was poor and we were back to playing in straight lines, unlike our mobile, developing Arsenal team. We thought we were fine just because we beat the Germans 1-0 in the summer.

Kevin could also have had the best physiologists, nutritionists and experts in biomechanics to fill in for his weaknesses. As England coach, you have access to them. He could have brought in a tactical expert. It would have been brave, for example, to have brought Glenn Hoddle back into the fold, to tap his expertise and experience of France 98. We may have had some differences at that tournament, when I thought him a bit too regimented in his approach, but I always believed that Glenn had a good tactical brain. Terry Venables was the last one to be brave, and not worry that people might take his job. Kevin had his mates around him.

I knew more about European football than they did. I was in an environment at Arsenal that was tactically superb; a passing team with great movement. One that kept the foundations of defence and did not overplay, knowing that 60 per cent possession would win you the game – but that too much more could be detrimental, with sides growing used to defending and the team in possession becoming predictable.

After Kevin came Sven-Goran Eriksson, which I think was the Arsenal vice-chairman and FA councillor David Dein's appointment and had the added bonus of keeping Arsène Wenger away from the job. David had got to know Sven when we played Sampdoria, the team he was then managing, in a Cup Winners' Cup tie. Not that I think Arsène would have taken the England job then. He was building another great Arsenal side and would have missed the day-to-day involvement.

We missed a chance to reassess our football after Euro 2000. At a time when we should have been coaching the coaches, we simply hired an expensive foreign manager. Public opinion would probably not have allowed Glenn to return, but I don't see why we didn't turn back to Terry to finish the job he had started at Euro 96. When Fabio Capello later took over after Steve McClaren's short and ill-fated tenure, it meant a decade of doing little to change the system while paying a lot for a man at the top.

I wouldn't have wanted Arsène to become England manager – and not just for selfish reasons of keeping him at Arsenal. While I can see the value of an overseas technical director, having a non-native coach is something I do not believe in for England. After all, none of the other World Cup-winning countries has ever hired a foreign coach. Personally, I would make it a rule that national coaches have to be from that country. UEFA and FIFA say they can't dictate to countries, but why not? They are the governing bodies. International football is different from club football and should remain so.

People – the FA mainly, and the media were buying it – were talking about a golden generation emerging at that time, and while it was true that we had the Manchester United group of Rio Ferdinand, David Beckham and Paul Scholes coming to maturity, I thought it was a bit of a myth and couldn't see that the new crop were any better than 1982, 1990 or 1996. Given his quick, explosive style of play, I always thought that Michael Owen was going to struggle with injuries. That said, they were a good group compared to what we have these days, with certainly more depth in the squad.

There was no temptation for me to stay on after Kevin departed. It wasn't quite a shambles but it certainly wasn't great. England were far inferior to my club team and I was finding it increasingly hard work, physically and mentally. The captaincy issue was also going to surface again under a new manager. On top of that, I am an all-or-nothing character, and could I commit, at the age of 34, to another two years? Could I make it to the World Cup of 2002 and sit on the bench? I am not that kind of player. I am a main man who likes to pull his weight. It was the end of my international days. I wanted to go out at the top.

Besides, Rio was coming through and could form a good partnership with Sol Campbell. Let the next generation have a bash. It felt clean to go now. I had done my bit and was not going to do myself justice with my body packing up on me. I guess it comes down to personality and style. I was never really the sort of player who would be a candidate for the club Man of the Year award by doing a job in playing out of position, like right back.

The bottom line was that I didn't want to let my country down through being off the pace, and I knew I would struggle if I wanted to play for Arsenal for another couple of seasons. I owed it to my employers and the supporters, the people who paid the bills.

In politics, there is a saying that all careers end in failure. It can be true in football, too. I guess Kevin's with England had. I never felt that mine with my country had ever got properly started. After the disappointment of not making the final squad in 1990 following a tricky baptism at Euro 88, I was given a chance by Graham Taylor, Bobby Robson's successor as manager, but he dropped me for Euro 92 before restoring me to the side. England didn't make it to the World Cup finals of 1994, however.

The only time I really had any momentum was that spell under Terry Venables as his captain in a team that had a plan. He selected and integrated leaders, such as myself, Paul Ince and Stuart Pearce, and had us playing a fluid, mobile style of football, blending solidity at the back with creativity further forward. Again, I was comfortable because a manager had made me the main man and I always responded to that. In their wisdom, though, the FA refused to give Terry a contract beyond Euro 96 ahead of the tournament. Terry famously said he didn't do auditions and quit after it, and that was that.

Eventually, my decision to retire came out in the following weeks, probably after the caretaker manager Peter Taylor left me out of a squad to face Italy. When I bumped into Peter some time later, he told me he had left a message on my phone explaining that he wanted to give some younger players a chance, but I said I'd never received it. We both agreed that was odd. Only years after, when the *Daily Mirror* admitted to hacking my phone between 2000 and 2005, did it become clear why. Apparently, messages can get deleted after someone has tapped into your phone. I was big enough to deal with not hearing anything at the time but, without an explanation, it can feel like you have been bombed out.

When Sven took over early in 2001, I met him in a players' lounge somewhere at an away ground. He introduced himself, I wished him well, and there was never really a discussion about me coming out of retirement to play for him. I think the decision may have been taken out of my hands anyway because of his desire to have a fresh start, and he would have felt vindicated by that amazing 5-1 win over Germany in Munich.

Besides, there was something going on in my personal life that probably coloured my thinking, something that required my urgent attention.

In the four years that had passed since my last drink, I had learned that pain was the touchstone for growth. It was necessary in my development as a person. Any pain I was feeling with Arsenal underachieving and my England career having ended was as nothing, however, to watching my mum, Caroline, suffer with illness. A terminal illness. In fact, it was the most horrific thing I have ever had to deal with and tested every last ounce of my faith and my sobriety.

Back in the spring, before Euro 2000, I went to France with Mum and Dad. I had got to like the country very much during the 1998 World Cup, had taken French lessons, and had decided to buy a villa there. Having consulted Patrick Vieira and Thierry Henry about a good location, I had settled on Mougins, just inland from Cannes. It was a beautiful spot.

We were staying in a hotel in Cannes, having appointments with estate agents and lawyers, and were going out one day when Mum, as she got in the car, broke her arm. After being treated at a hospital there, it just wouldn't heal properly when we got back to the UK, even though the local NHS hospital told us all was well. In the end, I took her to see my old friend John King at the London Independent Hospital, a doctor who had often treated me in the past, and he ordered some tests.

I remember where I was when I heard Mum had bone cancer. It was on a pre-season tour in Austria and our physio, Gary Lewin, pulled me out of the dining room. He'd had a call from John King. X-rays had revealed the extent of the disease.

Over the next six months, I watched her die. On my days off, I would drive over from Putney to Mum and Dad's in Essex to be there with her. She was in agony, poor soul. She was a good woman, a simple woman, who loved her family, and she didn't deserve that. She lived for her grandchildren. Sometimes I would take Oliver over. He was still young and she was more concerned for him and his wellbeing, even when the cancer was unbearable and she kept having to be moved because of bedsores.

When she died, she was skeletal, her head just a skull. There was no soul there. It is an image that I retain to this day.

I was angry initially, wondering why the Higher Power I had discovered in recovery had done this, and immediately after her death I went into a decline and couldn't get out of bed for three or four days. I was duvet-diving, immobilised, wondering what the point of life was, having experienced the death of a loved one. It is fair to say it was the darkest time in my life and sobriety.

Eventually, an acceptance kicked in and I managed to get myself up and to her funeral, which was even an uplifting affair. We played one of her favourite songs – Elvis Presley's 'The Wonder of You'. It was odd. It would later become the run-out music at the Arsenal.

I began to recall and implement the basics of Alcoholics Anonymous, living by the cornerstone phrases – 'one day at a time'; 'this too shall pass'. Getting out of bed to struggle to AA meetings in Wimbledon and Putney kept me going.

During these days I was feeling everything without the anaesthetic of alcohol to numb me. My only real experience of death previously had been years earlier when my dad's young office lad Cliff, to whom Dad had grown close, died. One day, Cliff, who was only in his early twenties, left the Squirrel's Heath pub in Romford, where we had all been drinking, and was hit by a car as he crossed the road. The poor woman in the car was distraught. Our way of marking Cliff's death was to have a drink and drop our trousers to 'It's Not Unusual' by Tom Jones, as it was his favourite record.

I had no desire for a drink through all the pain surrounding Mum, thankfully. I also wanted to honour her death and the feelings it provoked rather than self-medicate. Still to this day I miss my mother. I want her to make me better, to comfort me, when I am ill. I want her to make me scrambled eggs on toast and put a glass of water by my bedside. But I guess it was time to grow up.

There was another death around this time which shocked me. At the end of March 2001, after a short illness, my fellow youth-team graduate David Rocastle succumbed to non-Hodgkin's lymphoma at the painfully young age of 33. We went through so much together, having been at Highbury as 14-year-olds, not least the time when, on a tour in France, he and another youth-teamer, Greg Allen, were fighting and I had to separate them and then stay awake all night to keep them apart in the dormitory, with them wanting to prolong things. David could handle himself all right, as I recall him doing during a fight on holiday in Cyprus once.

Rocky was a lovely lad and rightly an Arsenal legend, even though he was a Crystal Palace fan as a kid. He was a talented player, strong in the tackle, a great up-and-down midfield player. He was, in fact, probably the player of the season the year we won the league at Liverpool in 1989. It was all the more remarkable given that he was as blind as a bat and needed contact lenses to play. They would often fall out.

So many happy memories of him . . . like a great night dancing at the Camden Palais in 1987 after we had beaten Tottenham in a League Cup semi-final, him smoking one of the thin cigars he liked every now and again. Then, by contrast, came the most poignant memory of all, going to visit him in Northwick Park Hospital in Harrow shortly before he died. I felt so sorry for his young children, Ryan, Melissa and Monique, as well as for his wife Janet.

Amid such sadness that season, I threw myself back into my football, which had ever been my salvation, and Arsenal were in the middle of an excellent campaign. My old mate Nigel Winterburn was gone, to West Ham, along with Manu Petit and Marc Overmars, who were now at Barcelona. In had come another full-back in Lauren and two French players, Robert Pires and Sylvain Wiltord.

By now we were a better European side. At times previously we had looked like a team built to win at Stoke City, but now we really had the makings of a modern Champions League outfit. Robert Pires in particular would develop into the sort of inventive player that made a difference, often from wide, like Rocky had in '89, Anders Limpar in '91 and Marc Overmars in '98. This despite Robert never really learning or speaking English. He mostly kept himself to himself. So clever on the ball was he that Lee Dixon used to hate going up against him in training. Sylvain, meanwhile, went back to France most weekends after matches.

This time our home games in the Champions League were back at Highbury, which had been upgraded, and I really think we could have won it that season. The fact that we didn't was probably down to a moment when I could and should have done better, I have to admit.

We weren't in the toughest of groups and beat Sparta Prague twice, and Shakhtar Donetsk and Lazio at home as well. Our away draw in Rome, when I travelled but was injured, also meant we topped the group, even though we lost 3-0 in the Ukraine.

At that time, there was a group stage in the second phase as well, and we were in with Bayern Munich, Lyon and Spartak Moscow. I particularly remember the away game in Moscow. It was a bitterly cold Russian night on a synthetic surface and, although we took an early lead through Sylvinho, some of the boys clearly didn't fancy it and we lost 4-1. Still, we won the home game and also won in Lyon and were able to finish second behind Bayern Munich to reach a quarter-final against Valencia.

We went a goal down, a valuable away goal, in the first half but should have won the home leg by more than 2-1. After the break, Thierry got us back into the tie and two minutes later Ray Parlour drove home a good goal. Unfortunately, Thierry missed a great chance late on to give us a real cushion.

In the Mestalla, it took just one moment for all that hard work to be undone. The big Norwegian international John Carew, all six-foot-five of him, was a good player at that time and just got in front of me to head home a cross for the only goal of the game and take Valencia into the semi-finals on the away-goals rule.

I had forgotten the first rule of captaincy: do your own job first before you focus on other people. Sometimes as a captain you can be looking around to make sure everyone is doing their job and you switch off for a moment. That's what happened and it shouldn't have.

I was annoyed with myself, and afterwards in the dressing room just said: 'Sorry, lads. Sorry, Arsène.' We were a good side – no, a great side – and that was the closest I came in the Champions League. Blowing it was a regret, the more so because Valencia drew Leeds in the semis and won through comfortably to play Bayern Munich in the final, losing on penalties. I would really have loved another crack at Bayern that season.

After that, we were the nearly men again. In the Premier League, we were once more runners-up to Manchester United, though we got closer to them this time and only finished 10 points behind. We even beat United 1-0 that season and had 6-1, 5-0 and 6-0 wins over Leicester City, Manchester City and Queens Park Rangers respectively. We were improving.

In addition, we reached the FA Cup final after a satisfying 2-1 win over Tottenham, who had just recruited Glenn Hoddle as manager, in the semi-final at Old Trafford. We went a goal down early on but we dominated after that, with Patrick and Robert scoring the goals. It came just a week after Rocky's death and was some small tribute.

In the final, we also outplayed Liverpool for long periods at the Millennium Stadium. We took the lead through Freddie Ljungberg in the second half, something we should have done earlier, having been denied a clear penalty in the first half when Stephane Henchoz handled. It would be remembered as Michael Owen's final, though, as he struck twice to win it for Gérard Houllier's side. It was the first time two FA Cup final sides had overseas managers.

Afterwards, Arsène threw his runners-up medal in a dressing-room bin. He does have a temper and it hit him deeply, though usually, being a clever man, he would take himself out of the room to vent his anger. I'm not a great loser either, but by now I could take it better, having become familiar with Rudyard Kipling's poem 'If', which talks about treating triumph and disaster the same. The twin impostors, it's said.

I picked the medal out of the bin and put it back in Arsène's hand. 'Look,' I said to everyone, 'let's remember how this feels. Let's come back and win it next year. We've had a great year but let's make next year greater.'

It has always been a character trait of mine. I seem to need pain as motivation. If I had had too much success in my footballing career straight away as a young player, I think I might have got complacent, maybe got bored. I need stimulus, need defeat sometimes. After the Littlewoods Cup defeat of 1988, we went on to win the league in 1989. That was my pattern. My body was aching but I knew I had, and wanted, at least one more year. It just didn't feel like the end.

Arsenal did not exactly smooth the path for what would prove my final year, however, I have to say.

At that point, the club were putting all their older professionals on one-year deals. I went to David Dein's house in Hertfordshire to talk to him and Arsène about a new contract and was a little surprised to see a well-known senior agent,

Jerome Anderson, whose agency had handled the deal for my autobiography *Addicted* a few years earlier, waiting outside for me. Jerome had been well connected at Arsenal for many years and close to David, having first represented Charlie Nicholas. He had rung me to suggest I talk about a new contract with Arsenal as I didn't have an agent, but I still did not expect him to be in on the talks.

In the early days, my dad accompanied me into meetings just to look out for me and I always ended up signing my contracts. Now I was being offered a basic sum and then a sum for each game played. What I really wanted was a one-year deal with a guaranteed salary. I was shocked. In fact, I felt embarrassed for the club. Arsenal were not paying what Chelsea were at that time, as shown when Ashley Cole moved there, but what I was being offered was around half of what I was getting 10 years earlier.

This was so different to that time when I met with the then club secretary Ken Friar and Danny Fiszman back in '96. I know I had aged, would reach 35 during the following season, but I thought I had done enough for the club over the years to warrant a salary rather than what I saw as a disrespectful appearance-based contract. Being sober meant I now had some self-esteem and could stick up for myself. David was a decent man – I have a memory of him enjoying himself like a kid at Wet 'n' Wild in Florida on a club tour back in 1989 – and a good partner for Arsène in transfer dealings, but that day I did not think they covered themselves in glory.

Arsène said very little. He never has liked confrontation. I recall a time when Ian Wright was coming from Croydon and getting in late for training most days. Arsène simply made training later but the boys were fuming. We as players then told Wrighty to get his act together. It was the big players who policed the group rather than Arsène.

Then there was a time when Manu Petit walked on to the training ground after a session had begun. I asked Arsène if he was going to do anything about it but he just shrugged his shoulders. I went mad. Standards needed to be set and followed. In frustration, I picked up a plastic cup by the side of the pitch and threw it at Arsène. A bit comically, the wind took it away from him and it didn't hit him, but the point was made to Manu and Arsène.

There were other run-ins. Arsène made us play a training game without offsides but I wouldn't have it. It was not what we were about as a back four. And he wanted to do a one-versus-one session with Thierry Henry up against me. I walked off the pitch. I told him I had spent a career not getting isolated against the opposition's quickest player due to my positional sense and wasn't going to start now. I guess I was a big enough figure at the time to be able to make my point. In Arsène's later years as manager, I couldn't envisage any other player having the authority to challenge him like that, which would worry me.

Anyway, that night I told David and Arsène that I foresaw a problem. I told them that I had always been fair to the club and always given them my all. In these later years, when my body was not standing up to 40 games a year, I would try to get myself fit and ready for the big games to be of best service to the club – off the pitch as well, by continuing to be an influence in the dressing room and around the training ground.

With the deal on offer, the temptation might be to play games I shouldn't because I would be chasing the money. In fact, that situation would come to pass in the upcoming season, my final one, after I was given little choice but to accept the contract.

It was a game against Charlton Athletic, when I was selected but decided on the morning of the match to be honest with Arsène. I told him my back was sore, that I could play, but I thought I might be better saving myself for a Champions League game that was coming up in midweek. I told him I was concerned about losing my appearance money, having been picked for the side, and he said he would get it for me anyway. In the end, Igors Stepanovs took my place, Arsenal lost the game and I never did get my money.

I would play only 13 games in my last season, 2001/02, and I suppose Arsenal would say they were therefore justified in paying me game by game. I just felt it was cheap, however, and not really in keeping with the club's tradition of fairness to its employees. Nor was it at the end of that season, when the players were all given Muller watches to commemorate their achievements during it. Except me. It may well have been because I was no longer at the club when they were handed out – perhaps at some end-of-season function that I was unaware of after retiring – but I hoped mine might have been sent on. I do think I contributed plenty to that season on and off the field with my presence. I knew the club's standards, helped to establish them indeed, and made sure they were maintained.

I remember two games in particular from my final season, neither of which I played in. The first came on that fateful day that will forever be etched on everyone's mind: 11 September 2001. We were away in the Champions League against Real Mallorca and I went to see Arsène, who was watching TV in the lecture room of the hotel. 'My back's not good, boss,' I said. 'I don't think I can play.'

Then I saw that Arsène was preoccupied, horrified, with the TV. I joined him in his shock as they replayed the planes hitting the twin towers in New York. Arsène soon got up and turned the TV off. We had a game to play. We would lose 1-0 and the atmosphere was eerie. Somehow we got permission to fly home that night when all other flights were cancelled. I think we were all pleased just to get home safely, especially when the enormity of the tragedy hit home the following day.

The other memorable date, and a much happier one, was Sunday 20 January 2002, when the team was away to Leeds United. After watching the game – a 1-1 draw – on TV, I decided to go out for dinner to the Embassy restaurant in Mayfair with a couple of friends. One was Peter Kay, who I had met at AA and with whom I had hit it off so well that he had become my chief executive at Sporting Chance, the charity I had not long established for sportsmen and women with addictive illnesses. The other was Steve Kutner, an agent I used now and then for personal appearances and suchlike. I remember Carl Fogarty, the motorcyclist who went on to win *I'm a Celebrity . . . Get Me Out of Here!*, being at a nearby table.

As was a woman by the name of Poppy Teacher. She approached our table, introduced herself and said that she hoped I didn't mind but she was an Arsenal fan and was wondering when I would be fit to play again. She had been due to go to Leeds that day, apparently, but – as I would later find out – had been having problems with a boyfriend she was splitting up with and decided against it.

Not long after she had returned to her table, her friend came over to me. 'Look,' she said. 'Poppy really likes you. Why don't you go over and talk to her?' And so I did. She was an attractive, single woman and I was a single man, after all.

It turned out that Poppy had been working as a personal assistant to a football lawyer and agent by the name of Richard Glass and was based in Holborn. We clicked and that day a relationship was born. Gradually, that click would turn into a certainty and that relationship would grow into a marriage.

Naturally, we made the papers whenever we stepped out after that. It was not lost on the media that I was a recovering alcoholic and Poppy came from the Teacher's whisky family. It was an irony that she found amusing, though her name had not even registered with me at first. Later, I would be able to joke that I may be teetotal but I still woke up with a Teacher's in the morning.

There's an old saying that when the pupil is ready the teacher appears. This one was literally a Teacher. Actually, at that time, I had almost given up on the idea of a relationship, and they also say that when that happens, one often materialises. It certainly did in this case.

I had been living on my own for six years, had had lots of fun and several short-term relationships, but it had been almost three years since my relationship with Caprice had ended. I had just got used to the idea of being alone, if that was what my life was supposed to be about, and was content in my solitude. In fact, I remember walking on Putney Heath one day and thinking that very thought. There is, after all, a difference between being alone and being lonely. During that time, I had been tested as I got to know myself, warts and all. I think it does people good to live alone for a while. It did this alcoholic. I learned to be comfortable with my own company, and so not to feel lonely.

I had honoured the previous relationships and been adult in them, telling the women concerned when it wasn't for me, being honest and respectful of their feelings. Now I just seemed to be ready for Poppy. And nor was it purely about the physical. When you get the physical, emotional and mental aspects of a relationship coming together, you have an explosion, as I did with Poppy.

For her part, she would later say that she met a successful footballer and a few months later ended up with a has-been.

I got back to playing in the February, for an FA Cup game against Gillingham, which we won 5-2, and Arsenal embarked on a great run to the final. I also played in the quarter-final replay against Newcastle, which we won 3-0, though was injured for the semi against Middlesbrough at Old Trafford, which the boys won 1-0.

That took us to another final at the Millennium Stadium in Cardiff, and this time we would not make the same mistakes against Chelsea as we had against Liverpool the previous year. Goals in the last 20 minutes by Ray Parlour and Freddie Ljungberg saw us lift the trophy. I recall afterwards consoling John Terry, who was a young player then and had come on as a substitute, saying that his time would come but this was ours. I would be right about that.

What I remember most about the aftermath, though, was being in the dressing room with the cup when our chairman Peter Hill-Wood burst through the door. It was unusual for him to come in; normally back then it would be David Dein who liked to speak to the players. Peter would just send champagne.

Arsène at this point went to shake the chairman's hand but Peter just kept moving past him, leaving Arsène well and truly blanked. Peter then came straight over to me in a corner, with the FA Cup beside me. Most of us were thinking that he wanted to lift the cup, and the players were all now standing up to attention for the chairman, but instead he said to me, his voice booming:

'Tony. Met Poppy coming down here on the flight from Stansted. What a wonderful girl. Such a sweetheart. I knew her grandmother Rosie. Wonderful woman. We had some times. She was such fun. This is the best news I've heard today.'

Here we were, having just won the FA Cup, and the chairman was more interested in my love life with a woman whose family he knew well. That was Peter, bless him.

After that, we were playing Manchester United four days later with a chance to win the double, such was the run the boys were having, mainly without me, as they closed in on what would be a 13-match domestic winning streak to finish the season. Dennis Bergkamp and I were rested, though Dennis was on the bench at Old Trafford, expecting to be playing the following Saturday at home to Everton when we could clinch it.

In the event, the boys pulled off a famous victory with Sylvain Wiltord's second-half goal and we'd won another double, the club's third. I then didn't need to play against Everton but lifted the trophy, the first man to captain a title-winning side in three different decades. The painful end to the previous season had indeed been motivation.

As a postscript, I had a testimonial scheduled and Celtic came to Highbury and helped fill the place as they usually do, Martin O'Neill then the manager. It was an emotional night that moved me greatly. I had by now decided to retire although I did have a few doubts when the crowd started singing: 'One more year . . .' I knew my time was up, though. I didn't want to be a bit player again, dipping in and out, on the bench for some of the time. That wasn't my style. I didn't want not to be captain.

Arsène didn't ask me to carry on either; I don't think he wanted to tell me what to do with my life by this time and he probably knew he would be wasting his time. It might have been nice to have been asked, mind. We all like to be loved and wanted.

Nor did I want to go for a season to Leeds United or Rangers, both of whom sounded me out, just to pick up money. Major League Soccer in the United States wasn't a retirement option at that time. Besides, I wanted to be known as a one-club man. And that club was Arsenal. As a banner at the club held up by fans used to say: 'One Life, One Love, One Club, One-Nil'.

I had had six years of sobriety to prepare myself for this moment. I knew mentally, emotionally and spiritually that it was the right time to go. I was approaching my 36th birthday and knew my body well. Arsène had been a leader in English football in the physical conditioning of players and he had extended my career, but you can't keep going to an empty well. You see people who get stuck and can't move on and the decision is made for them. I wanted to be the one making it. Once you get a degree of consciousness, you know when things feel right.

On reflection, I might have been prepared to sacrifice a couple of the league titles I won with Arsenal for a Champions League success, or winning a major trophy for England, but any regrets could soon be banished when I considered what I had achieved. And if you are going to go, you can't do much better than winning, for a second time, the classic double of English football.

4

Leadership – 1

SOMETHING that sobriety teaches you is humility, which emerges from the humiliation of alcoholic drinking. It means accepting that you are no better than anyone else and that the Higher Power I talked about is now in control of your life and events more so than you yourself are. For addicts, who are often beset by a huge ego and low self-esteem, it also means that you are, too, no worse than anyone else and that you acknowledge your assets as well as the defects of character that contributed to your drinking. It is called right-sizing. It is about getting life in perspective but also realising that you have qualities to bring to your life in recovery.

I guess that one of the qualities attributed to me during my playing days was leadership and – without boasting, but acknowledging my attributes – it always came easily to me, to the point that I captained every team I ever played for, right from Dagenham United as a kid up to Arsenal and England.

Whether it is nature or nurture I will leave to the anthropologists, but I am sure the contribution of my father Alex to my footballing education as a coach himself was key, alongside the drive, determination and will to win that I seemed to possess inherently. I just seemed to be born with a focus on football and an ability to be a positive motivator, and with the work ethic instilled in me by Dad, I had all the ingredients.

At school, for example, even at the age of 10 I loved nothing better than organising a game in the playground or after school at Pondfield Park in Dagenham near my home. Just give me three other players and I would happily lead them against all the rest – Jeff Fricker in goal, Marty Cooke as a defender and Richard Stout flying on the wing or up front. I loved the buzz of the four of us against the world, of upsetting the odds. I seemed to need the odds against me. And I loved winning, though it had to be by fair means.

It helped that I was taller than my peers from an early age and shot up quickly. I was a totem for the other players to look to and follow. Having an older sister who all the boys fancied did no harm either. It meant they literally followed me at times.

In all seriousness, I do think that – much as I hated it at the time – my discomfort and insecurity as a teenager, shown in my shyness around girls and my lack of academic ability, contributed to my personality as a footballer. I wanted to be the best. I wanted to please my parents.

Football was something into which I could put all my energies. I had found my 'thing' – and I always think it is important for kids to try all manner of activities to find out what suits them, what they are good at and what might be their path in life. I certainly have instilled that in mine. They all have different characteristics and interests and aren't necessarily sporty, though Oliver was a decent centre half for a while and Amber a good hockey player. I do see some of my own personality traits in Hector, my second son with Poppy, and he loves to throw himself into rugby.

He has what I had: an absence of fear on the field. It meant that I just loved getting stuck in, could get smashed, get up again and come back for more. It may have been – and I naturally didn't know this at the time – to mask all the insecurity I felt off the pitch, which is an environment to where you can escape and don't have to feel your feelings, an environment in which you can excel. When you can show that sort of fearless attitude, whatever the underlying reasons, players will follow you and your example.

I enjoyed stepping forward, needed to drive the bus. As a young player, if the ball was in the air and coming towards the defence, I would be the one to take command, shouting: 'TA's up!' Some people, especially on the opposition or in their camp, would take the piss out of me and that did hurt. But it also spurred me on. I wanted to show them, ram their words down their throats and head the ball back at them – with interest.

I became Arsenal captain at the age of 21, with the coaches at the time, notably Steve Burtenshaw, aware that I was a player and person who needed to be stretched. 'Just put him in and push him on,' Steve said. He was right. I needed to be allowed to run rather than held back.

I had a cockiness about me, I have to admit. 'All right, Son,' I would say to senior players such as Pat Jennings and David O'Leary. I guess they probably smiled at me, but I got away with it as I think I had the talent to back up that bit of swagger I had. I was confident and comfortable on the pitch. You have to be if players are going to look up to you. If you're going to lead at the highest level, you have to do your own job well or people will simply not respect you.

It actually became unnatural for me not to be the captain. I was happy to be captained by the great Bryan Robson when I first played for England but, later in my career, I thought Glenn Hoddle was wrong to appoint Alan Shearer above me. Terry Venables had it right – of course I would say that – and the result was the Euro 96 England team which the nation would love to have representing them now.

After I quit drinking, my change as a person was mirrored in the way I captained sides. I am sure, indeed, that I became a better leader when I knew more about myself. You've got to have something before you can give it away.

Before, it had all been about leading by example, unconsciously, instinctively. Now, I think I was more dependable and could employ some of the wisdom that I was acquiring and being taught in AA. I would think my style became more about carrot than stick. My words were probably equally as strong, but more softly spoken. I didn't need to shout so much in the dressing room. The growing number of overseas players coming in were unlikely to respond to that.

I could speak to Dennis Bergkamp in private, for example, to say with a smile that it would be a shame if he were not to win trophies while he was at Arsenal. I could tell Robert Pires that he needed to add toughness to his technical ability if he was to survive. Both took it to heart and reacted well. Dennis was magnificent as we won the 1998 double. Robert would become Footballer of the Year and star for the Invincibles of 2004.

It's not to say I threw the baby out with the bathwater. That hunger and desire, and – to paraphrase what they say in AA – being willing to go to any lengths to achieve, returned to me and underpinned all that I did in those six sober years as a player.

I also discovered a self-awareness and self-doubt that I probably had not encountered during my years as a drinking leader. There were times, in fact, when I have to say I was even scared.

Leaders, actually, in my opinion, are probably the most scared people in the world. They may exude confidence and often an arrogance, but underneath that – at least the best ones, I reckon – can be a questioning of their own position that may surprise people who only get to see a public face and don't think such people suffer from the same anxieties as they do. That is just comparing outsides with insides. They, we, are human too.

In fact, I wouldn't trust any leader who didn't have some

self-doubt. It shows an open-mindedness and willingness to embrace new ideas, to change and improve. But I do know that anxiety would manifest itself in leadership when the going got really tough.

I, for example, have been a bad flyer at various times in my life. I have got really anxious about getting on an aeroplane and have actually avoided it by taking trains or driving instead. But I am certain that if anything did go wrong, I would be the one up on my feet, wanting to sort things out, gathering people I could trust around me.

That is actually what the art of leadership is about – building and retaining trust, then empowering those around you. I may have changed as a leader, for the better, but that basic philosophy never does.

It was the same when I had Jeff Fricker, Marty Cooke and Richard Stout around me as a kid, through my early days at Arsenal with Pat Jennings, David O'Leary and David Rocastle, through the John Lukic, Steve Bould and Anders Limpar years, to the finale with David Seaman, Sol Campbell and Dennis Bergkamp. I picked my soldiers, led them and won. But, if it was to mean anything, it had to be fair.

5

A Sporting Chance

A hero is someone who understands the
responsibility that comes with his freedom.

BOB DYLAN

It was about two years into my sobriety when the truth of a saying in Alcoholics Anonymous really hit home with me. 'You've got to give it away to keep it,' it went. It is one of many wise sayings they have, apparent paradoxes, such as 'Surrender to win' and 'Hang in there – but let go'. For a professional sportsman, they were difficult to comprehend – surrendering to win, for God's sake? – but gradually their meaning became clear. Only by conceding fully that alcohol had beaten me could I recover from alcoholism.

The one about giving it away to keep it meant that to maintain your sobriety, you had to help others achieve it ...

I was getting plenty of phone calls from fellow footballers who had read my story in *Addicted* or in the newspapers and recognised something of themselves in me. It wasn't just drinking either. Many were worried about their drug abuse or how gambling was affecting their lives and those around them. Gradually, it was becoming understood that addiction was a disease, no matter the substance or damaging behaviour pattern. Calls also came in from players' agents, from family members and even friends of the family.

At this stage, around 2000, my playing career felt easy for me. I was in a great side at Arsenal. I was mentally and emotionally well, enjoying the single man's life and spending time with my children. Clare, my stepdaughter, was now nearly 16 and my two children from my marriage to Jane – Oliver and Amber – were eight and five respectively.

I was doing some really interesting things, like learning to play the piano and having French lessons. I began going to the theatre, and was asked to become a patron of a young writers' initiative at the Royal Court Theatre in London's Sloane Square. I was reading a lot, got to like JD Salinger's *The Catcher in the Rye,* read all of Nick Hornby's books after *Fever Pitch,* and took in all the classics I had missed out on at school – some Charles Dickens and Thomas Hardy, though I preferred non-fiction, such as biographies and autobiographies.

I was meeting people from all walks of life. I even went to see a modern dance performance featuring a friend, the daughter of Jerry Gilmore, the surgeon who had operated on my hernia a while back, and who even had a condition named after him – Gilmore's Groin. Well, it's good to be famous for something.

I was determined never to forget where I had come from, however. Given that I had been jailed for drink-driving, I was happy to get involved with a charity called RAPt – the Rehabilitation for Addicted Prisoners trust, which ran treatment programmes inside jails. I enjoyed going into prisons, telling them my story and trying to offer them hope. Naturally, I would get some stick from fans of clubs other than Arsenal. I remember walking through the blocks to the venue for the talk at one prison on the Isle of Sheppey in Kent and being given dog's abuse by some Millwall fans. Luckily, they were behind bars at the time.

I was also happy to become a patron of a charity called the National Association of Children of Alcoholics, having been put in touch by someone at AA with the Labour politician Mo Mowlam, who was their first patron and who wrote to me. Calum Best and Elle Macpherson were also patrons. While my mum and dad were not alcoholics, I wanted to endorse the message that it was important for children and young adults to know that they are not responsible for their parents' drinking.

Looking back, I felt like I was blossoming and I was finding new courage. Despite that anxiety of mine about flying, I took myself off to Japan on my own for a week's holiday during a close season. Arsène always talked fondly of the country, having been manager of Grampus 8 in Nagoya. He always said it was a spiritual country and that intrigued me.

I found Tokyo a bit manic, but hooked up there with a woman friend who was working in Japan and we travelled a bit. I enjoyed Kyoto. I was fascinated by Zen Buddhism and learned some basic tenets about meditating. It was all a far cry from the lads' booze-filled summer holidays to Magaluf and such resorts in the eighties, as was a beautiful and peaceful fishing holiday in Ireland that I also went on.

Naturally, I was staying close to AA and going to plenty of meetings in Putney, Chelsea and Wimbledon, encountering new people there as well, men like Ronnie the postman, Derek the tube driver and Pete, who was a musician, both of whom became good friends, and others who had good long-term sobriety. There's another old saying in the fellowship: stick with the winners; that is, those who are really walking the walk, not just talking the talk, and staying sober through the toughest of times.

These were special days for me and, as well as receiving wisdom from AA, I was having some fun too. I recall going to the Comedy Store in Leicester Square with a group of friends from the fellowship to see a woman member do an open-mike session. It was something she had always wanted to do, apparently, and now that she was sober, she decided to face her fears without any Dutch courage.

It was brave and it didn't really matter that she bombed. She did it. We all went out for a meal afterwards and she thanked us for coming, said she had got it out of her system. What could have been a depressing experience became an uplifting one.

I felt that, with a bit of good-quality 'clean time' under my belt, I had something to offer others now. When people in football were calling me about their drinking and asking for help, I tried to share my experiences with them. But while you can always pass on what you have learned, you can't get people sober. All you can share is your experience. Another old saying is true: you can carry the message but you can't carry the alcoholic.

I particularly remember a call from a Manchester City midfield player who I spoke to for a long time. I was also spending time with Paul Merson, who was then into his own recovery from drinking, drugs and gambling. I guess I was holding up a mirror to a lot of people and reactions were mixed. While some may have admired me, I'm sure others thought me strange. For many who have had a problem, there is often a sense of something being wrong inside but not being ready to confront it. It can be too soon for some.

Things began to germinate in my head and three events occurred which would prompt me into action . . .

Around that time, I met another pro footballer by the name of Alex, who had played in the Premier League. In fact, I was introduced to him while he was in a 28-day rehab at the Priory in south-west London. He was trying to maintain his fitness in there ready to go back to his club, but there was no special physical programme for him. He was just running round Richmond Park. That struck me as an oversight. I reckoned a player going back to his club after treatment needed to get playing as soon as possible to help him with his recovery, not have to get fit all over again mid-season and feel isolated.

Then, at an AA meeting in Richmond, I met this guy called Peter Kay, who was doing his 'chair'. He was a chef by trade and his talk was inspirational. He talked about how his drinking had led to him being in a coma, but when he got out of hospital he carried on drinking. Madness, but it made sense to an active alcoholic. He told of losing his pancreas and how close he had been to dying. Charismatic and enthusiastic, he had an amazing story and I talked to him after the meeting. We soon became friends.

Almost at the same time, I read something in the *Sunday Times* that confirmed to me that I had to do something. (Me reading the *Sunday Times*, who would have thought it? There were times when I would have been more likely to sleep under it.) The article was about a lawyer by the name of Ros Harwood, who was leaving her job at the Charity Commission to set up her own legal practice in York.

It felt as if all these experiences coming in quick succession were telling me something. There was this footballer who needed specialist help; a man with great communication skills who I reckoned could help me create a treatment centre for sports people; and a lawyer who could help me set up a charity that would finance it. I had also been impressed with how London Transport had helped my friend Derek the tube driver get into treatment and thought football could and should do that with its employees.

And so Sporting Chance – the name coming from Mandy Jacobs, wife of the guy at Arsenal who worked as a players' liaison and was in recovery at that time from gambling addiction – was born. In my head at least.

After that, it became about how I established the treatment centre and then paid for it. I had some money from the book deal for *Addicted* and, after paying off some of my parents' mortgage, I decided to put aside £165,000 to set it up. I managed to track down Ros Harwood and went to meet her. She said she would take me through the steps of establishing a charitable trust and she became the first trustee, to be followed soon after by my dad's accountant, Norman Ewen.

To acquire some credibility for the new venture, I also wanted to attract a well-known patron. About a year earlier, I had met Elton John at a Capital Radio awards ceremony, when he presented me with a London Sports Personality award – the idea being that I received it from a London station that was on 95.8 FM on day 958 of my sobriety. I was delighted when Elton, who had had his own problems with addictive illness and was now in recovery, accepted the offer.

The first administrator was a woman called Mandy Scott-Johnson, whom I had met at AA meetings and who had been clean and sober for a few years. James West, my therapist, became my clinical director. James would fret that he wasn't qualified enough at first, but he played a major part in getting me sober and I knew he would do the same with and for others. It was a giant leap of faith for him, given that there is a 50 per cent failure rate for new businesses in their first year. I was incredibly grateful to him for giving up a safe job with the West London Mission, a housing association that helped the homeless and those with addictions, and believing in me and the charity.

I, we, made expensive mistakes at first. I commissioned a report, for example, about the state and types of treatment in the UK ahead of deciding what I should be looking to establish. Basically, it cost me £28,000 to find out all about the business model of the Priory. And that was something I didn't want. The Priory got certain people sober, but I needed something different, something specific. I wanted something tailored specially for sportspeople. I needed a programme based on the Twelve Steps of AA, yes, but I also wanted an approach that was holistic and involved the physical wellbeing of athletes, as well as their mental, emotional and spiritual health.

I wrote to all the various governing bodies, such as the British Olympic Association and the Football Association, asking what they did for people with addictive issues. Not one association came back to me with a plan for how they would help athletes or players with problems. The BOA told me that they banned people for two years if they were caught having taken drugs. I asked what they did for them – and got the same answer: they banned them. They simply could not grasp the difference between doing something *with* a drug-taker rather than *for* them. And the distinction between performance-enhancing and so-called recreational drugs seemed lost on them. The Rugby Football Union, meanwhile, told us there was no problem in their game.

The Jockeys Association did let me in to give a talk and they did make a contribution of £10,000, which was very welcome, but it wasn't all about the money. It was about getting them to help us get their members into a treatment programme if and when they needed us.

This went on for some 18 months – me knocking on doors, being heard but not getting the message across – and while my motto had always been that if we helped one person, then we had been a success, in reality we helped very few. Meeting after meeting after meeting yielded nothing. It was demoralising at times and I just couldn't understand attitudes within the various sporting bodies.

I had always thought that if you played tennis at Wimbledon, rugby at Twickenham or ran and jumped at Crystal Palace – in fact, had given something to your sport – and then fell prey to addiction or mental and emotional issues when you practised or finished your sport, then your union should and would offer you guidance and even financial aid to seek help. It seems I was being naive.

By now, in 2002, I knew my playing career was nearing its end as I was injured a fair bit of the time. It meant I had more time to devote to the charity, but the harder I and the staff worked – the staff at that time being James and Mandy – the less Sporting Chance was happening, let alone thriving. My initial injection of capital was fast disappearing. We organised fundraisers, one at the Dorchester hotel, which did well enough in raising £25,000, but it was hard work and I just couldn't get past the feeling that governing bodies should be contributing to all this. Their members were the ones in danger and they should have a duty of care to them.

Enter Gordon Taylor, the chief executive of the Professional Footballers' Association. I had met Gordon previously at the FA's offices in Soho when Sporting Chance was just an idea, but now we were up and running – well, limping – he met with me again to consider what we could do for pros with problems.

They always say that the darkest time is just before the dawn.

This time, with some evidence to show him, he understood and grasped the concept that the PFA should be involved in helping its members when they encountered problems. And the timing was just right. Television deals were taking off and the PFA were receiving more income from them, so could thus allocate some to us. On top of that, Gordon had had some bad, and expensive, experiences with other treatment centres that weren't providing the holistic programme of physical training alongside the talking therapy that we were offering. He told me of one centre that had charged £36,000 for a 28-day stay, without the player concerned staying sober afterwards.

'So why not give us a go then?' I said.

We got a decision in a few weeks. Gordon pledged to help us help his members. Our crumbling charity was saved. He vowed that any player, past or current, who presented with addiction issues would be referred straight to us and the PFA would pay for them. And it looked like we wouldn't be short of business.

At the meeting, he presented me with a folder of papers. It contained details and case histories of a whole host of players with drink, drug and gambling addictions as well as mental and behavioural issues.

'Have a look at those,' he said. 'We've got plenty of players with problems.'

I didn't even need to look at them.

'I could have told you that,' I replied.

The encounters with Gordon gave me new impetus. Now we had some finance beyond my dwindling fund. It was time to find ourselves a chief executive officer. I took Peter Kay out for lunch – although actually the *Observer* magazine was paying. They had asked me to do some reviews of restaurants run or owned by footballers, and I took Peter along as he knew all about food, having been a chef at the Savoy and won awards for his cooking.

The idea was that I would interview the footballers – who were to include Gary Neville, who had bought an interest in an eaterie in Manchester, and my old mate Lee Dixon, who had a stake in the Riverside Brasserie at Bray – and Peter would brief me on the food. First stop on our itinerary was Gordon Ramsay's new restaurant at Claridge's in Mayfair, Gordon having been a young player at Glasgow Rangers before becoming a chef.

It seemed like a good chance to ask Peter if he was interested in becoming our CEO. He had some experience, having been involved with the Ark Foundation, a charity which helped people in the catering industry who had addictive illnesses.

Actually, I didn't really ask him. I just told him he had the job. I joked that I had asked two other people before him and they had turned me down so I was desperate.

Peter was flattered and honoured but wondered at first if he would be able to do it. It was typical, and the response I got from James too. We addicts always have that initial reaction of not being good enough, of not feeling we will be able to do the job. I think they call it 'impostor syndrome', where people with low self-esteem believe that they are going to get found out.

After thinking it over, though – and it didn't take him too long – Peter agreed and I knew I had a good man who shared the ethics and ideals of the charity, who knew the illness of addiction inside out but was in recovery himself, and knew me and how I worked. I had the spine of my team in place: clinical director, a CEO and an administrative assistant.

By now I had got to know Peter well and he had become a dear, close friend. A natty dresser with flamboyant blond hair, he had a real zest for life. We socialised together and any lingering thoughts I might have had that sobriety would be boring were dispelled around him. He showed me it could be fun as we had some laughs together, be it at jazz clubs in Dover Street or Chelsea coffee bars. He would also cook for me and arrange parties. He made me feel good about myself, telling me that I should be proud about what I was doing in establishing Sporting Chance.

He had quite a sense of humour, too. As a gift for my birthday once, he gave me a photo frame with pictures in it of the people he reckoned at that time were most special in my life – Caprice and him. Now, as we set about building Sporting Chance, that line from 'Moon River' seemed appropriate – we were two drifters, off to see the world.

Peter was especially good in the early years at forging a relationship with John Bramall, who would become Gordon's deputy at the PFA with special responsibility for player welfare, though I have to say our treatment was a bit ad hoc for a while. We would take players in, usually individually, at a place near Hook in Hampshire. It was owned by that surgeon friend of mine, Mr Gilmore, who was also an Arsenal fan, and he allowed us to use a coaching house in the grounds and the swimming pool.

We would bring in physios and fitness coaches to work with the players concerned and looked to help anyone who asked for it. It was mainly on a one-to-one basis and I would also go in and tell the guys my story and spend time with them.

The location and the one-to-one element were not ideal, however, and we needed more space to get more players through. So we moved to Sopwell House, the hotel near St Albans where England and Arsenal used to stay. There, we could get three or four players at a time through our programme if we needed to, given the good facilities and the availability of hotel rooms. The clients could also use the pool and we could train them in the grounds. In the evenings, they would go to nearby AA meetings, or meetings of other fellowships such as Narcotics Anonymous or Gamblers Anonymous.

It worked well enough for a couple of years but problems began to arise. The hotel was, of course, open to outsiders and we started to have concerns about our people being recognised and the press turning up. And though at times we would be getting small groups through, we were still mainly seeing clients singly. That was fine, as every person was valuable, but one of the essential elements of being in recovery is spending time with fellow recovering addicts. It is a disease of isolation and likes you on its own. You are more vulnerable alone, when you are left to your own thoughts and feelings. Easier prey. When people are in recovery together, they can talk things through and socialise as a group. With a common issue and bond, they are stronger.

This was where Stephen Purdew, the owner of the Champneys group of health spas, came in. Stephen was a big Arsenal fan, and in fact would take Box No. 1 next to the Diamond Club when the Emirates Stadium was built. Under George Graham, we players used to go to Stephen's Henlow Grange spa now and then ahead of big matches, such as cup semi-finals. After a conversation with him, he offered Sporting Chance a large, secluded house with the rooms we needed, in the grounds of his Forest Mere facility near Liphook in Hampshire. The clients could eat in the main building but had separate accommodation.

This was in 2003 and now James, Peter and Mandy could be based there. In addition, we would soon recruit, on a freelance basis, people coming in for specialist sessions, be they therapeutic meetings with counsellors or physical workouts.

Going out into clubs to deliver educational seminars also became a growing part of what we did. I would tell of my experiences and my recovery and Peter would give a talk on the physical effects of alcohol or drugs, using a dummy to show the damaging effects on the muscles needed to play the game and how recovery times after games and injuries would be so much longer when alcohol was a factor.

I particularly remember the seminar we held at Carrington, the Manchester United training ground. We must have looked quite a sight walking across the car park, Peter in his elegant tweed, waistcoated suit carrying the dummy, me towering over the pair of them. Often clubs would only let us talk to their academy players, but Sir Alex Ferguson made sure that all of the first-team squad attended – in fact, every player from the youth teams as well – and he himself was there overseeing it all. Of course he was.

It was a bit odd. I had had drinking sessions with some of the United players now sitting in front of me, either with England or on foreign tours. And here I was, telling them what life was like after some years of being sober. The whole room was respectful, such was the control Sir Alex exerted over them. There was no nervous giggling or laughing, except at some of Peter's gags. A few of them went, 'Wow!' Some would later come to see me and Peter privately.

Afterwards, we had lunch with Sir Alex and he took a real shine to Peter. From that day on, we were always welcome at United. I know Sir Alex has talked about issues he had with the likes of Bryan Robson, Norman Whiteside and Paul McGrath, and I knew that first-hand too, having had sessions with them around an Arsenal v Manchester United exhibition match in South Africa years previously. I recall Roy Keane having just joined the club and being out with us. In my state in those days, I kept calling him Kevin, after the old West Ham player Kevin Keen.

Indeed, Sir Alex asked me if there was anything he could have done differently to handle some of the players who were drinkers at the club. It was clearly something that he had thought a great deal about.

'Nothing,' I said. 'They were all going to go the inevitable way with alcohol without getting any help or treatment.'

Sir Alex became something of a standard-bearer for us. His huge influence within the game with other clubs and managers after more than 15 years at United at that time meant that doors now opened to us elsewhere, word having got round that we had been into United. We were very grateful to him.

Still, we were not breaking even, and the treatment of each person going through the facility was costing £8,000. That was fine if they were footballers, with the PFA paying for them on top of the core funding they provided, but other sporting people were coming to us with no funding and we were not about to turn them away.

We held fundraisers, one at the Guildhall in London, but didn't want to pay event organisers as we were a charity. We just about broke even on the night. We couldn't go on like this and I called a meeting of the staff and the trustees, the board who oversaw the running of the charity, down at Forest Mere.

We brainstormed for two or three hours. Peter, the controller of the finances, was his charming self. He reckoned that we were close to breaking even and that we should keep going as we were helping people. We all agreed with him but the cash flow was now a concern. We had let Peter get on with it, so enthusiastic a champion of Sporting Chance was he, and we had never got the sense that it wasn't working.

But I didn't think it should be such a struggle, and I didn't want us to fundraise any more. It was a lot of effort for little return, and I was tired of running around and calling in favours from mates for auction items, like signed shirts and days out at spas, for the events. It seemed that we were just keeping the place going to pay the staff salaries, which was not the best reason. Besides, we weren't really getting as many coming through and getting clean, sober and staying away from gambling at this stage of Sporting Chance's development as I had hoped for. There were a few relapsing back into drink, drugs or betting once they left us.

Overriding all my concerns about the effort going into the fundraising was my belief that sporting bodies should be financing all this. I had always felt it should be their responsibility. We would offer the facilities and the expertise, but they should be funding their athletes. That seemed to me like it should have been the deal. The PFA were great but their basic funding plus paying on top for individual treatments was still not enough to sustain us.

We also had a bit of a problem, I think, with the way we were perceived. As part of the charity sector, we were competing for funds with a whole range of good causes, but I am not sure the public would have seen us as a worthy cause at this time.

The illness of alcoholism and addiction was not really understood – many not even seeing it as an illness but instead merely a weakness. Nor was there an example of a high-profile footballer, or other sportsman or woman, who had been sober for some time and who could come out and say that they had been through treatment and that this programme of recovery based on the Twelve Steps of AA worked.

Most people, having read all about his alcoholic drinking in the latter part of his playing career, knew that Jimmy Greaves, the great England striker of the 1960s, had gone years without a drink, but his was his own sobriety. As far as I knew, he didn't go to AA and didn't use the programme. To me, that was a bit of a shame as I am sure he would have had so much to pass on to people who had newly stopped drinking.

And there were examples of people who just could not get the concept of the illness and the need to remain abstinent. Later, there would be Kenny Sansom, my old Arsenal teammate, and Paul Gascoigne, both of whom I and others tried to help on many occasions but who kept relapsing because they could not deal with all their issues and their feelings around them without a drink. Because they were alcoholics. Before them, there was George Best.

I met George on several occasions, the first in a restaurant in Dover Street in the West End. He was wearing a leather jacket with the word LEGEND on it. I thought that was sad. He didn't need to tell anybody that.

I was also scheduled to make a personal appearance with him once, along with Gordon Banks, but George turned up drunk an hour and a half late. Because of his lack of professionalism and no longer wanting to be around active drunks, I told the organisers not to book me with him again. People told me to loosen up but I was annoyed with them. They were all over George and that was the problem. Too many just condoned his behaviour and thus enabled him to keep drinking.

The final time I met him he was sober, down at Champneys at Forest Mere, next to the Sporting Chance premises in the grounds, with Stephen Purdew offering the facilities for George to dry out. George was charming, intelligent and articulate over lunch. That was his natural being when not drinking but alcohol robbed him of it. Too many people would tell him he was not an alcoholic and that's what he wanted to believe.

When I talked to him about AA, he said that he had been to meetings and was asked for his autograph, or to coach people's kids' teams. I'm not sure if that was the case. That never happened to me or to famous people I know who go to AA. But that was the ego and the denial of the active alcoholic who will find any excuse to keep drinking if they can. And it can drive them to their grave.

For me, it was vital to keep going to AA and to see people getting stronger in their sobriety, people from all walks of life. All people are different and have their own way of dealing with things, but this worked for me. I was grateful that there were people around willing to pass on their knowledge and experience to me, and I was now in a position where I could do that too.

It also helped me to see other people in the public eye – musicians and actors who performed in front of crowds for a living – managing to handle not drinking one day at a time despite all the scrutiny they faced. That is the great thing about AA – there is always somebody there you can relate to. Not only do you stick with the winners, as the saying goes, you win with the stickers.

I recall Paul Merson asking me around that time whether I

felt any pressure to stay sober, knowing that if I relapsed, it would be all over the papers and Sporting Chance would be blown as a credible treatment centre. But I never did. I was on my path and comfortable with myself. I was getting a lot of love from AA and other sources and I felt I had 'got' recovery – that I had found a power greater than myself who was walking with me and looking after me.

Not that I ever could or would crow about that. You never know what life has to throw at you and you can't predict the future. And my upbringing was that you didn't show off. I just had a sense that I could stay sober, one day at a time. It was a balance between being confident enough to spread the message publicly and not getting ahead of myself.

The Adrian Mutu case back in 2004 probably didn't do much for our image at Sporting Chance, either. The Romanian striker, who was then at loggerheads with the new Chelsea manager Jose Mourinho, tested positive for cocaine and the PFA asked us to take him under our wing and see if we could help him. It became a *cause célèbre* and attracted plenty of publicity that we did not seek and did our best to deal with.

Peter Kay worked very hard at doing that, and he also became something of a mentor to Adrian and indeed to other players who would come through Sporting Chance. He was very good at dealing with Chelsea and the FA, who would ban Mutu for seven months and fine him £20,000. Peter needed to be a diplomat as well as a good public relations man. In fact, he became the face of the charity for a time and while we were still in our early days, this was fine by me. His closeness with certain players also helped them, I'm sure, knowing that they had someone they could trust and turn to.

The problem in essence was that Adrian Mutu had very little interest in getting into any sort of proper recovery. This was mainly because I don't think he believed he had a drugs problem and it seemed clear to me that, when he came into Sporting Chance, he was doing what he was told to do without much personal willingness, as it would help him escape worse punishment by the game's authorities. We didn't really want to deal with anyone who didn't want treatment and recovery, but we were by now in a difficult position, as the PFA's go-to people when it came to drugs.

Indeed, they even wanted us at one point to become an arm of their work, to come under their umbrella. We were fierce about our independence, though. That's how treatment worked. Players needed to be anonymous at our facility, able to trust people who had nothing to do with their union or their clubs, so that they could talk freely about their issues. They didn't want to be going back to their clubs with even the possibility of private matters becoming public.

Thus – with the Mutu case an example of footballers' excess – a perception grew up around us that we were somehow simply a kind of safety net for people caught taking drugs, rich boys who had got into trouble of their own making. And, as rich boys, they should be able to pay for their own treatment. Why should it need subsidising?

Spoilt young men, who had everything done for them by their clubs these days, who went down the pub or betting shop and pissed or gambled it all away, just did not evoke much sympathy in certain quarters.

Those who advanced those arguments did not know two things, however:

First, anything about the illness of addiction. It is no respecter of status, wealth or power. It strikes at all sections of society, high and low.

Second, people like Adrian Mutu coming to us were few and far between. We weren't, at this point, getting the high-profile high earners who could comfortably afford the treatment themselves.

We were getting lower division and non-league footballers with their arses hanging out of their trousers.

Here we were, five years into Sporting Chance, having just moved into new premises, and I, we, were contemplating closing it down. Charities can be like that, I was told. Many do have a lifespan that comes to an end.

I hated the thought of shutting the doors, however, and I considered instead creating a foundation that would send players through treatment programmes at other centres, even if they didn't have the fitness and conditioning element that we had and which made us unique. Maybe, some people told me, it was time to let it go.

It was a tough call but, having got this far, I felt we just had to keep it going. What were sportspeople desperately in need of the sort of help I floundered about trying to find going to do if we no longer existed?

The decision was made to carry on, but we had to be more aggressive in securing funding. That would not be easy and there would be more transition periods before we got it right. Sporting Chance would come through and help get sportsmen – and women – sober, but there would be heartache and sadness along the way.

Indeed, what happened with the charity over the coming years would be mirrored in many ways by my own transition from player to ex-player to coach to manager. There would certainly be plenty of heartache and sadness, some of the latter very close to home.

6

Transition

Change will not come if we wait for some
other person or some other time.
We are the ones we've been waiting for.
We are the change that we seek.

BARACK OBAMA

Yes, endings do mean a chance for new beginnings, but after the conclusion of my playing career, I wasn't quite ready yet for a new start to the next phase of my footballing life – if indeed I was going to continue in football. I simply didn't know then. I just needed a rest from all the intensity of playing the game for 15 years at the top level and to do some of the things that I had wanted to do for a long while.

For many players, the transition from player to ex-player is painful and a huge deal, which is why the PFA's spending on education and welfare to prepare players for their retirement has increased so much. It is different for different people, but very often the retired player misses the dressing room and its camaraderie, which is why so many seek to stay in coaching, to be around training grounds and players and continue what can be a Peter Pan lifestyle.

That is not open to all, though, and those who don't stay in the game more quickly feel like a has-been and a spare part, getting in the way of the family at home. Having no real sense of purpose can lead to some players, morose, depressed, yesterday's heroes, seeking solace in drinking, drugging or gambling. There can be – have been – suicides among players with a void in their lives. Clarke Carlisle, who has endured depression and thankfully survived an attempt to take his own life, springs to mind.

I saw some statistics from XPRO, a charity for former players, from a few years ago which suggested that 40 per cent of players file for bankruptcy within five years of retirement. David James, the former England goalkeeper, is a well-known example. It surprised me the number was that high but they had the figures. In addition, they reckoned that four out of five ex-pros will develop some form of osteoarthritis. Worse, there were, they added in 2015, almost 150 former players in the prison system, many for drug-related offences, and 124 under the age of 25. I know this to be true. We've had some of them through Sporting Chance.

For the partner of the player, life can change dramatically too. At the top level, there is an undoubted glamour attached to being around a Premier League club and moving around the lounges at the stadiums, living in big houses with a network of friends at a club. Even lower down, players can be local heroes and their partners have some status.

Once all that goes, marriages and relationships can run into difficulties. Players and their partners are not used to being around each other for so much of the time all of a sudden and the dynamic between them changes. It is no wonder, according to XPRO again, that one in three players gets divorced within the first couple of years after retirement. That figure rises to 50 per cent after five years of not playing football for a living any more.

I felt very differently; I felt I was one of the lucky ones. I had had my rock bottom with alcohol back in 1996 and, ever since then, my life had improved. I had really appreciated the years I had left in the game and done my dream job, a privilege not granted to that many people in society. I did know that whatever I ended up doing next, I would not get the same sensation as playing, but I had learned that all things must pass.

It meant that I had pretty much prepared myself for retirement because I no longer defined myself solely as a professional footballer. I knew that if I did, it would leave a massive hole and I would find it hard to let go of the whole circus. Fortunately, I had a feeling of physical wellbeing and emotional euphoria due to my sobriety and I didn't need to replace the adrenaline of a match day. At the time, I have to admit, I thought that transitions were for other people.

Mind you, I still experienced 'football dreams' after I retired, and indeed can still have them to this day. Alcoholics will tell you they experience 'drinking dreams' for years after stopping, in which they are having a pint or whatever, in a bar or on their own, and the dream feels so real that, when they wake up, there is a moment of fear and shame before they realise with relief they have not actually had a drink and blown their sobriety. Usually, the dreams occur as part of a grieving process for a lost way of life, and as a reminder not to get complacent about what alcohol can do if an alcoholic takes that first drink.

For me, the booze was big – huge, in fact – but football was even bigger. My dreams were more often about me running around a football pitch kicking, heading, ordering and organising. I guess it was about being in control, doing something I was good at and knew inside out, when so often real life is about not being in control and needing to accept that. After these dreams, I would wake up with relief and realise I didn't have to go to training and punish my aching joints any more.

Physically, I needed to rest my body and certainly from that point of view I knew I had made the right decision. I watched the World Cup in Japan and South Korea on TV that summer of 2002 – applauded England reaching the quarter-finals even though I was never happy about Sven-Goran Eriksson, a Swede, being our manager – and saw Martin Keown on the bench. I knew that was not for me.

When pre-season came around in the July, it was actually a relief not to have to get up every day and have the stress of driving around the M25 into work. I guess I might have had some second thoughts if Arsène had let me just play games instead of having to do all the training – as Aston Villa did with Paul McGrath – but Arsène was not Martin O'Neill. Nor was he a Terry Venables, who gave me leeway when it came to training with England. Arsène was all about physiology. Arsène's way was to have all the players in all the time.

It was probably for the best. Some years later, when Zinedine Zidane retired, he came out with a memorable quote: 'It is better to go one minute early than five minutes late.' That sounds right to me.

In my last season, I did ask Arsène if I could train just on Thursdays and Fridays and do a bit of gym work on other days but he said no, he needed me out there on the training pitch the whole week. I did manage to persuade him a couple of times to give me time off, which meant I was able to play, rather than being injured due to over-training, but it made no sense to him really that I could do this. It was in conflict with all that he had learned and believed in. People prepared for matches by training with the team, not by resting.

It was the same for Lee Dixon, who also retired that season. One problem now was that, at the training ground at London Colney, the pitches were so firm. Arsenal liked a quick, hard surface so that the ball could be passed at pace. Lee and I would jog out on to the training pitch and be limping by the time we got there. Hard pitches seem to be the vogue nowadays because managers want firm, quick and slick surfaces to fizz the ball about on, but, because there is little give in them, I am convinced they contribute to injuries to players.

Indeed, Arsène would even come to accept some evidence of that and, more than 10 years later, Arsenal began to experiment at the training ground with a softer surface, with cork, sand and wool worked in below the turf to produce more give. It would still produce a quick surface but be kinder on the knee and ankle joints, and the aim was to install it at the Emirates if it proved effective at London Colney.

There were stories that summer that I was going into management, and, according to my Wikipedia page, I applied for the vacant Brentford job – and was rejected. I didn't, and so I wasn't. I was not ready for coaching or management, not yet. Not by a long chalk. I just had too much else I wanted to do.

I was now Tony Adams the human being, not just Tony Adams the footballer. I had changed and gained new interests during my first six years of sobriety. I played the piano – not that well, but I had learned to play a bit – and I had friends, a social life and AA. I had become involved with the Royal Court Theatre, having met the artistic director, Ian Rickson, a Charlton Athletic fan, who asked me to sit on a panel to judge a young writers' award. I was also recruited as a judge for a modern art competition backed by the *Financial Times*. I was now an avid theatre-goer and also enjoyed cinema and opera, going to Glyndebourne with friends. I even sponsored a new play at the Edinburgh Festival.

I was getting to meet some amazing people, too, including someone I really admired – Paul Weller, who was a fellow guest on that Ian Wright TV show where I first met Caprice. He had always been a big hero as I was a bit of a mod in my teenage years, with a parka and Hush Puppies and all. I was a massive Jam fan and later, for my 40th birthday, Stuart Peters, the agent who got me on to Ian's show with Paul, gave me a signed copy of the *Sound Affects* LP. They say you should never meet your heroes, though, and they are probably right. Some of the mystique and magic went when I found out Paul was a Chelsea fan. I liked his band more. They were all Gunners.

It was all a result partly of experimenting and finding out what I liked and partly of reading the Susan Jeffers book *Feel the Fear and Do It Anyway*, which always stuck with me. Her theory was that your life should have nine pillars – among them children, family, profession, leisure – and if you were to take one away, your life would not crumble. For most of my life I had had just two pillars: football and booze. Maybe I took the title of the book too literally: I did a parachute jump, down in Wiltshire, just for the hell of it. It was hell, too. Never again.

Anyway, maybe someone got the story about me applying for the Brentford job because I'd been seen in the area some time before. I did go out with a girl who had a flat there. That, though, was long before I met Poppy in those few months before my retirement, which was just before another woman came into my life in an episode I was not very comfortable with. In fact, her behaviour was very strange, as you might expect of someone who I can only describe as a stalker.

I had met her on Putney Heath near my home while out walking my Dalmatian dog Harry in the spring months just before my career ended. She was about five years older than me. We got into conversation but I was only being civil; it was no more than that – for me at least. The next thing I knew, a dozen red roses had arrived for me at Highbury from her. I actually gave them to Poppy, who laughed about it and still reminds me of it to this day.

Not long after, I was walking Harry on Putney Heath and I

ran into the woman again. This time, she had a Dalmatian. It was now getting a bit creepy and became more so when I decided to get another Dalmatian, which I named Sally – so I now had when Harry met Sally. She also got a second one.

One morning, I went to the door to pick up the post and there was a letter on the mat from her. She had read in the paper about a back injury I had, she wrote, and was recommending some homeopathic tablets. The next time I was on the heath with the dogs, there she was with a package of tablets for me. There would also be times when I would look out of my window and she would be driving down the street, slowing down in front of my house. A few minutes later she would be there again, driving around the block several times.

I suppose if it had been the other way around – a woman being stalked like this by a man – it would have been scary, but it never really frightened me, which was probably why I never did anything about it. I didn't want to be unkind. In some ways, it was touching and I even felt a little flattered. At first.

Then an article about Poppy and me appeared in the news-papers and she backed off a bit. Poppy did tell me that the woman had come up to her when she was walking in the King's Road one day and introduced herself as a good friend of mine, which unnerved Poppy a little. When I moved into Poppy's flat just off Sloane Square and put the house in Putney up for sale, thankfully it all faded away, though only after almost a year of it.

Later, Poppy would say that she too had stalked me, being an Arsenal fan. I don't doubt she had called me a few names from up in the stands despite that. Her favourite player was Nigel Winterburn. A left back may seem like an odd choice, but he had a rapport with the fans on the touchline and, having come from Wimbledon, he had some character about him. Poppy also liked his windmill goal celebration. She had a long wait between those moments, mind you.

That summer after I retired was a magical time in many ways as I embarked on my new life and the relationship with Poppy. I recognised very quickly in her a woman who was good for me. It helped, for starters, that she was an independent woman with means of her own and comfortable in her own skin and with her own status. She was not after money or celebrity. I had moved on in my life to the point now where I was attracted to an intelligent woman who was emotionally well. Being an Oxford graduate, Poppy was also very educated. I soon saw that she was an exceptional woman.

Not only did she look stunning in the purple Pringle jumper she was wearing when I first met her, but she also had a beautiful smile. I thought she was a good-looking woman with a great figure. Spirituality works, but I'm human too. As my therapist James says, agreeing with one psychologist who expounded the theory, there's an inner chimp in all of us, which is the part of the brain that controls our impulses. It's just a question of owning up to and taming it.

With all this pleasure also came pain, however. The summer also marked the death of the man who had been the biggest single influence on my life and career, my father Alexander – also my middle name – Adams.

In the June after my retirement, we went down to the villa I had bought at Mougins in the south of France, taking Dad with us. By now he was very ill with emphysema, and we travelled down on the train as he needed an oxygen tank always by his side to provide an airway and help him with his breathing. It was a special time with Dad. We were now closer than ever. The previous year he'd come down to Mougins a lot to help me buy the place, accompanying me to meetings with estate agents and architects.

Dad was the one who'd coached me in my early years and done most to develop my football career. He was the man who'd told me back in the mid-nineties that everyone around Romford, where I was doing a lot of my drinking with his clients and mates from his roofing business, was calling me a drunk and that I needed to do something about it. He had shown me love and tough love.

It was strange, though. He and Mum were always uncomfortable with me calling myself an alcoholic in recovery. A couple of years after stopping drinking, I took them out for dinner to a restaurant by Putney Bridge. I wanted to make my amends to them, as suggested by the AA programme in Steps Eight and Nine, where it talks about drawing up a list of people we've harmed and then making direct amends to them – apologising, in effect – except where to do so would injure them or others.

When Dad first confronted me about my drinking, rather than accept it was my own fault and responsibility he and Mum blamed my first wife Jane and her drug-taking for me going off the rails. Mum's little boy could do no wrong in their eyes. It wasn't the reality but they loved me and that was how they saw it.

I told them then about how sorry I was for causing them so much pain and anxiety through my drinking. I was especially sorry that going to prison for drink-driving had brought so much shame on them. My dad cut me off, not wanting to hear it.

'Look, Son,' he said. 'There's no way you were an alcoholic. Not in a million years.'

To them, I had had a temporary drink problem and all this recovery stuff was a bit over the top, even if they were pleased I was living differently to how I used to. I had to accept their reaction rather than try to force across my point of view. For a long time I had not understood the illness of addiction, so they could hardly be expected to. I left it at that. I had said my piece and made my peace. Cleaned up my side of the street, as we say in AA.

Dear old Mum wanted to talk about my house in Putney, about how nice it was and that I deserved it for all my hard work. That touched me. 'Thanks, Mum,' I said simply and smiled.

One day at the villa, with Dad settled and comfortable, Poppy and I decided to have a day on the beach at the famous old Le Club 55 in St Tropez, which had become well known in the 1960s when stars like Dean Martin and Sophia Loren used to be seen there. Once we arrived, I could sense that there were paparazzi lurking and, as Poppy peeled off her top to sunbathe topless, I told her about my suspicions. She was surprised and asked me how I knew. 'You just get to know,' I said. She didn't believe me but when I looked around more closely, I could see a long lens about 50 yards away. I had got used to checking out my environment.

I was right. A few days later, an article appeared in the *News of the World* with the heading above the pictures of 'Four Four Phew'. Quite clever, I have to admit, but not very nice, especially as by now the internet was in full swing and she would be all over that. Years later, I would privately win a case against the paper for hacking my phone, when they found out via my voicemail that Poppy was pregnant. As part of the settlement, I managed to get the topless pictures of Poppy removed.

A spate of articles about me and Poppy soon followed. One was headed, above a picture of the two of us, 'Whisky and Sober'. That was OK, I guess, and was quite funny. Another amused both of us when it claimed we had split up (I think it actually said I had kicked her into touch – geddit?) because of the differences between us. She was a King's Road, jolly-hockey-sticks socialite and me an Essex boy with his football mates, and I apparently thought we were incompatible. She got some stick off her Oxford buddies for that. Mostly, Poppy took it all with a pinch of salt and laughed it off, as did I, though she would get upset with anything in the press that she felt was unfair about me.

Anyway, that day on the beach Poppy's mobile rang and it was a friend of hers by the name of Paul Goldstein, who at that time had his own skiwear brand before selling it to Mike Ashley's Sports Direct. Paul knew we were in the south of France, but where exactly were we now? He was on a yacht in the bay, he said. Why didn't he come ashore and meet up with us? Poppy asked in reply. Oh, and he had a friend with him. By the name of Caprice. To wind us up, he said he might bring her along.

In the event, he came ashore but Caprice didn't, perhaps because they had been on the beach earlier for a while and she didn't want to make the trip again, but maybe also because she thought it would have been a bit awkward. It probably would have been, though Poppy was a bit disappointed. She was intrigued and wanted to meet Cap. She always kept saying that I should give her a call.

The holiday was a lovely time of eating well and Pops and I getting to know each other, but Dad was not a well man and was in decline. He died, in fact, not long after we got home, on 30 June, in St Francis Hospice, at Stapleford Abbotts, Essex. He was just 66, though given what he had been through earlier in his life, we had thought he might go before he did. He had had a heart attack in 1977 and would later lose a kidney and suffer a thrombosis.

It was almost as if he felt it was his time to go, now my career was over, and with my mum, his wife, having gone just over a year previously. He had taken the keenest of interest in my career, watching pretty much every game either live or on TV, and I had so much to be grateful to him for.

He, like Mum, was a good person. They had their problems and issues, stuff that happened to them as kids which they did not have the good fortune to be able to address as I was able to in recovery and through therapy, and which you hope your kids will not have to deal with as well. But you can also get too analytical. They played their hand the best way they knew how, for themselves and their family, given the cards that life had dealt them.

It was a well-attended funeral, with many figures from the world of football whom Dad had got to know there to pay their respects. Also there were people from his own playing days and from the Essex FA. Lee Dixon and other Arsenal players came too.

Afterwards, I received a letter of condolence from David Beckham and I was very touched by it. David had got to know Dad when he and his parents, Ted and Sandra, were invited into our hospitality box at Arsenal, and David wrote about what a good man he was.

It was a sad time but one that I felt I could deal with. I now understood more about the rhythm of our experiences, the ups and downs that were graphically revealed to me that summer. If you look at a cardiograph, the rising and falling movement shows you are still alive. If you are flatlining, you are dead. The trick for a recovering alcoholic is to find enough balance in your life so that you can go through both joy and pain without the need for a drink either to celebrate your mood or lift your spirits.

Now I was a parentless adult – the word orphan sounds strange at the age of 35 – and it was time to stand alone. At that time, the loss of my father probably didn't really hit me as deeply as it might have done, perhaps because I had prepared myself for it and was convinced I was emotionally well. But, sure enough, it would hit me.

I had had a few months off now and, while I had enjoyed it, I began to turn my mind to what I might do next with my life. Being a driven and goal-orientated person, I guess it wasn't going to take long. On top of that, some of my old impatience came back. I didn't want to go into management straight away, but I did think I should find out if coaching might be for me, to discover what I liked and what I might be good at.

I paid for myself to go on a course at Warwick University to do my UEFA B Licence, which is the stage that ex-professionals are allowed to come in at, being exempt from the various coaching levels beneath that.

There were quite a few notable ex-players on the course, which was led by John McDermott, head of player development at Tottenham, assisted by Paul Bracewell, the former Everton midfield player. Also there was my old Arsenal team-mate Paul Davis, the man who had written me a very thoughtful letter all those years ago when I was in prison about his hopes that I would learn from the experience. It went over my head at the time, though I would come to recognise its wisdom years later.

In the other group from me was Paul Gascoigne, who was his usual manic and funny self. I could see that he was great with the young players he was working with. People held his hand through the course and if only he could have stuck at it when he left Warwick, things could have been different, but of course he didn't. His alcoholism was still active.

My most vivid memory of the course is of Roy Keane being there and John McDermott having to intervene in a dispute between Roy and a student who, Roy claimed, had annoyed him by not listening to instructions during his coaching session. I warmed to Roy, though not because of that, I should add. He was an honest guy with interesting views. We played together on the same six-a-side team, so our goalkeeper was well protected. I would have liked to have played some club football with Roy.

I enjoyed the week, found it fun, in fact. It wasn't like playing but it was close to it, and people, both among the coaches and the players brought in as guinea pigs, were receptive to my ideas. I definitely came away thinking I had something to pass on and possessed the skills to do so.

My old need to find something I was good at and to be acknowledged for it was still there, even if I did try to deny it sometimes. If I played backgammon, I had to win. If I played the piano, I had to do it well. Actually, that was part of my recovery – accepting that I didn't have to be the best at everything I took on. I soon discovered with the piano, for example, that I wasn't going to be a virtuoso like Evgeny Kissin, and that was OK.

Around that time, I was contacted by an academic by the name of Gary Armstrong, who had heard me talking about retirement and my feelings about it on a radio programme. He wanted, he said, to interview me for a project he was working on. Gary was a Sheffield United fan, author of books on the sociology of football and a lecturer at Brunel University in west London, where they had a School of Sport and Education. We got on well and he suggested I could do a course at the uni and get a degree in sports science. It appealed to me on several levels.

First, I could do my coaching badges alongside the course, having learned that I had enough drive and determination to want to do it, as well as look more deeply into football and its culture, in conjunction with studying biomechanics, physiology and suchlike.

Second, and practically, I had more or less moved in with Poppy, into her flat off Sloane Square, and I was selling my Putney house so that we could buy a place together in the countryside. We had identified a house we liked in Gloucestershire, near Cirencester. I could organise and help with the move and divide my time between the two places.

(When it came to the house we found, it would prove to be an example of what a small world it is. Joe Strummer of the

Clash had once written a song called 'Tony Adams' for his other band, the Mescaleros, which had the lines: *Who is that screaming in Lunar Park?/ If they make Tony Adams captain,/ We could all go screaming in Lunar Park.* It turned out Joe's parents would be neighbours.)

Third, I could prove to myself that I wasn't the ignoramus I had thought I was as a result of my experiences at school. There had been a bit of promise there, after all . . .

In my first year at senior school, the English teacher Mrs Roberts asked us to write a story about ourselves. I basically wrote about how brilliant I was at football. She gave me a mark of 95 per cent and a star and said I was the best student in the class. I suppose I was good at talking about myself even then. Unfortunately, it was all downhill after that. She put me in for English O level when I was 14, and I got an 'Unclassified'. I never did take it again the following year. It was the year I went to Hungary for that England Under-16 tour.

It was interesting first walking into a classroom at Brunel full of 19-, 20- and 21-year-olds. I was not really nervous but I did feel about 102 years old. On induction day, we broke into groups to get to know each other, and I went with a few to a coffee bar in nearby Uxbridge. They were great kids but busy in their own worlds. I must have seemed 102 to them as well.

I think that whole experience of going back to school might test anyone's ego, let alone an ex-footballer who had had the sort of career I had and a recovering alcoholic a lot older than them. It made me feel humble, and I was proud of myself for being able to show that humility and a willingness to try something different. I remembered that being the former Arsenal and England captain did not make me better; not having a host of academic qualifications did not make me worse. The AA programme is about ego deflation and this was part of my recovery.

I had also learned by now to have some balance in my life,

by seeking to ensure that I didn't get emotionally too high or too low. Or too intense about work. Yes, I had to acknowledge the part of me that had drive and determination, but you can't take that into your home life. It will drive you into an early grave. Footballers are competitive people but you don't have to be the best driver, the best husband. Nor do you have to expect the same high standards from others too. When I was tempted to question myself, worried about perfectionism and any need to be the best, I tried to ask myself: 'Who are you comparing yourself to?'

It did me good to sit still in a classroom and listen to different subjects and points of view to discover what I was interested in and what made me tick. I hadn't forgotten that, in terms of learning, I was years behind the likes of Arsène and Jose Mourinho because I had had a long football career to occupy my time and attention and they hadn't. I may have known football in practical terms but I didn't know much about all the theory I was hearing. I was realistic enough to know that I couldn't just walk into a big coaching or managerial job without a proper grounding. Too many players think they can because of their name, reputation and contacts.

Gary Armstrong was good in helping me through, and he was an excellent football academic with specialist interest in anthropology, the history of sport, sociology and social sciences.

I quickly found out that biomechanics – the study of how the body works and moves – was not especially my thing and that physiology was a difficult subject. Psychology was too much Freud, too much theory. I preferred the natural psychology employed by Sir Alex Ferguson, the art of man management, which accorded with my own beliefs about how you got to know your players, how you treated them as individuals and got the best from them. Anthropology and sociology interested me, though, the more so when I realised I could write about my own experiences.

I also read a lot, books like Harry Pearson's *The Far Corner*, about North-east football, and a biography of Joan – formerly Hans – Gamper, the Swiss who founded FC Barcelona. I wrote essays on subjects as diverse as whether chess was a real sport and whether sport was play or business. I didn't, I have to admit, watch much live football. I wanted to get away from it for a while.

I did do a case study of West Bromwich Albion, getting hold of the club accounts to analyse in detail how you could take a club up to the Premier League and stabilise it financially. Later, I would use it as part of my coursework for my diploma in management that the League Managers Association set up at Warwick University under Dr Sue Bridgewater. It was a good course, preparing you for all the off-the-field stuff – interviews for jobs, being interviewed by television and press, and talking with owners.

Sam Allardyce was a speaker on the course and he described his own experiences in football. He was full of anecdotes that reflected his longevity in the game and his battling nature. He came across as a survivor which is ironic, looking back, given that some years later he would lose so quickly the England job he had wanted for so long.

The Brunel course also gave me time to go skiing for the first time. In fact, I went twice that winter with Poppy, who was a big fan of the activity, to Val d'Isere, where her family had a chalet. As a player, you can't go skiing for fear of getting injured, but it was wonderful to get the bug, a fabulous cleansing experience. You eat well, sleep well and feel free, relaxed and healthy. I was taught to ski by a great guy called James Dealtry. Again, it was nice not having to feel I had to be the best skier around the place, though I was determined to get off the nursery slopes after a couple of days. This holiday was more about being on the piste than something that sounds similar . . .

With the university terms being short, at 10 weeks each, there was plenty of time for other things in my life, including holidays. In late June/early July, we went to the Amalfi coast for a romantic break, staying on the island of Capri, then up to Portofino near Genoa. There I was, in wonderful hotels with the woman of my dreams, soaking up the sun, eating beautiful Italian food, playing tennis every day. How could life have been better?

It was then that it hit me.

It was around the first anniversary of my father's death and I was conscious of the date. Suddenly, out of the blue, I felt very alone. On top of losing my mum, this was the double whammy. I had no parents to turn to any more. The twin links to my past, the two pillars of it, were gone and it had well and truly dawned on me. A year earlier, I had been bound up in my own stuff – my retirement and my new relationship – but now the realisation of that moved from my head to penetrating my heart, and my veneer of having it all together just crumbled. The tears came flooding out of me. It was uncontrollable for three or four days. I just cried and cried.

Poppy couldn't work it out. I hadn't cried at my dad's funeral and she wondered why I couldn't be like everyone else – grieve at the time rather than a year later. I do tend to hold things in for some time before they hit home and I then release them. Again, I had no booze to suppress things any more. I just had to let the process take its course.

In fact, Poppy did get angry with me one day on Capri when we ran into a group of people she knew, a whole host of around 25 very lively people from the Sanchez Junco family who own the Spanish magazine *¡Hola!* She wanted us to go out for an evening with them but I just couldn't face it. To her annoyance, I took myself off to bed.

The memories of my dad came flooding back, of how he used to get me out of trouble. I recalled a time when I was about 15 and Dad was refereeing a game at Hainault and I got roped in to run the line. There was this mouthy central defender, a real bully, and he kept shouting at me to put my flag up – as I would come to do in my career with linesmen, at least in the George Graham days. Perhaps that was where it came from, long before George instilled it in us. The defender was calling me every name under the sun. He was killing me. At one point, I have to admit, I did put my flag up when I knew the opposition forward wasn't offside.

Enough was enough and, after one particularly bad volley of abuse, I just put the flag down on the ground and ran away. I turned back to see Dad walking over to the bloke and giving him a shove. I immediately felt guilty that my father was fighting my battles for me, but I was also grateful to him for sticking up for me.

I guess I would want to do the same for my own children, but I know these days how important it is to let kids make their own decisions. What I really wanted to do in that episode was turn round and tell the bloke to fuck off rather than have my dad sort it out for me. At that time, in that moment, and in the world we moved in then, my dad was doing the best he knew for his son, as he and Mum did when they chose my first house for me rather than let me do it myself. God bless him. Bless them.

I had become a man when I got sober and grown enormously. Now I had to become a man who stood on his own two feet. It needed three or four days of having an emotional breakdown for me to get back in touch with the reality of my life and where I went from there.

Eventually, I left the hotel room and I did what the treatment at Sporting Chance suggested to people like me, addicts who were sportspeople too. I worked my programme, praying to my Higher Power, and I got active as well. At Sporting Chance, we keep players occupied and fit through physical activities. I played tennis with Poppy and hit my way out of my trough.

The realisation also hit me on that holiday that Brunel was fascinating me but it was not fulfilling me. The feeling was confirmed when a new term and year started and I began to contemplate working on my master's degree – 'The Development and Production of Top International Footballers'. I had become friendly with Robin van Persie at Arsenal and he was to become one of my case studies, looking at his characteristics and the environment in which he grew up and was hothoused at Feyenoord of Rotterdam.

Having completed my UEFA B Licence, my master's was to run alongside my A Licence. The issue with that was I needed a group of players to coach on a regular basis – and it is naturally so much easier to have access to them if you are part of a football club. My old team-mate Martin Keown was coaching the Oxford University side in order to gain access to do his.

I was also getting twitchy about not being involved in football. Now, pre-season is an ordeal for most players, particularly the first week when you return. I had not missed the first year of pre-season at all. But something about the familiarity of its rhythms and routines gets under your skin. The second summer without pre-season provoked a strange, masochistic nostalgia in me.

Late October arrived and a job in football that interested me came up. The club was also showing interest in me. I went to Gary Armstrong and told him I was thinking of getting back into the game. He told me to keep writing, get to 30,000 words if I could, and they would look at giving me a master's. Get it up to 100,000 and I might get a PhD. It was definitely something I could come back to, we both agreed, and indeed in the coming years I would go on to collect more research and data for it.

The transition that I thought did not apply to me had actually happened, almost despite me. Life is, after all, what happens to you when you are busy making plans. I had retired as a player and found a new relationship. I had buried and mourned my father. It had been another year of loss, but with the reward of something new and exciting as a carrot to go with the stick. And it was preparation and life experience for the next adventure and new challenge.

7

Under New Management

A ship in harbor is safe,
but that is not what ships are built for.

JOHN A. SHEDD,
American author and professor

The question I was frequently asked in the immediate period after I quit playing was whether I missed the dressing room, with all its bonding, camaraderie and – the blokey word that everybody likes to use – banter. For some professional footballers it is, after all, as well as a haven of loyalty, a seductive bubble where they can lose themselves and escape from the real world.

I had been a player for so long, and had always been a bit of a loner using the bravado that drink gave me to cover up my isolation, so I was never really going to miss that atmosphere. After six years of preparing for the moment, I was ready. I was, as they say in AA, under new management.

Football had been a job of work. The dream job. But it was just what I did. I didn't do it for the camaraderie and the banter, to make friends or get a social life. And I didn't even do it for the money. I was there to play the game I loved. I loved training, loved the matches, loved the fans, the defending, the tackling, the scoring. Once you have done that to the maximum of your ability and extracted every last bit out of yourself and the game, it is very simple. You find another life for yourself.

Nor did I worry about not being well known any more. My therapist, James West, our clinical director at Sporting Chance, would also ask me that question. He is not a directive therapist but he would challenge me and, having once wanted to be a rock musician himself, he asked me if I missed being out of the public gaze.

I had never seen myself as a celebrity, although footballers can become that, especially in the modern media, and social media, age, so it becomes easier to give up if you don't get sucked in by fame. As a young player, I was barely recognised in London, but in my later years I was naturally known everywhere I went. In fact, being asked for autographs – and selfies these days – has increased down the years. I guess one reason is that I was part of some people's youth and they like to romanticise your role in that. Bob Dylan talked about it in his book *Chronicles*. You can transcend what you did to become something or someone else and thus a memory for people. It's as Nick Hornby suggests in *Fever Pitch* – fans often judge and measure their lives by certain games. Players can too if they don't find something new.

I could honestly say I never had the feeling of being concerned about going into some kind of obscurity. I had the tools to deal with whoever I was now supposed to become – emotionally, spiritually, mentally and physically. I had no regrets about my career, even though the underachievement with England and not winning the Champions League rankled a little. It, my career, felt pretty clean now.

Actually, I had spent so long in the public domain that I was relieved no longer to be in it on a daily basis. We all like the pat on the back and to be acknowledged – and, for me, it took a long time to be loved and receive praise for the career I had, having been ridiculed and called a donkey as a young player – but I could live without it. Part of being an adult is giving yourself a pat on the back.

So it wasn't to experience the dressing room once more, and certainly not to be famous again, that I decided to go for the job as manager of Wycombe Wanderers. It wasn't because I was pining for the football environment, or needing something to do on a Saturday afternoon at 3pm to get me out of the house. Or to prove myself. Or to beat Oldham away.

Quite simply, I needed to practise my coaching, to get a foot on the ladder that might one day take me to the top rung and the best fruit at the top of the tree. Dad told me to go to Arsenal when I was 13 because they had the best coaches – Terry Burton in the youth development department, Don Howe with the first team. He told me to watch the best centre halves and I did – Willie Young and David O'Leary, Bobby Moore and Alvin Martin, Franz Beckenbauer and Rudi Krol. Among all of them I found a player called Tony Adams, who was a blend of the kid watching the greats and finding out for himself what suited best his natural talent.

One day I received a call from the agent Steve Kutner asking me if Wycombe was a job that might interest me. Indeed it did, I said. It could be the first phase in a new learning process. As with playing early on, it had a purpose. It could have been Brentford or Arsenal reserves, though I did hear many good things about Wycombe when I came to do my homework.

One of Steve's clients was Martin O'Neill, who had famously started his managerial career with Wycombe before going on to such success with Norwich City, Leicester, Aston Villa, Celtic and the Republic of Ireland. Martin was willing to put in a word for me, Steve said, both to help me and his old club.

I also spoke to Martin before I went any further. He told me that it was a friendly club, with a great chairman in Ivor Beeks, who would support me.

'There'll be no money but you'll get a free hand,' said Martin.

When I came to meet Ivor and his board that October in 2003, it was almost as if I was interviewing them. They had just sacked the former Wimbledon player Lawrie Sanchez – who had had some good times with Wycombe, including leading them to an FA Cup semi-final in 2001 – at the end of September after 10 games without a win. I asked the board if they would stick with me if I went 10 games without a win.

'Absolutely,' Ivor said immediately. He was a lovely guy and it seemed a good fit. Even the ground, at the end of an industrial area on the edge of the town, was called Adams Park.

I had done my homework on the current squad and gave them a rundown, and I think they were impressed. They must have been, I suppose, as a week or so later they offered me the job, on a contract for the rest of that season and the following two.

When I took over on 5 November, Wycombe were bottom of Division Two of the Football League – now League One – with 11 points from 17 games. It was a precarious position but, knowing I would be given some time and would be allowed to learn properly on the job, I didn't feel under pressure. Ivor made it clear they were willing to give an inexperienced coach a chance and I appreciated that.

It started well enough, with a 4-1 home win over Swindon Town in the FA Cup in my first game. Afterwards, I spoke with Andy King, the old Luton and Everton player, who was then managing Swindon and who would sadly die prematurely of a heart attack in 2015 at the age of 58.

'What have you done?' he asked, smiling. 'Welcome to hell.' I could only smile back.

It would, however, be another six weeks before our next win,

2-0 over AFC Bournemouth in the league. In between, I would find out about the reality of the job and life in lower-division football.

That first game was also memorable for me noticing that the groundsman, Jim, was drunk when he came into my office to talk about something regarding the pitch. I recognised the signs pretty quickly, having had, shall we say, a fair old bit of experience of it myself in the past, though it didn't take too much working out. He could hardly stand up, in fact. I told him he'd better not let the chairman see him like that and that he should get his head down under a blanket in my office to sleep it off before someone else noticed.

Early the next week, I called him into my office and suggested that he might consider going into Sporting Chance to get some help. Luckily – and wisely – Jim chose to go, acknowledging that he did have a problem and, as I recount this story more than 13 years later, he is still sober not having had a drink. I look back to that time and think that I was supposed to be there, if only to point Jim in the right direction that day.

He was not the only staff issue I had to confront. I was walking into a political situation internally as I inherited John Gorman as my assistant and he had been the caretaker for a month. He had wanted the job himself and had the backing of the players. I had no problem with John, having worked with him when he was Glenn Hoddle's coach with England, and he was a good guy, but it was all a bit awkward.

So too was Terry Gibson also being on the coaching staff. He was definitely Lawrie's man, them having played together at Wimbledon, and he didn't want to be part of my set-up. He was off ill for a while and that became another difficult situation, though one not uncommon at football clubs when new managers take over and there is conflict between the old and the new regimes.

Sure enough, and soon enough, both John and Terry departed. With the club looking to make savings after paying them up, there was no money for replacements, people I might want to bring in, and so I promoted the reserve-team coach, Pete Cawley, who had all his coaching badges, to be my assistant. Actually, I didn't really want to bring in people from outside. I wanted to see all aspects of the job and do it myself. I would certainly get my wish.

Indeed, the job was an eye-opener. Over the winter I would come to see what the life of a lower-division manager was like and just how demanding it was. My salary was £70,000 a year, many times less than I was earning in my pomp as a player but for many more times the hours I had to devote to the job.

I quickly found out that the club was in some financial difficulty, losing £6,000 a week, which for a club like Wycombe Wanderers was huge. ITV Digital, which had signed a big deal with the Football League, had gone bust 18 months earlier and the club was still feeling the effect, probably having budgeted for the money, like so many clubs that had been left with holes in their projected finances. It was why I never claimed any expenses. I didn't want to add to their woes. I didn't even have a club phone.

Soon Ivor was asking me to build him a new team as so many players were coming to the end of their contracts. I would have a budget of £800,000 a year, around half of what Lawrie Sanchez had been given and much less than many in the division below us, or even the bigger spenders in the Conference. It might have got me Thierry Henry for a few months. This was new territory for me. I didn't know anything about budgets then and just got on with it.

I would spend my life on the road in the Mercedes that I had bought when I left the Arsenal and which would do 300,000 miles over the ensuing six years. Early in the week I would take training – opening and shutting the training ground myself – then head off to a match in the evening to scout players, mainly in the reserve teams of clubs such as Arsenal, Chelsea and Reading. It was all done with a view to the following season, as I sensed the players we had were not going to keep us in this division and I needed to prepare for a promotion push if we went down.

Most of the time, it became more about issues off the field. One of the earliest was when I arrived for the first time at the training ground about five minutes away from Adams Park and discovered there were not enough chairs for the players. This was just a little bit ironic. Wycombe is a town once famed for its furniture-making industry. Wycombe Wanderers are known as the Chairboys, in fact. But they didn't have enough chairs. I went out to a furniture shop and spent £500 of my own money on some second-hand armchairs so that the lads could have somewhere to sit down at the training ground.

I also quickly ran into some rivalry I hadn't been aware of. Just before Christmas, only a month into the job, we were playing Colchester United at home in the Football League Trophy, sponsored by LDV. Alan Hutchinson in the media department called it the Look, Duck and Vanish, after the old wartime joke that that was really what the LDV of the Local Defence Volunteers stood for. Anyway, it was not a competition that was a priority for me, let's put it that way.

In fact, I was planning to play some of the squad players who needed a run-out and to keep people fresh for a league game at Notts County on the Saturday. Word obviously got out about that and Pete Cawley, who had once played for Colchester, came to see me to say that the academy physio Terry Evans wanted to speak to me about fielding a weakened team. Imagine that at Arsenal – somebody trying to talk to Arsène about a team he might be selecting.

'Fuck off, Pete,' I said – it doesn't take long back in the

environment of football to pick up the language again. 'The academy physio is never going to talk to the manager about that.' But he did. And I asked Pete to sit in on the meeting as Terry was a big bloke.

It seemed that the Wycombe and Colchester fans did not get along too well. There had been dislike growing over the years and it really took off in the 1991/92 season when the two clubs fought it out for the Conference title. Both sides finished on 94 points, but it was Colchester who went up on goal difference, the crucial moment being their win in Wycombe's home game with a freak last-minute goal.

Terry informed me of the rivalry and advised me not to upset the supporters by refusing to pick my strongest side. 'With due respect, Terry,' I said. 'I am the manager of the club and nobody tells me how to pick the team.'

I suppose he would say he had the last laugh. We lost the game 3-2 – to another last-minute goal, in extra time – and Terry would go on to become the personal trainer to a new owner who would eventually take over at the club, thus lasting longer at Wycombe than I would.

There were some triumphs of recruitment. I got Nathan Tyson out of Reading reserves and the club would go on to sell him to Nottingham Forest for £700,000, which would sort out their debt. I also later got in the central defender Mike Williamson from the Southampton academy and he would go on to Watford, for £150,000, then Portsmouth and Newcastle United. It was a close-run thing, though ...

I had seen Mike playing at Torquay as a 17-year-old and made a note of him. He was now 19 and had just been released by Southampton. We gave him a club flat – with the poor old groundsman, Jim, getting kicked out to make way – and Mike came to me saying he was bored and asked if we could get him a TV. I went to Ivor and left it with him.

I was then called in by Keith Allen, the club secretary, who was a good guy and always really supportive of me. He said that Ivor had refused the request and had insisted the kid should buy one himself. Keith had communicated this to Mike, who hadn't signed yet, and Mike had reacted by saying that he wouldn't now be joining the club. I saw both sides of the argument – that of a player in a club flat, and a chairman who thought players were paid enough and should buy their own TVs like average people – but I couldn't afford to lose Mike. And so I went out and bought him a TV myself. Managers at lower levels often do that kind of thing and dip into their own pockets just to get the players they want or to keep them happy so that they will stay.

I do believe in miracles, having experienced personal ones in my own life in being saved from drinking myself to death, but not really in footballing ones like keeping Wycombe up that first season. There were false dawns like a 4-1 win over Grimsby, when I managed to get in Steven Taylor, then a kid, on loan from Newcastle and Luke Moore, who scored a hat-trick, from Aston Villa, but it was a grind.

I did make the side harder to beat by doing simple things like sending out a 4-5-1 formation for when we didn't have the ball and converting to 4-3-3 when we did. I got the side to reduce the gap between midfield and defence and tried to use the pace of Nathan Tyson and Danny Zenda on the break. We did limit damage so that we lost only two of 13 at one point, but unfortunately we drew nine of the 13; not enough points to climb clear of the relegation zone. I was pleased with points we got at Sheffield Wednesday and at home to Brighton, having lost 4-0 away to them.

In fact, that day at home to Brighton was doubly memorable.

Poppy was pregnant at the time and Keith Allen came to the touchline to tell me that he had received a call to say she had gone into labour. I left 15 minutes early to beat the traffic and make sure I was there for the birth of Atticus later that night. He was a bonny boy. We would attract some media comment for his name, which came from one of Poppy's favourite books, Harper Lee's *To Kill a Mockingbird*, with its central character and hero, the lawyer Atticus Finch.

Anyway, when I got back to work I could sense that, while I could organise a team, I was going to struggle to improve players who were just not up to it. We laboured on as spring arrived and duly went down. The fans were naturally disappointed but they didn't turn on me. The chairman also understood that this squad needed to be rebuilt.

I could only reflect on the irony at season's end of Arsenal going unbeaten all year, with 26 wins and 12 draws, to become the Invincibles while I was getting relegated to the Football League's bottom division.

That summer, I had to let around 20 players go. Calling them all into the office and releasing them is one of the tough parts of the job. I actually said a prayer before each day of having to do it, asking for the courage to see it through. It helped me to be honest with people. I always gave reasons.

Some were easier than others. Ian Simpemba came in to tell me that he had been offered the same money – £500 a week – to go part time with Crawley and he could also work as a gym instructor. It sounded for the best all round.

Another lad, Andy Reilly, came into my office with his dad. I had given the boy his first-team debut at the age of 17 and he had done all right, but they were looking for a three-year contract. Now, the lad was a straight-A student and had been offered a place at Cambridge. I told them I was going to do them a favour and not offer him a contract because he should go to university. They weren't happy but I believed it was for the best.

It was a draining period but it had to be done, and I knew that at the end of it I would have a blank sheet of paper. Hopes were duly higher for the following season as I cleared some players out and got some in, even if they were cut-price. We also had a new investor in Steve Hayes, who bought 25 per cent of the club for a £250,000 stake. He was more of a rugby fan, who would later bring Wasps to Adams Park when he became the full owner of Wycombe, but it fitted with the feeling of it being a fresh start.

In fact, we started well and had 17 points from our first eight games, though I suspected it might not last, given where the club still was and some of the things still occurring. For example, I had a centre half I was often at odds with in Roger Johnson. After that heavy defeat against Brighton the previous season, when he was sent off for a rant at an assistant referee, I asked him if he wanted to pay a fine or go for help to manage his anger. I think he thought I was nuts. He was decent, if not quite as good as he thought he was, and would go on to play with Cardiff City in the Premier League before moving to – and falling out of favour at – Wolves and Birmingham City, but he wasn't the most open-minded of people at that time.

With all the scouting and off-field duties, the problem was that I simply wasn't getting enough time to coach the players properly, which was, after all, the reason I had taken the job. They also weren't good enough, frankly, to absorb what I wanted of them and it became frustrating.

There was a day when I invited Lee Dixon down for lunch and he took the chance to watch one of my coaching sessions. As it happened, I laid on a session with my right back, a Dutch player I'd signed from Chesterfield by the name of Gus Uhlenbeek. It was a simple phase of play, involving the centre half playing the ball wide to the full-back, who would then take a soft touch to tee the ball up for a second touch that sent it forward into the channel between the opposition's centre back and left back for Nathan Tyson's run. That was the session in a nutshell and I was on the field showing them how I wanted it to be played out.

On the first attempt, Gus took a touch, then a second to drag it out from under his feet before a third to send it into the channel. I stopped the session and asked Gus to do it again, just using two touches as Nathan was struggling to know when to time his run. The same thing happened. I gave it one more try. Yet again, Gus needed three touches. He just could not tee the ball up properly to send it forward with a second touch. You might think a Dutch player would have good technique, but he had come to England early in his career. Besides, a lot of Dutch down the years have lived on Johan Cruyff's reputation.

On the UEFA B Licence, they tell you that if the drill doesn't work, you should simply throw the ball into the channel for the striker to chase. I ended up sending the centre half and Gus away and working with Nathan myself.

Later I went over to Lee on the touchline.

'Have you just tried to tell a professional right back how to control and pass the ball?' he asked in whispered tones.

'Welcome to my world,' I said.

'Unbelievable,' he replied.

No wonder Lee never went into coaching and preferred the world of TV punditry. It would have driven him nuts.

The temptation to compromise was always there. If you had a player with a long throw who could launch it in behind the opposition down the line, for example, it was very tempting to use that weapon. I always wanted us to play football and keep possession, but then things happen that make you question what you are looking to achieve.

For example, at Oldham, who were managed by the old Arsenal midfield player Brian Talbot – or Turn 'Em Talbot, as he was known – my right back threw the ball infield to the centre back, who slipped over and let the opposition in for a goal. Now you have a question to ask of yourself and a decision to make: do you stay with your philosophy and persist with players who can't pass the ball or do you play the percentage game?

Not surprisingly, in the lower divisions especially, so many do the latter when jobs are at stake. They start to coach the easy, safe option. I was concerned about becoming that coach.

It came to the first anniversary of me taking the job. Despite Steve Hayes now being a major figure at the club, Ivor remained chairman and he had a tradition of taking the manager out for dinner on the anniversary of his appointment. We went to a nice restaurant overlooking the Thames at Henley.

I told him where I was with the job. I had built him a team, costs had been cut and there was the prospect of selling players to wipe out any debt. We had also together overseen improvements to the training ground, Ivor's building company having come in to construct new dressing rooms and a top floor with a leisure area above it. There were offices and a gym, and we could eat there too. Previously the players had had to change at Adams Park and drive over and the meals had been brought across after training by dear old Jim the groundsman, who was now doing well in his sobriety.

The club was in decent shape, Ivor and I agreed, and the team was in mid-table, possibly, I reckoned, capable of a play-off push in the New Year with one or two modifications. I added that I wasn't particularly enjoying it, however. The club was not really going to progress much higher, I said, and I had gone about as far as I could with it.

Then, over the dessert – not wishing to spoil the meal entirely – I told him that I had decided to resign. I needed, I continued, to go away and be a proper coach somewhere, rather than just a solver of problems and mending and making do. I thanked him for the opportunity and for being such a good chairman to me. 'Let's just shake hands on it,' I said. I think Ivor was a bit shocked and he asked me to stay on. At the very least, he wanted me to sleep on it and see how I felt the next morning.

That afternoon, I was doing a chair at a prison near Oxford, so I drove up the M40. I had a few of the old doubts: Had I done the right thing? What would people think? I recognised that it was just the old voices from early recovery. I knew that I needed to find a new path.

Then my phone began to buzz with calls from the press. How they'd found out that I had resigned I don't know. These days, it could have been somebody in the restaurant overhearing, or Ivor having a private conversation with somebody at Wycombe and it being leaked.

Anyway, I was not going to lie and so I confirmed when asked that I had quit. It would duly come out that night and be in the papers the next morning. Ivor was upset that it came out the way it did, rather than the club handling the announcement, and looking back I could have managed the situation better by refusing to take any calls from the press. It was the first time I had been in this situation, though, and it was a learning experience.

I went in to the training ground the next day, said goodbye to the players and that was that. I think some Wycombe fans were upset with me, as was Ivor, but it was just their knee-jerk reaction. I wasn't doing the job – or now, not doing it – for affection or approval, though the fans had always been pretty fair to me.

I think I was fair to them, as well. In the end, I shook hands with Ivor and we parted on good terms. I didn't ask for the 18 months left on my contract to be paid up or anything like that, as some managers do by almost engineering their own sacking or in negotiating an exit package when they want to go. I took responsibility for my resignation. I had never been doing it for the money anyway.

I surely could have stayed on, could probably have remained there a long while indeed, as they were good people and Ivor would not have sacked me without giving me plenty more time. In fact, when Martin O'Neill later heard I had quit, he rang me to say that I should have given it another two or three years and I might well then have got a job higher up the scale.

My problem was that I just wasn't learning how to be a coach, although I had at least managed to get my UEFA A Licence while at the club. I had done the residential course at Lilleshall, this time with my old mate Steve Bould – then coaching in the Arsenal academy – Graham Westley, the Stevenage manager, and Marieanne Spacey, the former Arsenal Ladies captain among others. (Steve, as I recall, failed it on that occasion because he got annoyed and swore at a goalkeeper during a session. Which of us hasn't done that? And he would surely do it again when he became assistant manager to Arsène years later.)

I also came through the practical, when the course leader travelled down to Wycombe to see a session I put on. I was pleased with the way it went, with two attacking players working on a drill designed to improve their movement. In getting my A Licence, I had at least made some progress in my career.

I was, though, learning only how to be a lower-division manager – which is not the same as a top-flight manager – and was worried that I might get stuck, pigeonholed, at the level. I was not working enough with players, and good enough players, to enable me to develop and operate at a higher level one day. Some of them weren't as dedicated to their craft, or as aware of their standing, as they should have been.

I remember coming back from an away game at Wrexham, having drawn 0-0. We had not played well, with the game having been there for the taking. Had that been me as a player,

I would have been upset and brooded about it on the coach journey home. Instead, the players were having a dance-off in the aisles, laughing and joking. In the end, I just couldn't help but laugh myself and come out of my own gloomy mood.

I turned to Pete Cawley. 'It never seems to hurt them, does it, Pete?' I said.

'You've got to remember, Tone,' he said, 'we're dealing with broken toys here. There's always something missing with a player at this level. Either they're not quick enough or they can't head a ball, or they're one-footed or they've got a bad attitude.'

He was right and I understood that to a degree. I just wanted players who were teachable but, believe it or not, I didn't find too many at that time. There was very little inbuilt criticism of their own game. Their perception of how they played was always different from how I saw things.

Some also appeared more like fans than professionals. Roger Johnson always seemed more concerned with how Chelsea were getting on than with what was happening at Wycombe. Then there was an episode during my first week at the club . . .

I decided to get three senior pros into my office, as Arsène had done with me and a couple of others in his early days at Arsenal. Keith Ryan was a legend at the club, Frank Talia a decent goalkeeper and Michael Simpson a good, honest midfield player.

I wanted them, I said, to be my leaders on the field. I was looking to build a relationship with them and we spent 20 or 30 minutes chatting things over. As they left, Michael turned round and attempted a joke: 'I don't like you. I support Manchester United.' He giggled then made for the door. It was a strange moment, as if he hadn't bought into the mood and what we had just been talking about. Wycombe was his club. Not Manchester United. I was just gobsmacked.

Against that, there were some successes, which showed,

gratifyingly, that I was making a difference to some young players. I gave a start to a 16-year-old called Ikechi Anya from the youth team, making him Wycombe's youngest ever debutant, and he would go on to play for Watford, in the Premier League, and Scotland. In the summer before my departure, I also took on Russell Martin, an 18-year-old defender from non-league Lewes, after he had been released by Brighton. He would go on to become Norwich City's captain in the Premier League and lead Scotland. And send me this text out of the blue in 2016:

'Hello boss . . . I just wanted to say thank you. I don't think I ever got the chance to say it. You gave me a chance, a start in professional football. I'll never forget it and will always be grateful. I hope you've watched from afar and are pleased to see me, Mike [Williamson] and Kech [Ikechi Anya] go on to do what we have done (still lots more to come I hope!) and you are proud of the part you played in it. You're probably a bit surprised as well, ha ha!!' It was very sweet of him and lovely to receive.

And I guess I was still regarded reasonably warmly at the club as they would ask me, also in 2016, to record a video message to mark the 500th appearance of club stalwart Matty Bloomfield, whom I signed from Ipswich Town.

Back in 2006, I had also returned to the club for the sad occasion of the funeral of Mark Philo, a 21-year-old player I had given a debut to, who was tragically killed in a road accident. Afterwards, Steve Hayes thanked me for finding Nathan Tyson and for a £40,000 sponsorship deal with Jewson I had brought in just before I resigned.

Finding and coaching players willing to learn was enjoyable but I just didn't do enough of it. I could deal with agents – although I was surprised how many of them there were even at this level. I would meet many at youth and under-21 games who were themselves looking for the next big thing or trying to sell watching managers a player. I could also deal with the regional media, and even got the local paper guy into my office at one point to say that I wasn't worried about criticism, having had it in the national press for years, but that this was for a local audience and they needed information and analysis, not just tabloid material.

In addition, I could build teams and perform all the tasks necessary on the management side of the job, but it was a struggle financially – and not just personally, as it was costing me money, what with all the travelling I was doing. Wycombe simply didn't have the resources to implement a lot of the sports science elements I wanted, to do with physiology and nutrition for example. I had help here and there, with a strength and conditioning coach we used at Sporting Chance called John Goodman coming in for some sessions occasionally, but essentially I was a one-man band with little in the budget for anything 'fancy'.

One example: I wanted some mannequins for the training ground to act as a wall for free-kick routines. They cost £500. It was around the same time – shortly before I resigned – as an away game at Darlington when I wanted an overnight stay on the Friday. Ivor told me I could have one or the other. I opted for the mannequins because at least they would be useful every day. We ended up going to Darlington and back on the day, a round trip of more than 10 hours. We lost 1-0.

Sadly, I think the lower divisions produce a certain type of manager/coach. It is a really tough environment, with people being sacked right, left and centre, and they do what they need to keep their jobs, rather than work on a style of play and develop teams. You have had Dario Gradi at Crewe Alexandra overseeing a club and a philosophy for a generation, being allowed to build something that would last, but that is rare, an exception indeed. More often the thinking is so short term. It is all about the next result.

My goal in life was not to win League Two, One, or even the Championship. My goal was to work with the best players at the highest level. I was learning how to go to Oldham and keep a clean sheet on a wet Tuesday, which saddened me and I didn't like that feeling. Fair play to those who can but I didn't want to turn into that kind of animal, driven by anxiety and doing what was needed just to survive.

I did find some of it fun, and certainly educational, but I do wonder sometimes about the organisation of the lower reaches of the Football League, with so much travelling and such little income. I understand the interest in Wycombe v Swindon or Bristol City, but in playing in the same division as Hartlepool, for example? It would be far better being regionalised into North and South to my mind, and I am sure Darlington would have agreed. They might not have gone out of business and had to start again.

It was time to walk away, time to say goodbye to some days that started at 5am and didn't finish till midnight. I can't speak for Ivor but for me it wasn't a painful ending. And I'm sure for the club finding the next man was a matter of routine, as happens in the game.

I did switch my phone off for a few days afterwards and pondered how, eight years into recovery, I seemed always to feel a touch of seasonal affective disorder in November. It usually prompted me into a change, as it had done one year earlier when I left university to take the Wycombe job.

I couldn't afford to be SAD for too long, however, and indeed I wouldn't be, as something joyous was on the horizon. In fact, I had something else now to focus on that involved a joining together rather than a break-up.

8

Going Dutch

The past is history, tomorrow is a mystery,
but today is a gift.
That's why they call it the present.

Saying in AA

Poppy and I were married on Wednesday 15 December 2004 at All Saints United Reformed Church, in the village of Tudeley, Kent. It was a beautiful, simple, candlelit winter wedding but it was modest, just the way we wanted. So too the reception in a marquee on the Teacher family's estate near Tonbridge in Kent.

Not that it got off to the most auspicious of starts. I was having lunch with my ushers in Tunbridge Wells and left there at about 3.30 for the 4pm ceremony. I missed the turning off a dual carriageway, however, and ended up being late. Poppy, meanwhile, had to go round the block again in the car, confirming her suspicions of me that I could be a bit rubbish. Then when I did arrive, she wasn't there, which only increased my nervousness.

There were many highlights, not least being inside that church, which is the only church in the world to have all its stained-glass windows painted by the celebrated Russian-French artist, Marc Chagall. Poppy had an art-loving aunt she never knew, Sarah d'Avigdor-Goldsmid, who was tragically killed in a sailing accident in 1963 aged 21, and Sarah's mother, Lady Rosemary (Poppy's grandmother), commissioned Chagall to paint a memorial in the East window. Chagall liked the space so much that he ended up painting all 12 windows.

Another highlight for me came during my speech when I recalled what my oldest son Oliver – then 12, and my best man – had once told me.

'No offence to Poppy, Dad,' he said. 'She's lovely and everything. But I think I preferred a cuddle from Caprice.' Poppy, being a well-balanced person, took it well. I know Ollie also used to enjoy playing on the trampoline with Caprice in the garden of my old house in Putney.

For some of the guests, the highlight in the evening was the Elvis tribute act, who even had me dancing. Unfortunately, he was just about the only person in the place who got drunk and he had a row with someone, which we had to calm down. Poppy and I spent our first night as a married couple at the Pool House on the estate. I felt very blessed. She had an amazing family, who took me into their hearts.

I remember the previous Christmas spent with them, overwhelmed by love. Poppy's mother Chloe – Lady Rosemary's second and surviving daughter – came to me privately with some papers. They were the deeds to the flat in Sloane Square which she felt Poppy should have safe. I thought they were for Poppy's stocking and was taken aback that they were giving each other central London flats for Christmas. It turned out not to be the case, though. They were actually an unostentatious family and Lady Rosemary often gave them all plastic toys as jokes.

I compared it with the last Christmas before my father died, just a couple of years earlier and the year before I met Poppy. I wanted to make things nice for Dad, knowing that it could be his last. He was in a wheelchair at the time. I booked the Four Seasons hotel in Canary Wharf for dinner, and my three kids, Clare, Oliver and Amber came. My younger sister Sandra turned up on her own, having just split up with her partner, and the older one Denise arrived with her new man. It couldn't have been nice for my dad seeing his three children all divorced. It was all very fragmented, a bit sad.

We didn't have a honeymoon at the time – as Poppy frequently reminds me – but instead went up to stay with Ray Parlour and his new wife in the North-east for a weekend as they hadn't been able to make the wedding due to his football commitments. Ray was playing for Middlesbrough at the time and I went to see them play against Aston Villa, and win 3-0.

That night, Ray suggested that he and his wife Jo, me and Poppy and two friends went to a nightclub in Yarm. And so off we headed. When we arrived, there was a queue so we stood in line, with Ray suggesting I distract the bouncers and they all run in. Then a young girl in front of us in the queue was sick. I had gone with the flow but that was enough for me. 'Come on, Ray,' I said. 'Let's go home and have a cup of tea.' And so we did. All very different from a night out with him in Hong Kong . . .

After coming back from the North-east, we had a lovely time at our new home with Clare, Oliver and Amber all there for Atticus's first Christmas. Then it was skiing in the New Year. I was enjoying the good life.

I watched football, kept my eye in, and started on my Pro Licence, having finished the A. I watched that amazing 2005 Champions League final between Liverpool and Milan in Istanbul when Liverpool came from 3-0 down at half-time to draw, then win on penalties. In fact, it was partly as a result of that game that I found my next port of call.

Having become friendly with Robin van Persie at the Arsenal through my study of international players, it came up in conversation that Holland might be a good place to go and work. Robin was close to the Dutch football writer Marcel van der Kraan, who in turn mentioned it to Wim Jansen, previously manager of Celtic. Word of mouth and 'networking' are often how things happen in football.

Wim then put in a word for me with Henk van Stee, who was the academy director at Feyenoord, and I was invited out to Rotterdam for an interview at the De Kuip stadium. They had a vacancy in their set-up for a figure like me, Henk told me. They had taken note of Liverpool winning that final against impossible odds. 'Only an English team could have made a recovery like that,' he said. 'We need to instil that in our players.'

Henk outlined the set-up at the club: Mark Wotte, who would go on to manage Southampton briefly and work with the Scotland national team, was the technical director and Erwin Koeman, Ronald's brother, the head coach. Erwin had been brought in to succeed Ruud Gullit and been left with a lot of players, so the reserves had a big squad. Henk wanted me to assist Henk Duut with the reserves – the *Beloften* – as well as work across the club, helping with coaching sessions and the various age groups. Mario Been had just left to go to NEC Nijmegen and I was to be his replacement.

It suited me down to the ground, even though there was no salary, though they would pay my hotel and travelling costs. There would also be the logistical problems, of time away from home, but I could learn more of the art of coaching at a club – and in a country – where football was so technically conscious. I could finish my Pro Licence without being in any media spotlight. It meant I could just get on with the job without being scrutinised and having my results analysed, so that Tony Adams the coach was not compared with Tony Adams the player.

And so began another adventure, or a new one every fort-night, involving me leaving my Gloucestershire home on a Monday morning at 5am, driving to the Eurotunnel for 8am and being in Rotterdam for lunch ahead of a reserve game on a Monday night. Sometimes, for a change, I would drive to Harwich and get the boat to the Hook of Holland so that I had less of a drive at the other end, but in the winter the crossings became too rough and I would get seasick.

I have had many periods in my life when my fear of flying kicked in and this was one of them. In the Arsenal days, my fellow aviophobic — as the scientific name has it — Dennis Bergkamp and I had been known to keep each other company on a train while the rest of the team travelled by plane, and I would rather drive for eight or nine hours than take a one-hour flight. It also made sense to have my own car with me out there to get around.

I would then stay in Holland for 10 days, taking in games also in France, Belgium and Germany at the weekends, and work on weekdays on the Feyenoord training ground, with its excel-lent facilities and investment in youth, before going back home for my one weekend in two.

Away from the job, I also had plenty of AA meetings nearby, in The Hague and Rotterdam, which had the benefit of being in English. There were plenty of Americans around and where there are Americans, there is AA.

My time at Feyenoord was as educational for me as I hope it was for them. It was a remarkable set-up. The reserves and under-18s were in every day and I worked with them and their two under-18 coaches, Henk Fraser and Igor Korneev, who called me simply 'English'. Then the younger age-group teams would come in during the evenings. On Saturdays they would all play games. Also on Saturday mornings, once a fortnight, they would have trial games for kids invited by the 16 Feyenoord scouts around the country, which all the coaching staff would attend and note.

Now I had real talents to work with at the age levels, young players like Royston Drenthe, who had a spell at Everton, and Jonathan de Guzman, who played for Swansea. Then there was Bruno Martins, who would go on to play in the first team and the Dutch national side before joining Porto, and Evander Sno, who would join Bristol City. Martins' partner at centre back, Stefan de Vrij, would make his debut for the first team at 17, go on to sign for Lazio and play for the national team. He would also, touchingly, do an interview some time later in which he cited me as being a help and influence on his career.

It was a remarkable, formative time for me and I learned so much about techniques and the creation and use of space. Feyenoord had huge training areas so there was room to work, and they showed me how to put on sessions for offensive play, which I appreciated as I wanted to be seen as something more than just a defensive coach.

Holland opened me up to new ways of thinking, and not just about the game. It seemed to be appropriate to the master's degree that I always intended to complete and fostered the interest in sociology I had developed. In fact, a fascination with foreign cultures would, I soon discovered, become very important to me.

In tactical terms, I even learned some new stuff about defending, though while they wanted to find out more about that side of the game from me, I wanted from them more about offensive tactics. I had been used to the old George Graham style of a zonal back four yet now I was working with the Dutch preference for man to man. Sometimes, they would also play a third man as a central defensive sweeper.

I learned 4–3–3 properly as it was the system played right through the club. Away from home, it would be two holding midfield players and one attacking. At home, it would be one holding and two attacking. It was the only versatility they allowed. They liked 4–3–3 as it meant all areas of the pitch were covered. They also liked a libero, who played in front of the back four, not behind, like Ronald Koeman did for the Dutch and Matthias Sammer did for Germany.

If a team is losing, the English answer is often to put a big man up front – whether throwing on a striker from off the bench or pushing a defender forward – and to get the ball up early to him. It often looks good to fans, as if the coach is really going for it and doing something to turn the tide of a game.

Not in Dutch football. Statistics showed that it was much more effective to go 3–4–3 and put a centre back into midfield to make an extra man there. At Feyenoord, they would change the lines and shape of the team and that gave me another new insight. They liked wingers and players who were good one on one against opponents. They spoke of players by numbers rather than positions: a two was obviously a right back, three and four the centre backs and five the left back. The substitutes wore a plus-one number on their shirt, so 12 was also a right back.

I also liked what they did with goalkeepers. They wanted to make them footballers first and goalkeepers later, so often didn't choose the best person to go in goal until they were around 12 years old, making sure they learned all the basics of control and passing first. Even in the later age groups, they made sure goal-keepers were included in all the warm-ups and the drills before they went to their separate sessions.

My work there showed me I was right to leave Wycombe. The Dutch perception of the English coach was poor and they thought we were all kick-and-rush. I remember going with a group of Feyenoord coaches to watch Wolves, then managed by Glenn Hoddle, play at Den Haag in a pre-season friendly. Glenn had a reputation as a passing, possession coach but the Feyenoord guys couldn't see it in his side.

'The English don't want the ball,' one of my colleagues said to me. 'We pass, pass, pass and try and score a goal. Then they kick it back to us and we do it again.' The Dutch like to think of themselves as great thinkers on the game and indeed they are, though they can be a bit elitist about it. I couldn't really argue with them, though. I needed to learn differently, not get pigeonholed with that reputation, and I was in the right place to do it, to absorb a lot of knowledge and find my own best practice as a coach.

I was also in the right place to do some scouting, both for my own personal development and also for Arsenal. Steve Rowley, the scout who had discovered me on the playing fields of Dagenham and had now risen to be head of their scouting operation, had asked me to cast my eye over players for them. On my weekends not going home, I would travel round what is a very productive area for scouts – probably the best in the world after Brazil and Africa – that north-western corner of Europe.

Often I could take in a Friday night game in Belgium, maybe at Anderlecht, then head into Germany for a Saturday afternoon game and be back in Holland for a night kick-off. On Sunday, I would regularly head over to France, to Lens or Lille, for a game. It was a great grounding and I made a lot of friends and contacts.

I recall Steve sending me to Bayer Leverkusen to watch Dimitar Berbatov, but he was deemed too languid, even lazy, for Arsenal and it was Tottenham who took him. Then there was Simon Rolfes in Werder Bremen's midfield, whom I liked, but Arsène thought that, at six-foot-three, he was too tall to fit the criteria he was then looking for. At that point, after Patrick Vieira's departure to Juventus, he was preferring little guys in midfield. A memo had gone out to scouts asking them to look for players good at combination play and who would run 10 kilometres a game box to box. They were usually smaller and quicker.

I did text Arsène after watching Emmanuel Adebayor for Monaco at Lille and he agreed with me about his qualities. Another I took special note of was Manuel Neuer at Schalke, but Arsenal were unwilling to pay £25 million for a goalkeeper, even if he could have been persuaded to come to England.

I began to acquire some respect in the Dutch footballing community, and a game I took with the reserves against Ajax certainly helped mine and the club's cause. They are Feyenoord's big rivals and it goes beyond a tale of two cities. Ajax are the fancy dans from Amsterdam, Feyenoord the working-class club from more blue-collar Rotterdam – the dockers' club. I began to feel a lot of affection and affinity for a club known as 'The Club of the People' and *De Trots van Zuid* – The Pride of the South.

I experienced first-hand how intense the rivalry was, even at reserve level. When I parked my car at the Amsterdam ArenA, I was recognised and shouted at by a group of Ajax fans, who looked a bit menacing. I thought a bit of a run to the stadium was in order. Fortunately, they were long gone by the time I returned – Feyenoord having won 5-1, with Jonathan de Guzman outstanding.

Then, around Christmas time, I was approached by one of the club's directors, Jan Willem van Dop, who was about to leave to become president of FC Utrecht. He said he had taken note of my work at Feyenoord and would like me to go with him and become first-team coach at Utrecht.

I had little hesitation in accepting and said my goodbyes at the De Kuip at Christmas. I had worked with the kids and the reserves and learned much from being in the system and observing it in action: how they developed technique with the six- to

12-year-olds and tactics with the 12- to 19-year-olds. After that grounding, and having experienced the culture for half a season, I reckoned I had enough knowledge for a step up.

Two problems were soon to present themselves, however. First, Mr van Dop, known as Willem – nice guy that he was – was not the money man at Utrecht and, second, he had not informed the head coach, Foeke Booy (yes, that really was his name), that I was going to be joining the club in the New Year.

Not knowing this at the time, I went to see them play a game at Den Haag then drove over to Utrecht ready for work the next morning, as agreed with Willem. When I turned up, Foeke and his assistant John van Loen, the old Holland centre-forward, just sat in the office looking at me in an awkward silence that seemed to last for ever.

In fact, it would last a month. The two of them were used to doing things their way and they made it plain that it was not going to change, closing ranks and refusing to involve me in anything. I basically stood on the touchline watching training every day. I tried not to take it personally and I could understand their position – basically, another coach they had not asked for had been foisted upon them.

I was enjoying the country and the experience and so I looked to see if I could find another job. A head coach's job came up at NAC Breda but they wouldn't consider me because I didn't yet have the UEFA Pro Licence. In England, clubs are allowed dispensation for people who are working towards the qualification. I phoned Andy Roxburgh, who was technical director at UEFA, and his counterpart at the FA, Trevor Brooking, to see if anything could be done, but they told me the Dutch were very strict about it.

I talked it over with Pops, told her of my frustration and explained my belief that if I wasn't going to be able to get a head coach's position there for a while, Holland had given me everything I was going to get for now. She reckoned I should come home. She was by now seven months pregnant with our second son together, Hector, who would be born in the April of 2006. And so I did, feeling a bit like I was leaving with my tail between my legs. I got back into family life again, spending time with Atticus and enjoying another skiing holiday.

I also worked that spring and summer towards finishing the Pro Licence that I needed in order to complete my set of coaching qualifications, taking in a club youth tournament in France to study players, formations and patterns of play as part of the theory. Being on holiday in the south of France, I went on a study visit to Toulouse FC, then managed by Elie Baup, watched them train and with Elie's consent even gave a 10-minute presentation to players on some of my ideas.

It would be the following year when I completed the course with a residential week at Warwick University, where David Moyes, then Everton manager, was a speaker. It was more of an open discussion and a debate than a lecture and took in such topics as dealing with agents and star players, along with media and public relations. Hearing from him was fascinating.

Part of the course involved putting on a presentation and mine was a video session on how to counter the Watford team then playing direct football under their manager Aidy Boothroyd. The aim was to instil a strategy in a group of players that they would be comfortable using and which gave them a belief that they would win the match. For that, I used the Chelsea way of doing it, which had brought them a win and which involved switching the ball from wing to wing to stretch Watford until they opened up.

I passed the course and was awarded the Pro Licence, which meant that I was a fully fledged, fully qualified coach. I was one of fewer than 200 in England at that time – compared to five times that number in Germany and 10 times more in Spain.

As can be seen from those statistics, it seemed that English football did not set much store by the qualification. In fact, it was often mistrusted, with management by instinct and intuition more the mentality. When the Premier League stipulated that the Pro Licence was necessary to manage one of their clubs, often executives at clubs would find loopholes to employ the personality they wanted anyway.

Those who had been managers for 10 years were exempt when the qualification was first introduced, but they are offered little refresher courses from time to time in these days of more structured organisation. There is nothing like learning on the job but it's a bit like the modern driving test compared with the old, less intense one. It provides you with more detail more preparation for all the pitfalls ahead. There have been some old-fashioned managers who resented having to get any qualifications at all, of course, which meant that those from overseas were often better qualified.

I thought about getting back into the game in England, though was wary given my Wycombe experience. I wanted to be sure I would have a good chance of succeeding at a club, and also have plenty of time to coach players – and decent players – properly.

I also needed to be thinking about earning some money again soon. I had had two years now – at Wycombe and in Holland – of being out of pocket through my involvement in the game. We were comfortably off, don't get me wrong, but I had begun to eat into the savings I had built up while a player.

The Reading job came up and I texted Nicky Hammond, who was director of football there. I had played with Nick, who was a goalkeeper in his playing days, in the Arsenal youth team. He got me in to see the then owner, Sir John Madejski, and the chief executive, Nigel Howe, nephew of my old Arsenal coach Don.

Unfortunately, I made a mess of the interview. I began talking about a certain player, saying that he wouldn't play for England, at which point Nigel told me that he was Welsh. I should have got up and walked out there and then. I was never going to get the job after that. In the end, they gave it to Steve Coppell again.

I found the whole experience difficult. I was embarrassed to have made the mistake and it hurt me. I tried to tell myself that the interview was good experience for future job applications, and that I still knew I could coach players into being a good side. I had all the credentials and knowledge. The episode took me back to being a failure at school, though. All the echoes of the past crept in, of the kid ashamed of himself for pronouncing 'really' as 'wheally'.

It is that sort of memory that can be dangerous for an alcoholic. If he or she does not have the tools to acknowledge what is happening – that it is just a feeling and an echo of the past – the shame can take them over and lead them back to a drink just to drown it. When you drown sorrows, though, they have a habit of learning to swim. Thankfully, my sobriety was solid enough to own the feeling and share it, either by going to an AA meeting and talking about it there or with my therapist James.

I retreated to my Cotswold sanctuary but was tempted out in the spring when I received a phone call from Robbie Williams, ex-member of Take That and mega pop star. He was putting on a new charity event in aid of UNICEF and wanted me to take part. I would be playing for an England XI against a Rest of the World team, the sides a mixture of former players and celebrities, in a match that was to take place at Old Trafford.

Now, I was in two minds about it. I played seriously for 22 years and, when your last games involved winning the double with Arsenal, you don't really want to be playing over the park with your mates. Or even in celebrity games. Being the professional and perfectionist I always was when it came to football, I didn't want to risk my reputation while memories of me at my peak were still reasonably fresh.

And I didn't want the public to recall an overweight 39-year-old or for the media to poke fun at me. I didn't want to feel that sting of ridicule again, the hurt I experienced when some fans early in my career would throw carrots while yelling 'Donkey!' at me. I wanted to do myself justice. And I was still competitive. I wanted to win and wasn't going to play if I didn't think we could.

Perhaps at that time in my sobriety I looked at things too deeply. You can indulge in analysis to the point of paralysis instead of just doing things that appeal to you. And this did. In years gone by, I'd wasted too much time in my life worrying about what people thought of me, and I had made a lot of progress in just doing what I wanted to do and letting people think what they would. And of course it was a great cause.

And so I said yes. I thought it would be nice to be around some of my old Arsenal and England friends, like David Seaman, Les Ferdinand, Bryan Robson, Jamie Redknapp and, of course, Paul Gascoigne, who had all also agreed. No, I wasn't missing the camaraderie of the dressing room but a bit of nostalgia wouldn't hurt a few years on. And Terry Venables was coaching, my favourite England boss to play under. To add to all that, I was, to be perfectly honest, searching around for things to do.

Above all, I wanted to do it for Robbie.

Robbie has himself spoken of his alcohol and drug addiction, so I'm not betraying any confidences when I talk about our friendship. He is another who has had to live it all in the public eye. I got to know him when he got clean and sober and we met at an AA meeting just off Oxford Street in London and went for a coffee afterwards to share our experiences.

We would also have another, very powerful, conversation a few years later.

It was back in March 2001; I was nearly five years' sober, and we were playing Bayern in the Champions League in Munich. I got a call at the team hotel on the day of the game. It was Robbie. And it was one of those instances that may look like a coincidence to some but for people like him and me, it was a meant-to-be moment.

He was in Munich playing a gig that night, one of his first sober, and was nervous about going on stage without some form of alcoholic drink or substance to take the edge off, as he had often done in the past. Could we talk? Of course, I said. And for the next hour or so, we shared about performing in front of big crowds in big venues, about the butterflies and the self-doubt.

We all get scared, I said, but we have been given a talent by our Higher Power and I believe that my HP never puts me in situations that I can't handle. They may be challenging but I do have the resources to succeed in them. I communicated that to Robbie. The God of my understanding, I said, wants me to achieve and gives me the wherewithal to cope when the time comes.

'What if the audience don't like me?' Robbie asked.

'That's a possibility,' I said. 'But if it does happen, I now have the emotional equipment to deal with that situation.'

I told him I was a better player after I stopped drinking. That had been my belief and my experience and it would probably be the same for him. He would be a greater performer clean and sober. Nobody wants a shy legend, I added. Now go out there and give your paying public the superstar they want. Perhaps I was practising team talks.

Anyway, it must have helped, as sharing always does. It certainly helped me. I saw from watching TV replays later that

Robbie was in the crowd before going on stage later. He apparently wowed his audience in the Olympiahalle.

So it was that I wanted to support Robbie in the first year of this Soccer Aid venture. I wanted people to see what could be done by a couple of blokes who were free of drink and drugs. And I wanted to show that I could have some fun without putting anything mood-altering inside of me.

Once upon a time, I would have been scared of all the show-biz stuff, would have been a bundle of nerves and shied away from it, but I enjoyed all the build-up during the week, with Ant and Dec hosting nightly shows. And I enjoyed travelling the 45 minutes each day from the Conrad hotel in Chelsea where we were based down the A3 to the Fulham training ground at Motspur Park. After all the lonely travelling to Holland for much of the previous year, it was good to have company.

I was now 10 years sober and it was great to talk to Robbie and David Seaman and others. Gazza was still struggling, still a lovely guy but still scared. He hadn't been ready to get sober back in '98 before the France World Cup, when I tried to talk to him on the plane back from a friendly in Morocco and during that infamous time at La Manga when Glenn Hoddle cut him from the squad, and he wasn't ready now. There's nothing you can do if somebody doesn't want it. Ronnie O'Sullivan was due to be with us but he pulled out, all over the place emotionally at the time.

When we got to Motspur Park, I became almost Terry Venables' assistant. I felt in my element on the training ground now. It was good to be working with Terry again and exchanging ideas with him. I put on a couple of sessions, did the warm-ups. I was trying to show Terry what I had been doing in Holland and I guess I wanted to impress my old England mentor.

And I organised the back four. I put David Gray, the singer/songwriter, at right back and Robbie at left back. Ben Shephard, the TV presenter, looked like he could run so I put him alongside me in central defence. My idea was to get the defence sorted first. It was my environment and I could do that. Terry watched me and, more importantly as it would turn out, so too did Jamie Redknapp.

Then we needed legs in midfield, and Jamie was still fit, so you could work around him. The actor Damian Lewis also went in there. He was a nice guy, keen to mix with the group of football folk around the place, so wanting to be part of it all and fit into the environment. Up front we had big Les Ferdinand and there was also Robbie's mate Jonathan Wilkes, who was not bad.

We took it seriously while the opposition, under Ruud Gullit's management, looked as if they were winging it. I always thought we would win and we duly did, beating the Rest of the World 2-1, with Les and Jonathan scoring early on. The crowd – an amazing 71,960 – loved it when Diego Maradona pulled a goal back. He had some weight on and I was grateful he made me look like I was still in reasonable shape.

I would, by the way, receive a curious phone call about Diego around that time. It came via an Argentine journalist, Maria Laura Avignolo, who was close to him. Diego, apparently, was struggling with his own addiction issues, with his cocaine use well documented, and he had heard about Eric Clapton's treatment centre in Antigua. He wondered if I could arrange for him to go there. In the end, Diego didn't go but that was typical of the grandiosity of addicts – he had to go to somewhere exclusive (although in reality it wasn't; the treatment would be tough anywhere) set up by a superstar. Not for him mixing it with the lowly at some more basic place.

Anyway, after the game, there was a party at the Lowry Hotel in Manchester, which I enjoyed, pleased that I could these days be sociable without the need for an alcoholic drink. When I was drinking back in the day and confused by people who didn't drink, I thought them a bit weird. I'm sure drinkers thought the same about me when I gave up.

That's the thing about the illness of addiction – it wants other people to think we are weird because it is trying to keep us sick, fighting for its life. It wants us to turn away from people who are happy, joyous and free in an effort to make sure we also don't become those things. Most people who don't have drink problems, however, don't even notice or care, I have come to realise.

I found myself next to Jamie Redknapp and having a conversation about what had been a really enjoyable week and football in general. He had been impressed with my coaching, he said. 'You have got to give my dad a hand at Portsmouth,' he added.

'Interesting,' I replied. 'Tell him to give me a ring.'

9

Pompey Times

*Coaching is taking players
where they can't take themselves.*

JOSE MOURINHO

The phone did ring not long after the Robbie Williams match
at Old Trafford and it was Harry Redknapp. 'All right, Tony,
Son? How you doing?' he asked in that cheerful, bouncy way
of his. 'Jamie said to give you a bell. Come and help us at
Pompey. Come and have a cuppa tea and we'll have a chat.' It
was one of the first things I would find out about Harry. He
had the common, personal touch and was great at meeting
people. He liked to see them face to face, to get an instinctive
feel for them. He did it with players too.

I met him a few days later in London, at the Churchill hotel
in Portman Square, with Peter Storrie, the Portsmouth chief
executive, also there. At that point, I didn't know Peter and
barely formed an opinion of a man who would come to be so
controversial at Pompey. He mainly sat, observed and smiled.

'So you want to come and give us an 'and?' Harry asked.

I had pretty much decided that if the chance was offered I would indeed give him and Pompey a hand. I was grateful for such a big opportunity. It was a step up, a chance to work with Premier League players. I needed to get back in the swim. I'd not been around the top flight since 2002, and was thus unfamiliar with a competition, and its players, that was changing rapidly. Besides, I wasn't doing anything else, was I?

I said that I would love to have a 'practice' – that was to get some more experience of coaching, and in the Premier League. I told him what I had been up to, told him about Wycombe, Feyenoord and Utrecht, but I'm not sure he was that interested. He was more concerned about what I could do for him and Pompey than what I had been doing elsewhere.

One thing I emphasised to Harry was that I would not be coming in as his defensive coach. I made it clear that I couldn't be known purely as that. It was an easy label that people would stick on me, given my playing career, I said. I wanted to be fully involved on the training ground and I would need to access all areas.

'There's no point me coming down to watch you work,' I said, determined not to repeat the Utrecht experience. I needed to be hands-on, working, and developing as a coach, with a group.

'No problem, Tone. I'll give you enough rope to hang yourself, mate, don't you worry about that,' he said, and laughed.

Peter Storrie was ready there and then with a contract and I signed it straight away. It was for one year at a salary of £100,000. My title was to be assistant manager, the job having come up because Harry's previous number two, Kevin Bond, had gone to Newcastle United as assistant to Glenn Roeder, who had just been appointed at St James' Park.

I went down to the training ground on the day before the players reported back for pre-season and found Joe Jordan, Harry's number three, there along with Paul Groves, the reserve-team manager. Harry wasn't there at that time, and while he did come in during the first week, he took a back seat. He said the players were best left with the fitness coach, John Dalziel, for that period. There was no point doing much technical work with them if they weren't fit.

I was surprised by the ordinariness of the training facilities, which were rented from a school and sited adjacent to Eastleigh Football Club. This was a Premier League club but, with its Portakabins for changing rooms, it was hardly any better equipped than Wycombe. The club's stadium at Fratton Park, nestling in the middle of streets crammed with terraced houses, was charming and homely, but it was also outdated and lacking in modern amenities, certainly way behind the big clubs.

What made up for these deficiencies was the atmosphere and attitude that Harry fostered. It definitely made for an enjoyable pre-season which was a breath of fresh air to me. At Arsenal, it had been very regimented under Arsène, though naturally highly professional, while during my most recent experience at Utrecht, Foeke Booy had just been dour. This was a new way of working. And a lot of fun.

In fact, over the next couple of years working under Harry, I would have a ball. It was shambolic at times, it has to be said, but more often that was overshadowed by the innate professionalism that Harry possessed. Harry and I shared the belief that you could be focused on the job but could still enjoy your work. Over the next three seasons, I would come to see that Harry was passionate and erratic, ruthless and compassionate, kind and charming. And while I would also see an angry side that was rarely exposed in public, he did not hold grudges and had a heart of gold.

At first, we were all feeling each other out, defining what our roles were and how we would work best together. We also very quickly had a new man in the mix who altered the dynamic.

Harry was not best pleased when he heard that the owner,

Alexandre Gaydamak – known as Sacha to us and whose Russian-born father Arcadi, it was believed, had bought the club for his son to run – had hired as technical director a guy called Avram Grant, who had been national team manager of Israel, where the Gaydamaks were based.

It prompted Harry to fly out to Israel for talks with the owner, but it was soon smoothed over as Harry came back reassured that Avram was not going to interfere with his management. Just a few weeks with Avram revealed that he would never be a threat. He was such a lovely, warm, charming man who was not looking to stab anyone in the back. And, anyway, Harry was never going to let him get close enough to be a threat.

In the year Avram was there before he went to Chelsea and became director of football for his great friend Roman Abramovich, he mostly stayed out of the way, sat in his office and ate a lot, and offered advice about recruitment. He was also friendly with the 'super-agent' Pini Zahavi, which helped him. I got quite friendly with Avram and liked him. In fact, part of my role would evolve into being the staff coordinator, the man who would move comfortably from person to person liaising with everyone.

Soon, I had formed quite a bond with Joe Jordan, who was never a resentful man and made me welcome despite the fact that I was coming in over his head. He came to me to talk about his son Andrew, a decent centre back who had played for Bristol City, Cardiff and Scotland Under-21s but whose career had been ended by injury. Andrew, he said, was having a problem with alcohol – relatives often put it delicately out of a sense of loyalty – and needed some help. Could I do something? I thought about the best thing to do and gave Joe Peter Kay's number. I told him that Andrew had to ring Peter. It is important that alcoholics make the first move, as an important step in showing that they want to get into recovery.

Andrew did, and spoke to Peter. Soon he was going through Sporting Chance and it would prove providential for all of us. After coming through the programme and getting into good sobriety, he would train as a counsellor himself and end up working for us. Great guy. In 2016, he celebrated 10 years of sobriety.

Without treading on Joe's toes, I took over most of the training, doing all the possession and technical sessions, except on the days when Harry fancied it and he'd come out, take over and instil whatever message he wanted to at that time. I got in plenty of practice as a coach, as he promised I would. He never told me what, or what not, to do. Once the season got under way, on the day before a game I would leave the team to him to prepare, which was only right. I would have my input with the goalkeeper and back four on set pieces, while Joe would do the technical analysis of the opposition, as he was more experienced in that than I was.

I did wonder at one point in pre-season how we would ever get a side out for the opening day as Harry seemed always to be in the middle of overhauling the squad. Pompey had finished 17th the previous season, just four points clear of relegation having confirmed their escape with a 2-1 win over Wigan on the penultimate weekend, and there was certainly work to be done. He had taken over for a second spell only the previous November after an acrimonious departure from Southampton, the big local rivals, and now wanted to make a team in his own image.

At one point in June, we had 11 players at training but five of those were leaving. Harry said not to worry about it. He had some big players coming. Joe also told me not to be concerned. Harry liked a lot in and a lot out, said Joe, who had seen it all before. Harry had also recruited the well-respected Ian Broomfield as chief scout from Aston Villa and he was bringing his input to bear.

It became one of football's best-used lines when Harry would say that his squad was 'down to the bare bones', but we genuinely were at that moment. I actually think he loved building teams from scratch. To describe him as a wheeler and dealer was too simple a tag, but it was in reality a compliment, although he hated the phrase. He was a master at getting players to come and play for him, a superb recruiter. He makes you feel fantastic. He makes people like him when they meet him.

He was as good as his word about some big players coming in. Back in the January, he had taken a bit of a gamble with the Zimbabwean striker Benjani Mwaruwari for £4 million from Auxerre, which looked to have failed when Benjani went 14 games without scoring. The crowd took to him, though, for his willingness to work hard. Then two goals in that big win over Wigan cemented his position.

Now, before the transfer window closed at the end of August, Harry brought in David James and Andy Cole from Manchester City, Sol Campbell from Arsenal, Glen Johnson on a season's loan from Chelsea and Kanu from West Bromwich Albion. From overseas came Niko Kranjcar, from Hajduk Split, and Roudolphe Douala on loan from Sporting Lisbon.

Here and there, Harry felt he was picking up second-hand goods, with players either past their peak or cast-offs from other clubs, but they were certainly better than I was used to. The fees weren't enormous – around £2 million for David and Andy, while Sol was a free agent – but the wages were decent, I'm sure. I didn't really get involved in that, but Harry had the backing of Peter Storrie and the owner, that was for sure.

In fact, Sol's wages were a sticking point for a while. He was arguing with Harry about money to the point where Harry asked me to have a word with him, as I'd played with Sol at Arsenal. 'I can't believe it,' Harry said. 'He comes from Newham, for God's sake. But we need him.'

Finally, Sol signed and Harry felt that a big part of his work was done. 'Relegation avoided,' was how he saw it. Tactics and formations may have played a part in successful football teams but, for him, it was all about the quality of players.

I know there are many ironies about Harry, not least that he will probably have been well paid in his managerial spells, while hating players who were in the game just for the money and didn't love it. He will say, I'm sure, and I would agree with him, that he was good at what he did and deserved his pay. And nobody could say he didn't love the game. He always loved a footballer, one who could play a bit.

He got them in, I worked with them, along with Joe, and after a pre-season that seemed to be a tour of Harry's old clubs and a stay at Nigel Mansell's estate in Devon, we started in the Premier League like a train.

We had a good back five now, with David James underpinning it. He was an interesting character and I talked to him a lot. I didn't need to work on much with Sol, who was already accomplished and established, so took on Linvoy Primus as my pet project, trying to make him a better centre half by keeping his game simple. He responded well, leading to Harry telling him he was the real player of the season despite David James officially winning it that year. David kept clean sheets in his first five games and that season he would surpass David Seaman's Premier League record of 142 in total. He was exceptional but it helped that he now had a solid, organised defence in front of him.

On either flank we had Gary O'Neil and Matt Taylor at their career best, along with Sean Davis in midfield with the Portuguese Pedro Mendes. I worked a lot on one-v-ones with Glen Johnson, who made a lot of goals from right back for Benjani and Kanu. These were good professionals with whom I enjoyed working and, while Portsmouth may have seen some players of similar high quality in its past, such as the legendary Jimmy Dickinson who led them to two titles, in 1949 and 1950, I doubt they had seen so many in one team.

We were a very workmanlike, high-intensity team, who pressed hard and closed sides down. The statistics showed that if we covered 7,000 metres of high-intensity running as a team, we at least got a point. If we dropped below that, we lost.

We found this out by using, as was becoming more prevalent in the game, some very sophisticated computer programmes. Most people will have heard of Prozone without quite knowing what it does in any detail. We used a French company called Amisco, who were rivals, though the two companies would join forces in 2011.

The idea was that using TV footage from Premier League fixtures, a game was fed into a computer and would provide data both on the team and individual players, tracking them throughout the 90 minutes. Nowadays, players even wear special vests in training that provide data so the intensity of the sessions can be varied as the week goes on. Harry may not have always have relied on data, often using his intuition, but it was something a modern club had to employ.

By mid-September, we were top of the Premier League, having won four of our first five games, drawing the other at Manchester City. We knew it was a comfortable start – with the wins coming against Blackburn, Middlesbrough, Wigan and Charlton – and that it probably wouldn't last.

We had a good team but not a deep squad and, as soon as we suffered our first defeat at the end of September at the hands of Bolton, another three in five games followed, though they were all away from home. At traditional Fratton Park we were formidable. It was a compact, old-fashioned arena, with fans who made a lot of intimidating noise, and we were a tight team.

I enjoyed going back to Arsenal – now in their first season at the Emirates – and getting a 2-2 draw. In fact, we achieved some great results, also drawing at Liverpool and winning 2-1 at West Ham, as well as beating Manchester United at home by that score. Even a 2-1 defeat at Old Trafford in the FA Cup fourth round would prove a valuable experience for another day . . .

In fact, both personally and collectively, it was a fantastic season. Pompey finished a more than creditable ninth, just two points off a European place, with Sacha Gaydamak getting carried away at one point in asking Harry if we were going to make the Champions League.

I learned so much, too, not least about analysing the opposition. We had two exceptionally good guys working in our technical department, Michael Edwards and David Woodfine – Eddy and Woody – and they supplied data and video on opposing teams and players, which really furthered my education. They would also boost my ego by letting me and Paul Groves beat them at head tennis in the afternoons after Harry and Joe had gone home.

Harry was an old-school manager for sure and, for a while, I think it was difficult for him to adapt to and adopt more modern methods using technology that were second nature to a new generation of guys. He hated seeing his old mates in the game, those he looked after like all his scouts, being made redundant and losing their £100 a week pin money for looking at players and opponents when it was now all done on computer. They included his lovely old assistant from Bournemouth, Stuart Morgan, with whom he had a very touching relationship. Stuart would sometimes come and join us in the coaches' room after training, chewing the fat, telling football stories.

But Harry was clever enough to know he had to change and smart enough to let people he trusted get on with their jobs, allowing Joe to prepare the detailed analysis of the opposition with the tech guys and giving me a free hand in certain coaching sessions, which not too many managers would do. I felt sure Arsène wouldn't, so in control on a daily basis was he.

There were frustrations. Sometimes I would be sitting next to Harry on the bench and suggesting he make changes, perhaps going to 4-3-3, perhaps to make a substitution. Sometimes he would agree and act, sometimes he wouldn't. Whatever the outcome, the manager would always learn something from the game. But as an assistant, if it doesn't happen, you can't learn from it. Then again, while learning may have been my agenda, I accept that it wasn't Harry's. Results were. His head was on the block. Mine wasn't.

The flipside of that is that, as a number two, you are protected. If you lose a game it hurts, but not as much as for the manager. It means equally that, if you win a game, you don't feel quite as triumphant. I knew at some stage that I would want to get my own team again, to be in charge. I have always found it difficult to take orders and prefer giving them out. I am an addict, after all. And, I like to think, a leader.

I'm sure Harry saw me as a bit aloof. Maybe even a bit strange. In fact, I know he did because that was the feedback I got from somebody I knew who was close to Milan Mandaric, the former Pompey owner who then took over at Leicester and with whom Harry still spoke.

I don't think it was anything to do with me not drinking. I like to think he was respectful of that and, also, he probably wasn't even interested. I must admit it was not something I ever talked about in front of him. He was my boss after all. No, I think he just found me different to what he'd expected me to be. Now, I was more composed, a more calming influence than I had been when he saw me as a player in the up-and-at-'em days.

The game had changed and I had changed. As a young player, I was brought up in a tough school. I always remember the

Arsenal caretaker manager Steve Burtenshaw making the phrase 'Kick, bollock and bite' part of his team talk, as an exhortation before we went out. It stuck with me but it was just no longer relevant. All that hairdryer stuff – the term used to describe Sir Alex Ferguson standing in front of a player and giving him a blast of verbals – was changing. Sir Alex himself knew it.

I never had any trouble motivating myself, but I was simply much less noisy about it in my latter days as a player. I know fans like to see passion and pride in the shirt – and I do too – but it's not always about being showy. More often you need to keep a clear head, rather than be too wound up and make mistakes. A lot more players nowadays just want to be quiet in the dressing room to prepare mentally, and gradually in my career I learned about delivering messages more effectively. It was a case of strong words, calmly but firmly spoken. And for all his own old-school reputation, I only ever saw Harry deliver one bollocking and that was in a pre-season friendly, as will be seen . . . Credit to him. He changed as well.

I often made my own way to away games, which would also have made me look a bit of a loner. The team were flying to pretty much every away game north of London, even to Birmingham, on a Friday, out of Southampton airport. I preferred to go home to the Cotswolds then drive to the ground on the Saturday, ready to sit at Harry's shoulder for pre-match.

Over the summer before my second year at the club, Harry had another busy period of developing his squad, shifting some on and bringing in another consignment of very good players. Out went Andy Cole to Sunderland. Gary O'Neil went to Middlesbrough while Lomana LuaLua left for Olympiacos and Dejan Stefanovic for Fulham. Plenty more further down the pecking order left too.

Against that, Glen Johnson signed permanently from Chelsea,

while John Utaka came from Rennes, Sulley Muntari from Udinese, David Nugent from Preston, Sylvain Distin on a free from Manchester City and Papa Bouba Diop from Fulham. Plenty more to bolster squad numbers arrived too.

The deficit in dealing was around £25 million, but the club seemed to have it to spend. It was part of Harry's desire to push the club on from that ninth place that both he and the owners wanted. We certainly looked like a Premier League squad now, deeper and with much more quality. It would show as the season unfolded into one of the greatest in the club's history.

We went from the high-pressing, tough-to-beat team to one that could dictate the play and be on the front foot rather than sit back. David James had a back four in front of him of Glen Johnson, Sol, Sylvain and Hermann Hreidarsson, both full-backs capable of bombing on. Sylvain was not the best on his right foot but improved us, while Hermann had a great attitude.

We looked more like a natural 4-3-3, as I said to Harry, with Papa Bouba Diop, Pedro Mendes, who could keep the ball, and Sulley Muntari in midfield, while further forward there was Niko Kranjcar coming in off the left on to his right foot, John Utaka on the right and Benjani or Kanu centrally up front.

Despite starting off patchily, taking only nine points from our first seven games, I knew we would be all right. We were just too good not to be. Then came a 7-4 win at home to Reading, setting a Premier League record for the number of goals scored in one game. I remember nothing about it. I refuse to. I have blanked it from my mind. I hate games like that.

I can recall more easily the game early on at Chelsea, where we lost 1-0, which is more my type of result, though naturally I would have preferred it the other way round. Afterwards, Jose Mourinho, in one of his final matches before the end of his first spell at Stamford Bridge, invited me into his office. There he produced that Arsenal shirt he had retrieved from our laundry basket that night at Wembley when we played Barcelona in the Champions League. And he asked me to sign it. I was very flattered.

By the turn of the year and the midpoint of the season, we were comfortably mid-table and we were thinking of Europe. Come January, we were also thinking of the FA Cup, being in a good position for a run with no danger of relegation, though Harry had a few bits of business to do before then.

Benjani had done well for us in the first half of the season and he attracted the interest of Manchester City, then managed by Sven-Goran Eriksson. They offered £7.5 million for him with all the add-ons and Harry took it. The only problem was that the player did not want to leave. He loved it on the south coast. In fact, Benjani was in tears when Harry told him he was selling him and that he had to go.

That was where I saw Harry's ruthless side. Benjani's tears counted for little. Harry knew the money was good and it would also enable him to do other deals, most notably the signing of Jermain Defoe from Tottenham for £7.5 million. He also took Milan Baros on loan from Lyon as Jermain was cup-tied. Matt Taylor left in that window too, for Bolton, while in came a player from Arsenal who would prove great business.

We got Lassana Diarra because Arsène wanted all his players to do 1,000 metres of high-intensity running during a game, out of the average 10,000 metres that midfield players cover. 'Lassie' never achieved that at Arsenal and so was sold on, in this case for £5 million. In fact, with us early on, the stats showed that he was doing just 400 to 500 metres. He was decent over five or 10 yards, but he simply couldn't do the distances at high intensity. Still, I liked him as a player for his ability to protect the ball and the back four and said to Harry that he could just sit in there and do a great job for us. We would play to his strengths and perhaps in return he would increase his distances.

Harry loved the FA Cup almost as much as a transfer bargain, and this year he wanted to give it a good go, knowing that we were strong and the bigger clubs were never as bothered about it these days due to the European competition they were usually involved in.

The third round sent us to Ipswich and it was a tricky tie against a Championship side. David James had a great game, though, and we clung on for a 1-0 win. It brought us a home tie against Plymouth Argyle.

Harry wanted to play his first-choice team. He always wanted to play his strongest team. Joe and I, though, pointed out that we had Manchester United four days later in the Premier League and we prevailed this time, sending out a smattering of squad players who needed to play. Thankfully, the team prevailed too, by 2-1, with Lassie, who needed the game time having not been playing for Arsenal, scoring a goal.

Sometimes Harry and Joe would have some serious ding-dongs and I found myself mediating on more than one occasion. Harry, for example, would want to play 4-4-2, Joe would want to go 4-5-1.

'Fuck off, Joe,' Harry would say.

'Harry, you cannot play that way. It's too attacking. We will get smashed if we play that way,' Joe would reply. He could be fearsome, as he was in his playing days for Leeds, Manchester United, Verona and Scotland, with that snarl of his made more intimidating by not keeping in his denture to cover his missing front teeth.

On it would go until I said, 'Enough' or it had run its course. It would depend on how Harry saw the game, with that canny intuition of his, as to who would prevail. Me? I would side with whoever I thought made the better argument.

The great thing was there were never any grudges and that has always been one of the good things about football in general – mostly – and Harry in particular. You would soon be back in each other's good books again. It was also to Harry's credit that he didn't just employ yes-men.

I enjoyed all those times after training when Harry would come into the coaches' office having changed into his civvies and want a chat and a gossip. He would relay stories, his phone going off all the time, often with agents calling him. 'No, don't like him, Athole,' he would say or, 'Yeah, love him, Pini. You've got to get him for us.'

I particularly liked a story he told about John Hartson at West Ham when he was fed up with him and his lack of contribution during a game.

'Warm up, John,' Harry shouted from the dugout. 'You're coming on, Son.'

As our cup run built, he would always be in there talking about the draw and how far we could go, loving it when a big team went out, as plenty were doing that season. His belief increased after the fifth-round 1-0 win at Preston, when we had that bit of luck all teams who have a cup run can point to, as David James saved a penalty and we nicked a goal in the last minute. It was an old Arsenal performance under George Graham based on a good goalkeeper, a solid back four and a striker who can take a chance, except at Deepdale we didn't need that as the winner was an own goal.

Because it is so rare in the modern era, I can remember the draw for the quarter-finals being made on a Monday lunchtime, though the fact that Harry was less cheery and less quick to come through to the coaches' office had nothing to do with any back-to-work feeling. In fact, we were in there, Harry was in his own office and we could hear him swear and kick the table when the name of our opponents came out of the hat. MANCHESTER UNITED. And we would be away.

This was a United team at the peak of their powers, and with a manager in Sir Alex Ferguson still the dominant figure in

English football. That year, they would win the Premier League and the Champions League and while, to our advantage, their eyes may have been more on those prizes in the March of 2008, they still fielded their strongest team, including Rio Ferdinand and Nemanja Vidic, Paul Scholes and Wayne Rooney, Cristiano Ronaldo and Carlos Tevez.

I don't know what added value I was able to bring to the game and the occasion as a coach, or what percentage of what happened that day was down to my input, but I do know that I truly understood how to handle those big occasions while most of the Pompey players didn't. Not even Harry had been to an FA Cup final. I hope Harry and I were a good combination at Old Trafford that day, me a calming influence, him passionate and using that instinct that would serve him so well.

Naturally we came under pressure, and I recall Sylvain Distin getting away with a penalty shout early on when Ronaldo went down. At half-time, it was 0-0. I backed up Harry, telling the players at the interval that we were doing well, not to worry about coming under pressure, to keep it tight and believe in the game plan of full-backs tucking inside to thicken up the midfield alongside our trio in there.

'Just stay patient,' I said. 'We will get a chance.'

I looked at Sol Campbell, one of the few who had also been there and done it, sitting quietly in the corner, and smiled at him.

We did get a chance. The boys were growing in confidence as they kept out all United's attacking talent, and then Harry made a fantastic decision in bringing Kanu off early in the second half and putting on Milan Baros to utilise his pace against defenders who might be tiring.

Now, Milan had done nothing for us since he arrived and he would do nothing again for the rest of his time at the club. But this was his day. Our day. I had sensed it earlier, knowing we had done our homework properly and our game plan was working. On top of all that, Harry had a bit of a jinx on United in the cup, having beaten them with Bournemouth and West Ham.

Soon Milan was running at the United defence and he won us a penalty when Tomasz Kuszczak, substitute goalkeeper for the injured Edwin van der Sar, bundled him over. Sulley Muntari drilled home the kick, soon after which, at the other end, Sylvain kicked one off the line before the post stopped a shot from Patrice Evra. We were through to the semi-finals. Pompey were at Wembley – for a last-four game if not yet for the final – for the first time since 1942. And Lassana Diarra had run an unprecedented 890 metres at high intensity.

We couldn't deny that the draw had opened up for us, with West Bromwich Albion now the opponents, but we deserved it after beating United at Old Trafford. I don't think semi-finals should be played at Wembley as I am an old footballing romantic and believe the national stadium should be reserved for the final, but it was a wonderful day out, especially for the supporters, I have to admit.

And it was another fantastic occasion, with 83,584 rocking Wembley. Again we nicked it, this time Kanu poaching the only goal of the game against his old club. Milan Baros missed a great chance to seal the win – normal service having been resumed – but we held out well enough in the end.

Pompey were in an FA Cup final for the first time in 69 years – and would have a great chance of winning it now. Championship club Cardiff City had won the other semi by beating Barnsley, who had beaten Chelsea in the quarter-finals, so we would be the favourites. And I would have been at the new Wembley more times than the Arsenal.

With the cup job done and us safe in the league, I asked Harry straight after the West Brom game if I could nip off for a few days' skiing with Poppy. 'Course you can, Son,' he said. 'You've done great for me.' And so we headed for Val d'Isere and had a great time, spoiled only a little by the team beating West Ham 1-0 without me to show how dispensable I was. It would be the team's only win for the remainder of the season as we lost four of our last six league games, with the cup now our main focus.

The only win apart from the final, that was.

It was a smashing week leading up to it. We stayed the night before at a lovely hotel in Windsor, right next to the racecourse, from where you could walk into town to the castle. It was funny, I had once stayed there with Caprice. And we were given smart Paul Smith suits, which I still wear to this day.

The game itself was a good battle of wills. Cardiff were managed by Dave Jones, with Terry Burton, my old Arsenal youth-team coach, as his assistant, two good footballing brains. I knew it would be tight, but I always sensed that a piece of quality would settle the game and believed that we had the greater quality in our side.

So it proved. Again, Kanu grabbed the goal, 10 minutes before half-time, and we saw it out to lift the cup. Harry was finally the manager of a cup-winning side, though it was not a typical Harry performance, more an old-fashioned Tony Adams one. One-nil to the Pompey once more. My old Arsenal boss George Graham would have been proud of me.

I was coach to a cup-winning side. I had a quiet satisfaction about that but I was not one for wild celebrations any more. In fact, I don't think I was in any of the photos. It was the players' day, the fans' day. I suppose, yes, I did feel aloof in many ways. I didn't want to build up my role too much. I felt part of it but didn't . . . I just didn't have the same buzz as the players and the fans. I felt that I had helped them a great deal to win the cup, but I was humble enough to recognise my part in it without having to shout about it.

I thought I had contributed a lot and I'm not sure they could have done it without me, but perhaps they could. I certainly believed I'd had some input into team selection for the final. The day before, Harry said he wanted to play Papa Bouba Diop, but I said, 'Not for me.' Pedro Mendes was the man, I said. 'Wembley feels massive. We need people who can keep the ball and Pedro is the one to do that.' Harry went with it and it worked.

There it was again, the trouble with being an assistant: you don't get the crap stuff but you don't get the good stuff either. Some people like not having their heads above the parapet. I didn't. I was always disappointed I wasn't making the calls. It was just a good set of circumstances and personnel – Harry, me, Joe and the players. I do remember Harry saying at Wembley: 'This club will never do this again.' Well, who can say, but there was a sense that it would never get better than this.

We all headed back to the hotel in Windsor, where Poppy and the kids were waiting for me, and we enjoyed the party for a couple of hours before heading back to the Cotswolds. I didn't go on the open-top bus ride around Portsmouth the following day. I told Harry that my daughter Amber was playing for Millfield School in an England Schools hockey final in Nottingham and I wanted to go to that. It's not every day that happens so I wanted to see her play and support her.

Besides, all that celebration and fanfare was unusual for the Pompey people, but it wasn't for me. I had done more than my fair share of open-top bus rides through Islington with Arsenal. I had won the cup as a player and now as a coach, but I didn't feel the necessity to take part in the celebrations. I can understand how Harry thought I was aloof, yes. I did feel different. Clean and sober, I did things differently, the way I wanted to do them.

It was strange. While there was elation at winning the cup, there was also that emptiness you feel afterwards once it's over, with nothing now to focus on for a while. One thing I do remember in the aftermath was Steve Rowley at Arsenal contacting me for the stats from the final for a young Cardiff player called Aaron Ramsey, and my opinion of him. Arsenal were thinking of signing him. I thought he was a good footballer, honest and hard-working; thought he could become more than just an up-and-downer, I said . . .

When it did come time to go back for pre-season training with Portsmouth, things didn't quite feel the same this time around, not as they should have been for a cup-winning club. There was a very real sense of something having ended, rather than this being the start of something big.

10

Premier Pressures

Take risks.
If you win you will be happy.
If you lose you will be wise.

ANON

It's hard to mention the name of Portsmouth Football Club around that era, from 2006 to 2009 when I was there, without the talk moving quickly from all the success of the time – embracing high Premier League finishes, winning the FA Cup and playing in Europe – to the state of the finances that would eventually lead the club into administration and acrimonious disputes about ownership and who owed what to whom before regrouping under a supporters' trust.

Did it not occur to me that Pompey were paying transfer fees and wages to players beyond what the club was bringing in through the gate and commercially? Of course it did, but it is the nature of football – and was even more so at that time, before Financial Fair Play regulations kicked in – that a rich man can bankroll a club if he so wishes. That is the market and, while it has become more prevalent since Roman Abramovich took over Chelsea, it has always been true, going back to the earliest history of the game, that owners and directors can finance footballing dreams. Even if they can turn into nightmares.

In Portsmouth's case, the promises that it would all be underwritten came from the owner, Sacha Gaydamak. People always pointed to his father Arcadi – who was tried in France for arms dealing, which was not proven, though he served a short jail sentence for tax evasion and money laundering – being the one who pulled the strings, but the Premier League said it was always satisfied that Sacha was the sole owner. Only later would it emerge that most of the money going in was loans, which would lead to all sorts of wrangles when the cash injections dried up and potential new owners emerged, only for Sacha to demand his money back.

All dealings with him were more Harry's issue than mine. It just wasn't my agenda and I hardly ever came across Sacha. I was gaining my Premier League coaching experience, working with the players who came in, so wasn't that interested in the bigger picture of the club. I was in my own footballing bubble. It sounds selfish but it was out of my control anyway. My energies needed to be concentrated on preparing and sending out the best side possible for the fans. A successful side drives revenue. And my line manager was Harry, not Sacha.

Harry did speak about it often, however, and was concerned by what was going on, if never fully conversant with where the money was coming from. 'Who is this guy?' he would say. 'What's he doing? . . . What does he want? . . . He doesn't really seem interested in football . . . He never speaks to me in person . . . Only phones now and then to say, "Well done, Mr Redknapp . . ."'

He was a difficult owner for Harry. Harry was used to having a personal relationship with Milan Mandaric. They would go out for dinner on a Saturday night after a game and talk it all over. It was almost the beginning of the time when relationships at the top changed, as the increasing number of new owners from overseas in the Premier League – a bit like absentee landlords – no longer had the same everyday contact with managers as the old-style chairmen did.

When we got back to work in pre-season, it became clear that Pompey were suddenly a selling club rather than a buying one. In the previous few years, around £180 million had been spent on the squad, but now those coming in were costing less than the money being raised by player sales. In hindsight, it is easy to see that the powers that be were reining in, with the money drying up, but at the time it was just an impression that things were changing.

Sulley Muntari went to Inter Milan for nearly £13 million and Pedro Mendes to Rangers for £3 million. There was lots of interest too in Lassie Diarra, which would culminate in him going in midwinter to Real Madrid for a then amazing £21 million. We would be losing the best-quality players in the squad.

There were signings. Peter Crouch came from Liverpool for £11 million, Younes Kaboul from Spurs for £5 million and Nadir Belhadj from Lens for £4.5 million – with all the movement, no wonder agents loved Harry. But he was uneasy in pre-season. We were now in Europe and he talked about needing a bigger squad and rotating. But the squad seemed to be getting smaller, not bigger.

'I don't know what's happening with the money,' he would say regularly, along with: 'I don't like this team. Don't fancy us at all.' He was unsure of formula and shape, was worried we were just going to knock the ball up to Peter Crouch, whom he had taken but seemed uncertain about. We discussed going three at the back. At times things would get a bit fractious. He was arguing more with Joe.

The club had been on a pre-season tour to Portugal, which I swerved – and this one was partly due to my fear of flying. I stayed at the training ground, meanwhile, working with the players coming back to fitness and was glad I didn't go as there were reports of some players getting drunk. And so Harry was not in a good mood when things were not going well in a friendly at Oxford United. He rounded on Martin Cranie, gave him a real volley of abuse. 'You're fucking shit, you're a fucking disgrace,' that kind of thing. Soon Martin would be out of the club, on his way to Charlton on loan. It was a result of the fallout from Portugal.

Such an outburst was not like Harry. This was that only time I mentioned earlier when I saw him do this kind of thing, despite all his old-school reputation or tendencies. It was another example of things not feeling right around the club, which was strange given we had won the FA Cup just a few months earlier. I think Harry was also deeply affected that summer by the death in the spring of his wife Sandra's sister Pat Lampard, Frank's mum.

I was unsure about my own position, too, amid all these negative signs. I wondered if I had gone as far as I could, as I wanted to become a manager in my own right. Should I resign with nothing to go to? Do I stay and wait till something comes up? I had also been offered a new contract which I informed Peter Storrie I couldn't sign since there was a compensation clause if I left. They wanted £50,000 – half my salary – if I went. That was surely going to put off another club from hiring me, if an opportunity arose.

Early in the season, a job did come up and I thought about going for it. It was at West Ham, with Alan Curbishley having resigned after disagreements with the then Icelandic owners. I thought the best thing was to talk to Harry about it, not least because he might be going for it himself. He said he wasn't; he'd decided not to go back, having already had a long spell there, so I asked if he could put in a word for me. I also asked him to speak to Peter Storrie to see if I could get that clause taken out of my contract.

'No problem, Son,' he said, on both counts. 'I know you want to have a go yourself.' But nothing happened. I don't know if he ever did put in a word at West Ham, but I didn't pursue my interest in the job and it would go to Gianfranco Zola. The stuff about my contract went on for weeks. Whenever I asked about it, Harry would say he had told Peter. Peter would say that Harry hadn't.

I was sympathetic to Harry's situation at the time, as I knew he was starting to have his doubts about the club and wondering whether to quit while he was ahead. He had been courted by Newcastle United back in the winter when they sacked Sam Allardyce and, amid a big media frenzy, I know he was close to taking it, even telling Mike Ashley that he would. In the end, his wife Sandra had a say because I don't think Harry could face long spells away from her and their home at Sandbanks near Bournemouth.

But it meant that he was open to offers and I began to wonder now where I stood. I didn't know if he maybe hadn't put in a word for me with West Ham because he didn't want to lose me . . . I was feeling a little isolated now, not as much a part of things as I had, and began to get more withdrawn. I wasn't sure I believed in what we were doing any more, either. I just didn't know what was going on so sat tight for the time being. Sometimes doing nothing is also a decision.

It was no disgrace losing to Manchester United on penalties in the Community Shield at the start of the season, but we struggled to get going in the league, losing to Chelsea and Manchester United before winning two then getting thrashed 6–0 at Manchester City. Harry and Joe went bonkers.

I asked Lassie into the office on the Monday and pointed out his stats to him. He had done just 240 metres of high-intensity running, almost three-quarters less than he had in the FA Cup quarter-final win against Manchester United. Against that, his opposite number at Manchester City, Stephen Ireland, had run 1,500 metres at high intensity, mostly off the back of Lassie, who was just not going with him.

'You've thrown the towel in here, buddy,' I said to him. 'It doesn't happen again. I like you. It's in you.' He nodded. He knew that he had let himself and the team down. But I think even then the talk was building. Real Madrid was beckoning . . .

The result was thankfully a one-off and might have been explained by us playing Vitoria Guimaraes of Portugal on the previous Thursday night in a UEFA Cup qualifying-round tie, beating them 2-0 ahead of a 2-2 draw out there a fortnight later and so going through to the group stages. We did not make a great start to that, losing 3-0 away to another Portuguese side, Sporting Braga, but otherwise we put together a decent run of form that also included wins over Tottenham and Stoke.

Something was in the offing, though. Spurs had been really poor when we played them and were bottom of the table after taking just two points from their first eight games. Juande Ramos, their Spanish manager, was duly sacked and the public clamour – and all the press speculation – seemed to be about Harry going to White Hart Lane.

Not having heard anything from Harry about Peter Storrie taking that clause out of my contract, I had written to Peter directly on a Friday, 24 October, to ask what was happening, as I was growing weary of things not being sorted. When my phone rang on the Saturday evening – we were not playing our home game against Fulham until the Sunday – with Peter's number coming up, I thought he was calling about the contract.

'Harry's going to Tottenham,' he said, though the public

announcement of the Ramos sacking, and Harry's appointment, would not come until later that night. 'Come in tomorrow and we'll talk about it.' He was short and to the point.

I thought things over. I would be sorry to see Harry go. He had given me a great opportunity and let me have my head with the coaching. In fact, he had adapted from being the old-fashioned manager who controlled everything to the modern guy who has to accept the input of others – from his chief scout helping with recruitment, through the tech guys doing the analysis, to me and Joe preparing the team.

If he hadn't let people have their heads, I don't think the club would have been so successful and credit to him for it. I also think that if he hadn't learned to do all that, he wouldn't have got the Tottenham job, where a lot of the transfer dealings were taken out of his hands and where they had a lot of staff. The game was changing and he knew it. The manager/head coach was still the kingpin of football operations at any club, but he had to work with more people than ever before and devolve some responsibility.

I would also miss Harry simply for his company. He could be calculating with people, I had seen that – like the way he would complain about a player in the office, then the player concerned would knock on the door and come in and Harry would be his best buddy. I would imagine he might be like that with me as well. But then he needed to be that way because he was the boss and his neck was on the line. He needed to keep people sweet in order to get the best out of them but had private opinions that would inform his longer-term actions. Anyway, you can't always be everyone's friend. You have to be a bit ruthless. Ultimately, I don't think he cared at all if people didn't like him. Results were what counted for Harry.

There's always been talk about his transfer dealings, which would come to a head in a court case a few years later, in which he was cleared, as well as his fondness for a bet.

Just after I arrived at the club, a *Panorama* programme aired about transfer dealings in the game and Harry and Kevin Bond featured. Kevin was even sacked from his job at Newcastle but resurfaced as manager of Bournemouth. The evidence against Harry did not seem solid, however.

I am often asked my opinion of all that and would just say that I think Harry was canny in probably having it written in his contract that if he made a profit for the club on a player transfer, then he was due a bonus or a percentage. It happens with many managers. It is designed to remove any temptation to take a bung.

As for the gambling, all I can say of my experience with him is that he was a product of his environment, growing up in the East End of London. He told me how he'd go round his nan's from school at lunchtimes and put her bets on for her, so he was around gambling in his formative years. He always did like horse racing. He was also brought up among Jack-the-lads.

I guess that was why I could relate to him in many ways, even though our paths in life took different turns. As an East Ender, he was one of my own, and football also got me out of my environment. I found him charming and fun and I have always thought, after my time with him down the years, that as a manager I would want someone like him alongside me: experienced and wise. He is an emotional, happy, romantic and passionate individual, and that worked alongside my serious side.

I was never going to go to Spurs with him, though. Not with my Arsenal background, even if Harry had wanted me. I knew that Kevin Bond would be rejoining him. I thought I would be leaving Pompey too, as I didn't have a contract in place and any new manager would almost certainly want to bring in his own staff.

So it was with a heavy heart that I drove down to Portsmouth on the Sunday, to join Joe and Paul Groves in Peter's office.

Peter asked us if we would take the team that afternoon. Joe and Paul seemed happy enough to do so, but I had some questions I wanted answering. I asked if I could have a word alone with Peter and he agreed. Joe and Paul left the room. I was confused and a bit angry.

'Hold on, Peter,' I said. 'I told you on Friday that I wanted my contract sorted. I don't even have a contract with the club but you want me to take the team? What's going on?'

His answer took me by surprise, and took the wind out of my sails.

'Why don't you have a bash at the job?' Peter said. 'You watch the game today, let Joe and Paul take the team, then come up to the lounge and talk about it.' Sacha was at the game today, he added.

I had been thinking this might be my last day at the club. Now it sounded as if I was being offered the job of Portsmouth manager. This scenario hadn't occurred to me.

'Come up and talk to Sacha,' Peter continued. 'Put yourself up for the job. You're asking about what's going on here at the club. Here's a chance to find out. I know you want to be a Premier League manager. Well, there's a job available here ...'

He had a point. It was a Premier League job at a club I knew well after two seasons there. I knew the players, the set-up, the culture of Pompey. For that minute, and that day, it made sense. And so, after the 1-1 draw with Fulham, I went up to the lounge to talk to Peter and Sacha.

Sacha told me about a new training ground they were going to buy and a new stadium he was going to build. He even got out all the plans. I had heard about them before because Harry told me he had seen them. I also remembered Harry telling me then: 'Tone. It's a load of bollocks.' And it did seem at odds with the implied messages of the summer's transfer dealings that the club was cutting back.

But I hadn't been a Premier League manager and I could see there was an opportunity here. It would be a risk but surely one worth taking. I needed my next experience in the game, that of being a manager at the top level, and here it was, being presented to me. Against that, I knew it might just be for one game, that football changed quickly, and I recalled my days as a young player when I had three managers in three months at Arsenal when that club was in turmoil. Or about as much turmoil as Arsenal ever got itself into.

I was thinking on the hoof. And I was thinking that I would never know if I was a potential Premier League manager unless I took this chance. It might be a big regret if I turn it down, I told myself. Someone else might get the job, and should another owner come in after Sacha who was prepared to invest and that manager had done well, suddenly it would look like the best job in the world. And Peter was saying all the right things.

I decided there and then that I would take the job and shook hands with Sacha and Peter. I drove back home to the Cotswolds and told Poppy. She was always happy for me to go with my instincts and accept roles that were good for me, but she was unhappy now at how impulsive I had been in saying yes. In fact, she was hurt.

'You didn't consult me,' she said. 'You've got children to think of here as well.' Hector was now two and a half, Atticus coming up to five. This on top of Oliver, at 16, and Amber, then 13, still being at home. She also pointed out that I'd told her I didn't exactly trust Peter Storrie.

She was right. I should have told Peter and Sacha that I needed to go home and speak to my family first, but I didn't. That was my first mistake and others would follow. I got flattered into it. I just saw the opportunity, not the storm clouds that were gathering over the club.

I went in to Fratton Park on the Monday morning and signed

a contract for the rest of the season plus two more after that. This one was for £700,000 a year, not the £100,000 one I had been wanting and waiting to sign a few days previously. It wasn't up there with what Harry was getting, but then he was an experienced Premier League manager. I was probably a cheap option for them but it was still a good salary, even though it was never about the money. Not for me, anyway.

It didn't start well, with two defeats in a week, away to Liverpool, thanks to one controversial set play, and at home to a late goal by Wigan. They say luck evens out over a season. I suddenly started to wonder if I would be there long enough for the luck to even out. Fortunately, we stopped the bleeding with draws against West Ham and Hull that followed a good away win at Sunderland. Roy Keane was their manager and just didn't look as if he was having any fun. I would come to know how he felt.

Not around a UEFA Cup game at home to AC Milan, however. It was the sort of night and game I was made for. I loved pitting my wits against a team from the highest level and a manager like Carlo Ancelotti, who would go on to win league titles with Chelsea and Paris St Germain and the Champions League with Real Madrid. Milan were a good side at the time, if not the great side of previous decades. They had Kaka, Gennaro Gattuso, Pippo Inzaghi and Andriy Shevchenko. At the back was Philippe Senderos, once dubbed the Swiss Tony at Arsenal, but I think it's fair to say he never quite emulated me there.

On the bench they had Andrea Pirlo – and Ronaldinho, who came off it to turn the tide after we had gone 2-0 up through Younes Kaboul and Kanu. The Brazilian's 84th-minute goal was followed by Inzaghi's in added time and it was 2–2 at the end of a breathless game. So good was the match that a poll among Pompey supporters in later years would vote it the club's best game of all time.

After losing to Braga before Harry went, the draw meant, however, that we were now struggling to get out of the group. It was all but up when we lost 3-2 in Wolfsburg in another good game, their striker Edin Dzeko having a fine match, as my tech guys, Woody and Eddy, pointed out to me in their analysis.

A 3-0 win over the Dutch side Heerenveen in the final game was too little too late and we duly departed the competition. It was always likely. The squad simply wasn't deep enough to sustain a European campaign. Still, they were pleasant interludes as the real business of the Premier League was proving much less enjoyable. The ground was shifting under my feet all the time. It was all getting a bit Harry Styles – going in One Direction.

I was trying to put my stamp on the side, trying to go back to the work ethic with the players. David James would later say that I did less coaching than before and, while later I was certainly distracted by off-field matters, I probably did even more coaching work with the players initially. I worked particularly hard on making the lines between defence and midfield, then midfield and attack, much tighter.

And I tried some new things. In seeking an assistant, I tried to get Terry Burton, but he was then secure in his role at Cardiff. I also asked Martin Keown if he wanted to help out, but he was by now earning good money as a pundit and didn't want to give that up to move into what could be an unstable situation.

I did bring in Johnny Metgod, once of Nottingham Forest and who was at Feyenoord with me before going to be technical director at Den Haag, to work on ball drills and warm the guys up. I warned him about the growing problems of the club but he still wanted to get back into English football. I promoted Paul Groves to first-team coaching from the reserves in a change forced on me after Joe Jordan had come to see me.

'Look, I'll stay if you want,' he said. 'But Harry has asked me to go to Tottenham with him ...' It was good of Joe even to think of staying, but I couldn't ask him to.

'No, Joe,' I said. 'I'm not going to stop you. There's a good chance this could go tits–up here anyway.'

It was clear that some of the players wanted out too, though they had a dilemma. Where else were they going to get the wages they were on now? They had lost Harry, then Joe, and I could see some hearts weren't in it any more. We lost games against Newcastle and Bolton. This was just not my team. If it went on much longer without changes being made, we were going to fail.

I said as much to Peter Storrie and talked about moving out some among the higher earners and getting in some new, hungrier players in January. I was preparing a list of targets with my tech guys. We knew Barcelona were willing to let Yaya Toure go, but he wanted £75,000 a week. It didn't seem ridiculous at that time, with some of the Pompey players being on sums not far off. I told Peter that I wanted Edin Dzeko and that we could probably get him for £8 million. A French agent had rung me up to say the player was available as he had lined up a replacement for Wolfsburg.

Now I was getting caught up in stuff going on away from the pitch. In fact, a lot of my time was spent dealing with players and their agents, and I was back in the Wycombe scene of more management than technical work. I could do it, but I realised I was lacking a coach, as I had been to Harry, to train and prepare the team.

Then, just before Christmas, I was called up to London, to an office in Berkeley Square, to meet with Sacha and Peter. There was also a financial guy in the office. It proved to be a bizarre meeting and one that pulled the rug from under my feet.

'Mr Adams,' Sacha said. 'I am sorry to have to tell you that I will not be investing any more money in the club and we are reorganising a few things. In fact, we will need to sell players. We need to find £6 million by the end of January or we may have to go into administration.'

I don't know why but I said, 'OK. Thanks very much.' I suppose it was because at least I knew where I stood now. I still thought that if I could ship some players out – though that might take some doing, with plenty of them on those high salaries – I could sign some with more stomach for the fight. We certainly needed a few, judging by the 4-1 defeat at home to West Ham on Boxing Day.

I looked at the team and I could see a majority simply weren't interested. I thought to myself that I just wasn't getting any respect here. I had never done it before – and never since – but once they got back into the dressing room, I gave them all a complete and utter volley. It wasn't like me and I don't really believe in it. You're not actually going to get players onside by giving them a bollocking. But I just couldn't help myself that day.

'You are,' I shouted, 'a fucking disgrace . . . Half of you are not trying and it's unacceptable . . . You're letting yourselves, the fans and everyone else down . . . You're going through the motions.' Nobody argued. It wasn't very Churchillian but it was honest.

Had I lost the dressing room, in the parlance of the phone-ins? I don't really know what it means but I do know I never actually had the dressing room. They were never my players. I was just in there as a figurehead.

I was particularly disgusted with Jermain Defoe and looked him straight in the eye when I said: 'If any of you don't want to be part of this club that I am building, then you can fuck off. Come to me tomorrow morning and we'll sort you a new club.'

Thank God the next morning Jermain did come to see me. He said he wanted to go back to Spurs. I guessed he had had a phone call with Harry, or maybe his agent had, but I didn't mind even if someone might have seen it as tapping up. By now in the game it was much less blatant: there were so many representatives and hangers-on around players, and so many means of communication without documentation, that any charge could be avoided. Actually, I was delighted. It meant we would get in the money that the club needed and which might finance some transfers of my own. I told Jermain I would see what I could do.

I was thus in a happier frame of mind two days later when I took Portsmouth to Arsenal and received a wonderful reception from the home fans singing my name. It just didn't feel right being Pompey manager as an Arsenal man. I suppose it was fitting it finished 'One-nil to the Ars-en-al', as the old song had it. David James had been brilliant for us but made a mistake 10 minutes from time in this one.

Come January, we did indeed do a deal to let Jermain go back to Spurs for £15 million having paid £7.5 million for him just a year earlier. And with that £21 million deal for Lassie Diarra's move to Real Madrid going through, I even thought I might have money to spend.

How wrong I was. And what an introduction as a manager to the Wild West of the January transfer window in English football it was.

It had begun after that meeting with Sacha and Peter in Berkeley Square. Peter took me to Les Ambassadeurs to talk strategy and make plans. When I got there, the 'super-agent' Kia Joorabchian – who had become well known as Carlos Tevez's representative through some controversial moves – was at the table.

Peter suggested that David Moyes at Everton liked David Nugent and that we might be able to get Leighton Baines as part of the deal. We had Djimi Traore at left back but he was prone to mistakes. Peter asked me if I would be open to that. I said, yes, let's do it. Baines was a good player.

Peter rang the Everton chairman Bill Kenwright, who in turn

rang David Moyes. Two words came back from him: no chance. Any information Peter had got was mistaken. I thought so. A deal like that always did seem fanciful to me. And so was set the tone for January.

I liked a big German defender I had seen play when I was scouting – one Per Mertesacker, who was then at Werder Bremen. His agent said he was looking for a bigger English club than us, but I tried – and failed – to persuade him he could use Portsmouth for a couple of years as a stepping stone. In came Arsenal a few years later . . .

Newcastle United had let it be known they were willing to let Joey Barton go, and I knew he was fit and in a good place as he'd not long been through Sporting Chance following his own problems. I met him and his agent at the Dorchester hotel in London, but the deal never came off, probably because I could not give Joey the assurances he was seeking about the health and future of the club. Being an honest man, I didn't want to mislead him.

I talked to Peter about Dzeko and asked him to go down to Seville, where Wolfsburg were in a warm-weather training camp during the German winter break. The deal was there to be done, the agent had told me.

Instead, at a meeting in a hotel in Kensington, I was presented with the 'opportunity' to sign Giovani dos Santos, who had been a teenage prodigy with Barcelona before being sold to Tottenham for €6 million in 2008. Spurs – where Harry was now the manager – wanted to unload him already, and we were being identified by his agent Pini Zahavi, it seemed, as the potential destination.

The fee would be £7 million and there seemed to be a lot of people involved in brokering this deal, from Harry and Daniel Levy at Tottenham, through Zahavi, to Peter Storrie at Portsmouth.

I made some calls. I phoned Pep Guardiola at Barcelona, who told me not to touch him. I rang Arsène, who called me back after talking to one of his players and dos Santos' Mexican compatriot, Carlos Vela. The word was that 'Giovani does not live well' and was not fit.

I told Peter the player was not for me. Peter insisted the deal had to be done, even putting Sven-Goran Eriksson, then Mexico manager, on the phone to tell me what a good player he was. And so I offered Peter a deal in return: if the player passed a bleep test – a way of determining fitness – then I would sign him. I was pretty confident he wouldn't.

Dos Santos turned up at the training ground with his father and took the test with our fitness coach, John Dalziel. John came to me with the result. It was a nine. Considering that in my last season with Arsenal, at the age of 35, I had recorded a 12, and I was the slowest in the team, then this was really poor.

The kid was in tears and I tried to console him by saying: 'Maybe in the summer . . .' There was no way I was taking him now, though, and I told Peter as much. Fortunately, he didn't force the issue and the deal was scrapped.

But the whole episode – when I wanted Dzeko, then up for grabs, and Peter wanted me to take dos Santos – showed me which way the wind was blowing. I knew then that I was the fall guy here. To use a newspaper industry term: I was a dead man walking.

I always did find dealing with Peter difficult. We had, shall I say, a different take on how business should be conducted. Take the time we were negotiating with our midfield player Richard Hughes about a new contract, with his expiring in the summer. I met with Peter in my office ahead of Richard coming in with his dad, who was his agent.

Richard was a decent player, not highest quality, I said, but a good club man who was worth keeping. Ideally, he wouldn't be a starter but he could do a job when we had injuries and sit in there in midfield. At the time, salaries at the club were huge, though he was not among the highest earners. Start low, I told Peter, and I recommended two seasons at a figure just above what Richard was then on. OK, said Peter, we'll keep him. And he called in Richard and his dad.

Virtually the first words out of Peter's mouth were a sum of money well beyond my suggested maximum. I was flabbergasted.

'Peter,' I said, 'was there even any point in having a meeting? I have given my recommendations and I am the head coach.'

This was all in front of Richard and his dad. I ended up storming out of my own office. Richard, who would later work as head of recruitment for Eddie Howe at AFC Bournemouth, was a great guy but he was never worth what was finally agreed.

We lurched through January, reinforcements thin on the ground. When once I was talking about bargaining Yaya Toure down a bit from £75,000 a week, I ended up with Hayden Mullins on £16,000, Pompey having paid Reading £1.2 million for him. I worked at getting in a Greek striker from Bayer Leverkusen on a short loan, Theofanis Gekas, but he was on £37,000 a week so I knew we would never take him full time.

With word out that Portsmouth were now a selling club, calls came in regularly. The final one I took in the madness of that January window came at 30 minutes before the 5pm deadline on Monday 2 February, the period having been extended due to the fact that 31 January fell on a Saturday. It was Mark Hughes, then at Manchester City, enquiring about Peter Crouch. It wasn't going to happen.

That night, I went to bed with a headache and the following day, a day off, I just duvet-dived.

At the end of it, with players like Diarra and Defoe gone, we looked like a side that was going to struggle to compete in the

Premier League – though at least the club was still in business, thanks to the sales. For now. I actually confided in a few people close to me that I thought the club might well go out of business soon.

Our defence of the FA Cup was weak. We won a third-round replay 2-0 at Bristol City after a 0-0 draw at home, but lost in the fourth round 2-0 at home to Swansea, who were then in the Championship. In the league in January, we also lost at home to Aston Villa. The only bright spot was a 1-1 draw at Tottenham. Harry Redknapp's Tottenham. David Nugent put us ahead – and Jermain Defoe scored the equaliser.

The final day of the month saw us go to Fulham and lose 3-1. It was a third defeat in a row so it wasn't entirely surprising. What happened next shocked me far more than the result, however.

As we got back on the coach afterwards, this one Pompey supporter began screaming abuse at me, calling me every name under the sun. Now, I shouldn't have let it affect me, especially given all the names I was called as a young player when I was less able to deal with it all, but it did. This was also an exception. The Portsmouth fans had always been great to me and still are to this day.

I wanted to shout back at him, to tell him that he hadn't a clue what I'd had to deal with for the last four months. I wanted to tell him what a pantomime the club was becoming with all the chaos behind the scenes. Everyone would come to see it later, but then few knew the extent of what was happening like I did. I guess, given what I was experiencing, I was just getting to the end of my tether and that final weekend of the transfer window was not helping.

After the Fulham defeat, I took the team to the Forest Mere spa for a few days for us to try to clear our heads. It seemed to have some effect come the Saturday when we led Liverpool 2-1 at home with five minutes to go. Familiar frailties resurfaced, however, and we turned victory into defeat when Dirk Kuyt levelled and Peter Crouch gave the ball away in a dangerous area in the last minute, leading to Fernando Torres grabbing the winner.

On my drive home, I mulled over the state of the team and the club and decided enough was enough. My belief that I was on to a loser with no chance of turning things around had been confirmed. My reputation was just going to get trashed the longer this went on. Peter had told me in January to hang in there and he would find me some money to get players in but nothing had happened. I knew it was doomed.

I phoned the agent Steve Kutner to get him to ring Peter to tell him I wanted out. I wanted him to tell Peter that he needed to sack me because I wasn't going to resign. After Wycombe, I didn't want to be labelled as a quitter; didn't want it said that Tony Adams couldn't hack management. I knew I had it in me to be a good manager at a high level, but not in this dire situation where I had no chance of succeeding. Anyway, Peter had put me in this, so he needed to get me out of it. Also, although it had never been about money, having walked away from Wycombe with nothing, I wanted to be paid some of what I felt I was owed.

Peter, who, I would later find out, had gone to Sol Campbell and David James to discuss my position, then rang me to ask if I wanted to come down to the club to talk things over. It was Atticus's fifth birthday party on the Sunday and I told Peter I wasn't driving to Fratton Park to get the sack and that he should – please – just do it. He agreed and I settled on three months' salary with him as a severance package.

The sacking was duly announced. I had been in charge for 21 games in total, winning four, drawing six and losing 11. In the Premier League, we had taken 10 points from 14 games.

Not a great return but, given what would follow, it could have been much worse. I knew we were in a relegation fight but we had never gone into the bottom three in my time. Who knows, the 10 points under me might have kept them up that season.

What I did know was that I had been set up to fail. In view of what was going on behind the scenes – which would culminate in ownership wrangles over the next few years and Pompey subsequently slipping down into League Two, finally to be taken over by the supporters' trust – I was not going to turn this ship around, whatever I did.

Paul Hart would be promoted from the academy to caretaker manager, but the job would do him no favours and he lasted till November. Nor would it enhance his successor Avram Grant's reputation much, though he did reach the FA Cup final again. Pompey had just enough decent players left to survive that season I went by seven points but it was a stay of execution. The next season they finished bottom with just 19 points, all the higher earners departing, some of them never to get paid.

Harry rang me to say he thought it was disgraceful that I was sacked before a run of less-demanding games, but that wasn't the point. Longer term it was going pear-shaped. Only one player rang me to say how sorry he was that I had been sacked and that was the gracious Richard Hughes.

Later, in the summer, Glen Johnson would text me after his move to Liverpool to thank me for my coaching, which helped develop his career. I would also later meet Fabio Capello, then the England manager, in a box at Arsenal and he would thank me for my work with Glen.

Other coaches rang me too, including some I had been on my UEFA Pro Licence with. Glenn Roeder, now at Stevenage, reminded me that all the greats had been sacked, most notably around that time Jose Mourinho at Chelsea.

There were one or two players less kind towards me. David

James did an article in one of the Sunday papers saying that I was not a good manager. The dressing room was too quiet, he said, and the team not well enough organised. He discussed a row we had after the Fulham game and added that he never felt we would win against Liverpool, despite leading, as we were too open.

That all disappointed me not only because he had been quoted in the press a few months earlier welcoming my appointment, but also because he wasn't seeing the bigger picture, the one outside of his world of being a player. He didn't know what was really going on in dealings with the hierarchy. And he wouldn't have seen me working hard with the team on organisation as he was a goalkeeper doing his own training, often away from the group. That said, I don't blame him really. I could be like that as a player – in my own zone. These days, the evidence of how it went south very quickly is there for all to see and he might have a different perspective.

Could I have done anything differently? Not taken the job, that's for sure. Otherwise I did the best I could in the circumstances. Some would say I paid a high price, with that unhappy experience of management being people's last impression of me in charge of an English club. I am, however, grateful for it. It taught me that I didn't want to be one of those managers on a roundabout of jobs, going from one to the other just to be in the game and earn money. I wanted to be working at a club where I had a chance of building something over a period of years and could win things, as I had as a player.

As I watched Portsmouth from afar over the next few years, I could see that their demise was coming. We as professionals could move on, though it was painful for some people after me who wouldn't get the money they were owed, and I saw several within the club struggling to get jobs afterwards. It was the fans who had enjoyed the thick but who would now be experiencing plenty of thin who would be really suffering.

And they were lovely fans, their world shattered by financial illiterates who destroyed their club. Some people who thought they could save the club were like those who end up going to Al-Anon – partners of alcoholics who believe they will be the one to get the addict to stop destroying themselves. The George Best story is an example of that.

I think most of the fans appreciated the job I did for them, but it was all a perfect storm of overspending and mismanagement that would have taken a lot of good people under with it. How to ruin a football club. It left me making a vow to myself that I would never work with idiots again.

For me, it was actually a relief to be out of the firing line at first, as I headed back to my sanctuary in the Cotswolds and the comfort of my family. Soon the assault to the senses that leaving a club in unhappy circumstances produces would kick in.

11

Loyalty

Being a one-club man as a player has its benefits but also draw-backs. As a player, I was often lauded for my loyalty. It probably ranks alongside leadership as the quality most associated with me and I am often cited as a rare beast, one coming close to extinction in modern football.

When it comes to wanting to be a coach or a manager, it can work against you. You don't, after all, have a lot of clubs where you are remembered fondly and knowledge of you as a character, along with your record and reputation, might give you a chance of an interview at least.

So what is loyalty? In my case, it could have been very different at Arsenal but for circumstances and experiences. I could have begun at another London club, for example, but chose Arsenal because my dad recognised what a good youth set-up they had and I liked the look of their facilities.

I then stayed with them out of convenience. The training ground was accessible from Essex and I could be near my family. Arsenal liked me and I liked them, and I was too scared to ask for any more money and create waves. I was no trouble to them – on the pitch at least. I guess because we were having success, they put up with the off-field stuff. It meant I could happily indulge my drinking for a long time.

It felt right; there was nowhere else I wanted to go. And we were successful. It was the same as when I was a kid at Dagenham United. The team scored 140 goals a season and conceded one. Where was I going to go?

You develop a feeling for your environment and colleagues when you start so young at a club. I was in that class of '82 with Martin Keown, Michael Thomas, David Rocastle, Niall Quinn, Paul Merson, Gus Caesar and Martin Hayes. We came through to the first team. We looked out for each other. There was also a great working-class, and work, ethic around the club that would be fostered later by George Graham.

So it wasn't hard to turn down any Manchester United overtures in 1991. I was simply too young and too scared to leave the comfort zone of Arsenal where I could do the two things I loved best: play football and drink. Although somewhere deep down I would have said that Arsenal was my club, that was masked by the way I was living my life. I think I would have to say I was probably trapped rather than loyal.

That all changed when I got sober in '96, when I turned down Manchester United for different reasons. It was then that I got in touch with my true self and my real feelings about the game, my club and my life. I was clear of mind and free of fear.

Then you can call it loyalty. In fact, over the final six years of my playing career, I became the most loyal man I knew in football. I realised how much I loved the Arsenal and wanted to win things with them.

At that point the loyalty that can get buried – and sometimes did in my drinking days when I was just acting on instinct rather than being aware of my bonds to colleagues and club – becomes significant, as it did with me.

I always felt grateful to George Graham and would have run

through brick walls for him, but that kind of loyalty was a product of the way I was then, of my upbringing and drive to succeed. I did consider leaving during the brief Bruce Rioch period, and even when Arsène Wenger arrived, as I was sceptical of change. Sobriety, though, is a great precursor to loyalty. Such was the respect that Arsène and I developed for each other that loyalty became natural to both of us.

So what did loyalty feel like then? It was a sense of wanting to do the right thing by those around me through being the best that I could and using my talents for the good of the collective. It was thanking the football club who made me what I am.

I never wanted to leave once that became established in me. I felt I would have been letting my team-mates down, primarily David Seaman, Lee Dixon, Steve Bould, Martin Keown and Nigel Winterburn, my fellow defenders with whom I had gone through more than 500 games. Steve and Nigel would leave in the end, but that was because they were being replaced. I don't doubt they would have stayed on at the Arsenal as I did if they could have done.

In football, you are obviously not facing the same kind of dangers as a soldier in the SAS, the Marines or other branches of the military, but it is the same principle: you are putting your faith – if not your life, as in the soldier's case – in the hands of someone close to you and he is putting his in you. You don't want to renege on your responsibility.

When you have such an intense attitude, and have been through so much together and seen each other warts and all, the defeats may hurt more but the wins are all the sweeter – which is why you become so determined to avoid the former so you can experience the latter.

Clearly, as a coach and a manager, I will never know the longevity of loyalty that I did as a player and that Sir Alex Ferguson and Arsène have enjoyed. They are extreme rarities amid the hire-and-fire culture nowadays, and being given the chance to stay at a club for a long period is unlikely ever to come along again.

All I as a coach or manager can do when fortunate to find employment is bring to bear all the experience and qualities learned through the times when senses were heightened. Such as in those six years at Arsenal after getting sober.

You are constantly looking to bring your loyalty of service to a group of players, your employers and the club, and hope that, by seeking to instil it, you have a chance of receiving it in return. For many coaches and managers that is a forlorn hope in the dysfunctional world of the modern game, but for your own satisfaction and integrity, you can never give up the search for it.

At least, whatever may have happened to me in the past during my management career, and whatever may happen in the future, I will feel forever blessed that I got to know intimately what true loyalty is.

12

Every Cloud . . .

Success consists of going from failure to failure
without loss of enthusiasm.

SIR WINSTON CHURCHILL

It took a while of licking wounds after leaving Portsmouth before I was ready to face the world and the game again. Leaving a club amid bitterness attacks every part of your psyche and your self-worth. It is not just the event itself but the aftermath. Players have their say – as I saw with David James – and it feels like your whole character is being examined; your talent and ability dismissed. It is especially difficult when you have had a playing career that has taken you to the top and won you trophies. Even as a coach, I had just won the FA Cup with Portsmouth eight months earlier. That, however, is a long time in football.

It was also hurtful to receive a call from Harry Redknapp accusing me of leaking stuff to the press. My co-writer on this book, Ian Ridley, was at the time the chief football writer for the *Mail on Sunday* and he wrote a column defending me and my time at Portsmouth, saying that I had inherited a sinking ship from Harry due to all the excessive spending at the club. Harry thought I had put Ian up to it but I hadn't – he had written it off his own bat. Ian also got a call from Harry, but he was big enough to fight his own battles, as was I.

The thing is, I could easily have leaked. I know how football and the media work. I could have done interviews, or rung up journalists, and given my side of events, blaming others. That's not my style, though. I have never played the media or public relations game. I prefer to walk with dignity. I felt clean with my role in matters, and other people could make their own judgements.

The time to set the record straight is – such as now – later, in the cold light of day when cooler analysis can be made. Then, Portsmouth Football Club was a shipwreck but people couldn't see the causes because it was going on out at sea, and so many must have thought it was the captain's fault, rather than the boat not being seaworthy.

I coped with any feelings of rejection or pain the way I always do: I went to AA meetings and shared how I felt, without going into the specifics of what I did for a living or the personalities involved, knowing that to do so would help me process it better and not to do so would lead to the feelings festering in me. That way, for an alcoholic, can lie a drink.

For recovering alcoholics, emotions and reactions can be extreme. If I am not careful, my head can run away with me and I can see myself as the worst in the world at my job, destined to drink again and die on the streets. Or I think that I am better than everyone else and they can't see it, that I should be managing a Champions League club. The answer is to get it all in perspective. Somewhere between two extremes you can live.

Also, I took solace in my assured belief that there simply wasn't much more I could have done. As a player, when I had

had a bad game, I would look in depth at how I could have done better. That's what separates the good pros from the also-rans. Doing that again now, while I might have made a different decision here or there, mostly what I could see was a set of mitigating circumstances. In coaching and management, it is not always about ability. It can also be about being in the wrong place at the wrong time.

I didn't want to dive straight back into the game but I knew that I had unfinished business. After a few weeks of soul-searching, I went into action, as the AA programme suggests, and started to make some calls to people to see where I might fit in. When the summer came, the job as manager of Celtic, in succession to Gordon Strachan, came up.

I received a call from a Dutch journalist I had got to know from my time both at Arsenal and Feyenoord, Marcel van der Kraan. He told me that Wim Jansen, with whom I had got on well at Feyenoord in his role as an adviser to the club, had been approached by Celtic to go back there. Walter Smith had not long returned to Rangers and it seemed to have planted a seed with Celtic that maybe they could get back a successful manager of their own, as Wim had been in the late nineties, to recreate the past.

Wim turned them down, Marcel said, but he would go back as a technical director if he could work with a young head coach like Tony Adams. Would I be interested in going there with Wim? Yes, I said to Marcel, if Wim wanted to call me.

A day or two later I was making a personal appearance at a press conference on behalf of Nationwide Building Society, sponsors of the England team, ahead of a Wembley international. It was at Nationwide's headquarters in Swindon, not too far from where I lived, so it seemed like a good idea at the time.

I was asked about whether I would be going back into management and talked about the Celtic job and the interest there.

That's the way I am. If asked a question, I am going to be honest and open. Of course, that was not going to be the end of the matter.

The next thing I knew, Celtic were denying the story and Wim was refusing to comment. I was disappointed with that. He could have backed me up. There was also an article in the *Daily Telegraph* by Paul Hayward suggesting I had gone a bit strange and must be hearing voices in my head. It was odd, because I respected Paul, who was a good writer and a good man, and so I got hold of a number for him. I asked him if he would meet me for a cup of tea.

He agreed and so we talked it through. He admitted that his piece had been a bit wide of the mark and said he would like to write another, based on our meeting, redressing the balance. I wasn't after that, I said. I just wanted him to meet me to see what I am really like. Let's be men and move on, I added.

Actually, Paul did write an article, this time from knowing me a bit better, and it was a fair piece. In years to come, I would even include it in my CV so that people might not judge me just on Wycombe and the Portsmouth mess.

After that episode, nothing really appealed as the 2009/10 season approached, even though I might have wanted to show people – and myself – that I could succeed at being a manager or head coach. I wanted to keep active, though. I'd been out of work after leaving Wycombe and Feyenoord, and I didn't want to get bored.

And so I looked to further my coaching education and took myself off on a road trip to Milan, where Jose Mourinho had agreed to see me. He was manager of Internazionale at the time and he gave me access-all-areas and was charm itself, open and honest.

I also had lunch with Patrick Vieira to catch up on things and we agreed that the 1998/99 side – unfortunate to find our

nemesis in a treble-winning Manchester United that season —
should have gone on to achieve more than win the double and
reach a UEFA Cup final in subsequent seasons. We also agreed
that side laid the groundwork for the Invincibles.

While there I met up too with Alex Manninger, then playing
in nearby Turin for Juventus; and I recall Jamie Redknapp also
being around the Inter training ground, needing a bit of help,
in fact, to get in with a film crew for a Sky programme he was
making about trying to take a player and turn him into a
superstar.

It was interesting watching Jose work on the training ground.
I thought he would be at the side of the pitch letting his coaches
work. But he was very much hands-on, and he knew his stuff,
empathising with players — among them Sulley Muntari, who
I'd had at Portsmouth — in a way that was unusual for someone
who had not played at the highest level. He had complete control of the group with his understanding of the game. It was
easy to see why players loved him and why he has been a success
everywhere he has gone.

He said to me: 'Tony, you have got a lot of catching up to do.
I was watching van Gaal and Robson 25 years ago. Your playing
career has got in your way of being a coach. You are going to
have to give it a lot of time and learning.'

I also talked to him about handling maverick players, Mario
Balotelli being at Inter at the time. It was simple, he said: I tolerate him when he is scoring goals and playing well, I don't
when he is not. You cannot let players drag down your squad,
Jose continued. If they are not going to give the team energy,
you let them go.

The way to get such players on board, he said, was to go to
their close family and friends and seek their help in keeping him
on the straight and narrow. The problem was, Jose added, there
was even less stability among Balotelli's support network.

When I got home and took stock, I came to realise that autumn that after Wycombe and Portsmouth, I had become a bit disillusioned with the UK. And I was realistic about where I stood. No big Premier League club was going to touch me after what had happened at Pompey. Actually, no Premier League club full stop was going to. I didn't want to go back to being a number two and I didn't want to go back to the lower leagues. The only place I hadn't worked was the Championship. That, in my thinking at the time, was a possibility. I kept my ear to the ground, went to watch a few matches.

I was running out of options, though. Here I was, seven years down the line in coaching, and I wanted a number one's job at a club that had money and a chance of winning, with a chairman I could work with and who would give me time. It was, in hindsight, no wonder I was running out of options, given those criteria – which are sadly all too rare in the cut-throat environment that is the Championship, where most clubs have revolving doors on the manager's office. And also given that those criteria form the wish list for pretty much every manager.

Added to that, I had to consider whether it was going to be worth moving the family up to Blackburn or Bolton or Burnley for a salary of £100,000 and a job that might last just nine months. And one that would involve plenty of abuse in those nine months.

And so I stayed patient and waited for an opportunity. I was in no rush, partly because by now Poppy was pregnant with our third child together, whom we would name Iris when she was born in the February of 2010. I wanted to support Poppy and also spend plenty of time with her and our new daughter.

I continued to watch games and do the odd bit of TV work, then received a strange phone call just around the time Iris was born. It came from Gary Stevens, the former Tottenham full-back I had known from England squads. He asked what I was doing these days and I told him that I was enjoying life: spending time with the family, working with Sporting Chance, going to therapy and AA meetings, saying yes to charity functions now I had the time and just trying to keep an interest in the game. I was indeed enjoying life, though I had to admit I was still unfulfilled professionally.

We talked about the state of the game and how it was spitting out coaches and managers. It was a long conversation. But even so, we both agreed that we would like to get back into the game, though there seemed to be little out there, with so many unemployed coaches going for so few jobs. Gary seemed more desperate than I was to be involved again.

'If you do get a job,' he said, 'I'd love to be your assistant.' I said I would bear it in mind, and I put the phone down wondering why I had had a call like that out of the blue.

A couple of months later I had another call, this time from an agent who dealt mainly in lower-league players and with whom I had come into contact when I was manager at Wycombe. I had known Lorenzo Paolo for a while, as he had worked with Steve Kutner before branching out on his own. Our paths crossed again in a Frankie and Benny's restaurant next to Oxford United's Kassam Stadium, where I was scouting a reserve game for any potential players I might recruit. Glamorous life, football. As it happened, I didn't take any players from him but we had exchanged details after he had reintroduced himself to me.

Now he was asking me where I was. I was a bit taken aback. 'In London,' I said, having just come out of a lunchtime AA meeting on Piccadilly. 'Great,' he replied and said he would meet me in a coffee shop nearby. I was intrigued.

'Tone,' he said when we got together. 'How do you fancy

Azerbaijan?' How did I fancy it? How could I say? I had never even heard of it. I told him I was open-minded, though.

'Well,' Lorenzo added, 'I know this bloke I used to have dealings with at Bournemouth when he was chief executive there. Name of Alastair Saverimutto. He's trying to build a club out in Azerbaijan, a club called FK Gabala, and he needs a head coach. Let me fix up a meeting with him and the club's top brass.'

I was curious and went away to do some homework, finding out that Azerbaijan was a former Soviet Republic with a population of around eight million, situated on the Caspian Sea between Russia and Georgia to the north and Iran to the south. Gabala was a town in the north of the country, the football club founded just five years earlier, in 2005.

A week or so later, I found myself, along with Lorenzo, in a meeting in London in Queen Anne's Gate, the headquarters of The European Azerbaijan Society (TEAS). Alastair, a smooth-talking guy aged around 40, told me about the Gabala club, which needed building up from the grass roots – the team, the club and the facilities. There would, he added, be ample resources available to do it.

I would soon come to see that the defining characteristic of Alastair, who had been a Premiership rugby union player and also commercial manager at Everton, was his salesmanship. He was so enthusiastic about the project (and while I don't like to use that word when it comes to football clubs, this was most definitely a project). It was a great little club with a young owner, he added, and he wanted to get me into a meeting with the guy.

Alastair pointed out that I was a manager out of work – though I hardly needed reminding – and that this was a brilliant opportunity for someone young like me in need of a new start in coaching and management. They had, he said, considered a couple of more senior figures, in Terry Venables and Sven-Goran Eriksson. However, Terry seemed to want to do the job by Skype, he added, and Sven wanted a £4 million salary before he would even go to the country.

I suspected Alastair was joking and doubted that Terry had even entertained the idea – though the Sven statement may have had a grain of truth – but what appealed to me was his assertion that they really wanted a younger man who would throw himself into the job. I was willing to do that, and I especially liked the idea of building a club from scratch, far from the madding crowd, where I could get on with my apprenticeship in management in peace.

At this point, we were joined at the large table by two men, who turned out to be Tale Heydarov, the Gabala club president, and his right-hand man, Fariz Najafov, vice president and a national sporting celebrity, having been seven-times Shotokan World Karate champion.

Tale was then just 25 years old. A well-dressed young man, he spoke excellent English, unlike Fariz who smiled and observed, and who I thought at the time was his security man. Tale was clearly well educated and I would discover later that he had been to the London School of Economics. He came across as sincere and respectful. I liked him.

'Thank you for seeing us, Mr Adams,' Tale said. I'm not sure many club owners would have said that. Normally you were expected to be grateful to them.

He told me about the Gabala region, where he was born, the town having a population of around 25,000 but with 90,000 in the surrounding area. He showed me the drawings for a 25,000-seater stadium with a training complex adjacent to it. There were plans also for a ski resort, new hotels and an international airport to be built there. It was a fantastic presentation.

'We need someone young and passionate to build the football

club and Alastair tells me you are the man to do it, Mr Adams,' he said. 'Come and help us.' It was nice to hear.

I asked some football questions, about the standard of the league and the players they had at Gabala – and also about the playing budget. At this point Tale turned to Fariz and I realised then that Fariz was more than the president's security man. Actually, he knew more about the club itself than Tale did, I would soon discover. It turned out the playing budget would be US $1 million, then about that of a lower Division Two club or mid-table National League (formerly Conference) club, but not bad for Azerbaijan.

Having had the experience of working with Sacha Gaydamak and Peter Storrie, and seen their fancy drawings and plans for training grounds and stadiums, I still needed some convincing. Not only did I need to think about it, I wanted to get out there and find out for myself, I told them, whether or not it could be done.

This time, I was determined not to do anything without Poppy's agreement, having learned my lesson from the Portsmouth episode. When I got back home that night, we talked it through and made arrangements to go out to Azerbaijan together. She could help me through my fear of flying as well.

Knowing that I had a six-hour flight ahead of me, I went to see a hypnotherapist in South Kensington for some tips. He had me tapping the pressure points around my head and face to try to reduce tension and told me to use that technique on the flight. It must have worked to some extent as I would get on the plane, but I must have gone to the toilet 10 times, so nervous was I.

We had to wait a few weeks, mind, due to the intervention of the ash cloud caused by the eruption of that Icelandic volcano, Eyjafjallajokull. We even went to Manchester to try to get a flight, in the middle of the Conservative Party Conference, without any luck. At least it gave me more time to do further research on Gabala, Azerbaijan, Alastair, Tale and Fariz. Along with Gary Stevens.

I had smiled when Alastair suggested Gary as my assistant. Gary had obviously known more than I did when he phoned me that time. It turned out that Gary and Alastair had met each other at an England Under-21 game that had taken place at Bournemouth, when they'd been introduced by a mutual acquaintance, as they shared the same lawyer. Clearly, I had been in the club's thoughts for a couple of months, even if Lorenzo Paolo had joked that Adams had come up first alpha-betically in their search. I was happy with Gary, and all of the people I might be working with, in fact.

The trip was, as might have been expected, an eye-opener.

The capital Baku – with its five million inhabitants who thus accounted for more than half of the nation's population – was developing fast on the back of oil and gas reserves from the Caspian, with the country keeping its own wealth since the break-up of the old Soviet Union in the early 1990s, though of course there were trade deals in place. Elegant buildings were going up all over the place. It was a Muslim state but a relaxed one. Due to its comparative sophistication, Baku, indeed, had always been something of a playground for old Russians with wealth able to travel. With its sweeping promenade emulating La Croisette, it had been described as the Cannes of the region.

Out of Baku was a different matter. Travelling the 130 miles north-west out of the city to Gabala, not too far from the Georgian and southern Russian borders, took more than four hours, such was the state of the single-track roads winding through the isolated small towns and villages to the Caucasus mountains. There would frequently be cows on the road and people alongside the tarmac, including small children, trying to sell you whatever fruit and meat they could to make a living.

When you got to within 10 miles of Gabala, you could see high on a hill two giant satellite dishes, apparently for monitoring communications, left over from the Soviet era and which would be dismantled some years later. In fact, the football team was known then as The Radars.

Gabala was growing, I could see that as Alastair showed me and Gary around, with luxury hotels sprouting up and factories being built, all with Heydarov family money. Tale's father Kamaladdin was a minister in the government – for what was called 'Emergency Situations' – and was also a prominent songwriter in the country, having apparently had several hits. He had given his son responsibility for running his company Gilan Industries, which was a trading and construction business, while he was in politics. The family were determined to make their home region of Gabala prosperous.

The football club, however, had very little except a huge patch of land close to town on which to operate. The only real facility was a huge green hangar, a remnant from when the site had been a military base, which had housed tanks and helicopters in the old Soviet days. It served as home to everything, from dressing rooms to offices, though they were basic. There were six teams, from first team down through age groups, playing on one bumpy pitch and a poorly laid 3G pitch. There were no seats or terracing.

I took in an Azerbaijan Premier League game, with Gabala beating FK Baku, who had won the national cup that season. A couple of hundred turned out to watch. Neither side was outstanding and I gauged the standard to be about the old Conference level. There was some potential there.

I also watched the final Gabala game in Baku, a 4–0 defeat by Inter, who had already won the league, which comprised 12 clubs playing each other four times. I thought there was scope to do something with this team.

Talking things over with Gary on the plane home – him wondering what was going on when I kept getting up to go to the toilet in my anxiety about flying – I began to think this might just work, though the situation had been far from promising. I was working on a mixture of raw gut instinct combined with facts and logic. In the end, it often comes down to the people involved rather than the circumstances.

I had been particularly impressed by Tale and I thought about the old piece of advice that Sir Alex Ferguson used to give to budding managers: 'Don't pick a club, pick a chairman.' In other words, work with someone who will give you a chance, no matter the status of the club. That crossed off a large percentage of people in England after my Portsmouth experience. From all the fuss around the English game, and listening to all the nonsense spoken, there weren't too many who impressed me. Tale didn't know much about football but he didn't pretend to, and I liked that at the interview. He was a quiet, serious man, one to be reckoned with.

Normally, managerial interviews take place in front of three guys – maybe the owner, chairman and chief executive – who all reckon they know more than you. They ask questions such as: 'Do you play 4-4-2?' or 'Are you going to work on the defence?' or 'We are a counterattacking team. You won't change that, will you?' They're supposedly interviewing you but really they would like to be doing the job themselves. Or at least the best parts of it, like picking the team.

With Tale there was a humility and respect for me and my career. He said he wanted my information and knowledge. He was on my side and that was important. That would give me the mandate I required to accomplish all the things that needed doing if a good club was to be established.

I also talked at length with Poppy. 'I think I can do this,' I said to her. 'I can build my own squad, play the way I want, and

I'm going to get time. I have the owner's backing and he has resources. On top of all that, I get to have input in building a club and a stadium. Where am I going to get a remit like that in the UK?'

When it all came out like that, what was not to like? I had been going round the M25 for the last 25 years and I wasn't getting anywhere in England any more. I was ready for a new challenge and new country where I could further my experience and learn more, far away from the judgements of people who often didn't know the reality of situations.

Was I running away from the real challenge of management in England? I didn't think so. It was about learning my trade properly, maybe to return to a good job one day, though that was being a bit of a Little Englander about it as there was plenty of good football, played by good clubs, all across the world. Anyway, I wanted it to be like it was when I was an Arsenal apprentice, learning in the South East Counties League on a Saturday morning, making mistakes but well away from the glare of the media and unforgiving owners and fans.

Above all, I was clean and sober and I had the mental and emotional resources now to be able to confront this type of challenge, out of my comfort zone. I knew I could do this. Poppy agreed. She knew how frustrated I was growing at home and that I needed to be active. She also liked an adventure herself. She thought it would be exciting and fascinating for her and the children to come out there too.

I was concerned about there being no formal meetings of Alcoholics Anonymous but I could make other arrangements. I would take tapes with me, by speakers talking about AA's Twelve Steps, and also tap into websites that had speakers. A friend also had a friend in recovery working in Baku and we could meet for coffee. I took comfort too from the fact that Azerbaijan was a Muslim state and, while there were bars and clubs, they were not widespread and it would be a help not seeing booze everywhere in your face.

And so I accepted the job, though before I went out for pre-season, I had one commitment that I had, and really wanted, to keep.

13

Why, Why, Why Gabala?

In return for a bottle and a hangover,
we have been given the Keys of the Kingdom.

ALCOHOLICS ANONYMOUS, *page 312*

I spent the June before pre-season began at the end of that month getting my Gabala team together. That month was punctuated by something that was a real privilege to do and provided huge enjoyment. I was honoured to be asked to appear on Radio 4's *Desert Island Discs* with Kirsty Young, and it was wonderful picking my favourite songs as a soundtrack to my life. It would also prove to be an emotional experience.

I included the first record I ever bought: 'Boy About Town' by the Jam, which probably said something about the cockiness of being 14 that I used, subconsciously, to mask my insecurity. I also picked 'Let's Groove' by Earth, Wind and Fire, which reminded me of being young and carefree and out on a Saturday night after a game.

Then there was 'Sweet Caroline' by Neil Diamond for my mum, and that track by Squeeze which was playing on the jukebox the day I got sober, 'Black Coffee in Bed'. I also just had to pick the Arsenal FA Cup final song of 1971 – 'Good Old Arsenal'.

In between, Kirsty asked me in detail about my life, based on my conversation with a researcher who came to my home to get a list of songs and some background on me for the interviewer. It is an intimate setting, just you and Kirsty in a dark studio, and I began filling up when she asked me about my mother. These days, I get less emotional when I talk about how drinking brought me to my knees, but that day I also welled up when I recalled it. From Kirsty's questions, I felt she understood a bit about alcoholism.

It was a cathartic experience, and down the years I have been gratified by the number of people who said they heard it and were moved by it. I was also flattered that my contribution was chosen as one of the castaways' choices in a book to mark 70 years of the programme in 2012.

I picked as my favourite track Monty Python's 'Always Look on the Bright Side of Life' and my luxury item was – naturally – a football. That would take care of my physical wellbeing. To nurture my spiritual self, I chose as the book I was allowed the Big Book of Alcoholics Anonymous. That too would be going with me to Azerbaijan, along with my hand-picked backroom staff.

The physio, a recommendation by Gary Stevens, was a Muslim who was born in Iran but lived in England by the name of Faraz Sethi. Though just 24, he had worked at Watford and Colchester and I thought that he would be perfect, as he could adapt to the environment and help me adjust to the religion there. He was tough and ballsy, though some would later find him a little too much so for their liking.

For my development coach, overseeing the academy we were going to build up, I recruited Daryl Willard, a skills coach in the Chelsea academy who had worked with Gary Stevens at a soccer school Gary had in Gibraltar. At first, the Azerbaijanis would think he was too young, as they preferred more mature coaches, but Daryl would do so well that he ended up becoming the technical director of the Azal club out there and would remain in Azerbaijan for more than six years.

I also took on a Turkish guy by the name of Fatih Kavlak from the Qarabag club to do our technical analyses and physical warm-ups. Otherwise, pretty much everyone working around the club – directors, drivers, stadium operatives – was from the vice president's family.

I asked Gary to go and watch the Azerbaijan national team so we could see who might be worth recruiting from among the best in the country. It was important to get good Azerbaijanis due to the regulations on the number of domestic players who had to be in a club team and squad. At that time, it was four in a team, which would a few years later increase to five.

When I arrived on 28 June for pre-season training, I resolved to give everyone a chance before making too many changes. The squad comprised mainly players from Latvia and Georgia, former Soviet republics too, but I did bring in some of my own, chiefly the Jamaica striker Deon Burton, who had been at many Football League clubs and had just been released by Charlton. He was a durable character up for the adventure, if a bit physical for the league. He would do well, go on to be leading scorer, though would get frustrated with referees.

An old friend, Gary Walker, who owned and ran the Palm Beach soccer academy in Florida, also knew of young Brazilian players developed by the Sao Paulo academy and I took three with potential. They were all gambles and only one, Silva, really went on to do well.

I also wanted to do pre-season in Gabala itself, to familiarise myself with our environment. Usually they went to the resort of Antalya in Turkey and I think I disorientated a few people around the club who didn't like change. It saved the club $100,000 which I thought could be better spent elsewhere.

It helped that Poppy and the kids came out with me – Atticus now six, Hector four and Iris six months – and we took six boxes of personal stuff to make the hotel rooms seem more homely. The first hotel we were in, the Riverside, looked from the outside like it had all mod cons, and advertised them, though it didn't quite work out like that.

It did have a new amusement park next door, but it was barely used during our time there. The kids loved it, especially having all the rides, the bumper cars, the waltzer and the skating rink, to themselves. The lovely young guy who ran it, Ismet, used to give me the keys so I could open and shut it for them myself if it was out of hours. It spoiled the kids for when they went to Chessington and had to queue.

Just as the hotel's professionalism in those days was a facade, so too at the club. Within days, I was wondering where to start with it all. In fact, that Tom Jones song 'Delilah' kept going through my head, though I would change the chorus to 'Why, Why, Why Gabala?'

On day one, there were no balls, bibs, or cones. It was like a Sunday league club. Then when the equipment did arrive, the next day the balls would not be pumped up properly. When I talked to people working around the training ground and the club about it all, they would just smile and nod, but actually they were showing me no respect.

Apparently, they were used to people shouting at them. And so I did. First, I made them watch as I kicked every ball out of the training ground. I then assembled all the staff in the hall – the hangar that served as the venue for everything at the club – and lost it with them, by design. I didn't wait for a translator to interpret my words. He was not needed. They got the picture. And from that day, the attitude changed.

We did reasonably well in the first four games despite the circumstances of the club. Against the top teams – Neftchi Baku, Khazar Lankaran, Qarabag and Inter Baku – we won one and lost the other three by the odd goal. I recall my first press conference at an away game, against Lankaran. There was one cameraman and one reporter there and the conference consisted of two questions:

'Do you like it here in Lankaran?' was the first.

'Yes, it's very nice,' I replied.

'How long will you stay in Azerbaijan?' was the second.

'Hopefully a long time,' was my reply.

And that was it. Nothing about the game, which we had lost 1-0. I would have tried to be gracious in defeat. That would not always be reciprocated during my time in the country, however. I encountered a few managers who had plenty to say for themselves.

Early on, I also held a 'fans' forum' at Gabala. Around 20 people showed up. The first question I took was about whether David Beckham and/or Roberto Carlos would be coming to the club, as had been rumoured. I tried to give them a long, detailed, honest answer about where the club was, the budget and what we were seeking to achieve. Then came a question from the father of the Azerbaijani centre-forward I had substituted the previous day during a 1-0 win asking me why I had done it.

It was all interesting stuff, learning about the local mentality, and I knew we would have a battle on our hands to build up the support, and the understanding, of the supporters. In those early days, whenever we went to an away game, we would take about 15 fans on a coach we provided and give them packed lunches. We also paid a few guys in the town to go around and drum up support for home games. Few stayed till the end of the match. They would certainly leave early if you were losing.

By now Poppy and the kids had gone home, which didn't

help when so much was going wrong and I had no diversion from it. Attitudes may have changed a little within the club after my outburst but logistics and efficiency hadn't. In fact, over the first six weeks of the season until the end of August, I made a list of things that needed to be fixed but took so long to get sorted – if indeed they did. The list stretched to 23 items.

For a start, six teams at various age groups would all often turn up to train on the two pitches at the same time. Everyone was in the same colour shirts when training as we had no bibs. So we had to play skins v shirts. There were no showers after training, but then there were no towels even if there had been. The 25 towels and 100 pairs of white socks I ordered somehow didn't arrive.

Some of it was trivial but intensely frustrating as I compiled a to-do and to-get list: no microwave in the team bus, the toilets being locked, no DVD player on the bus, no treatment beds, no defibrillator (and one player had a heart problem), no ice machines, no mats, hurdles or mannequins. There was no inter-net on which to scout players and our website was rarely updated. Nor was the food for the players good enough.

In addition, I had to sort out unpaid wages and cars for the staff that were promised. Deon Burton was not being reim-bursed for taxis. Our long-term visas had not been sorted out and, indeed, our passports were being held so we were unable to go home for a week's holiday during an international break.

There were some amusing interludes, such as the day we arrived for training to find cows on the training ground. Apparently, after the military had withdrawn from the site, a local farmer was granted grazing rights in return for conceding the land. The problem was that the cows were on the synthetic pitch trying to eat that, and leaving cow pats all over it. After they were cleared up, I think a deal was done for the farmer to graze them elsewhere.

I recall one game, too, when we were playing in the National

Stadium against Qarabag, who had to play all their games in Baku because their region was the subject of a bitter dispute between Azerbaijan and Armenia and the two countries were technically still at war. Before the game, there was dog mess on the pitch and I called the groundsman over. He duly moved it with a shovel – into a long jump pit next to the surrounding athletics track.

There was another time when, before training, we were doing a light weights session in the gym I had set up inside the hangar when we heard a loud bang. We all went outside to find out what it was and saw, about 100 metres away, a group of soldiers on manoeuvres. In fact, they were chucking hand grenades into large mounds of earth that had been created by the work on new pitches.

I was assured we would be fine to train but every now and then there would be a loud bang and the players hit the deck. After a while, we got used to it. At the end, I spoke to Fariz, the club VP. I told him that I wanted to respect the army's activities but could they let us know in advance when they might be coming? In the event, they didn't come back.

I felt like I was constantly problem-solving and growing more annoyed by the week. One day, I wanted some tea after training but there was none. And so I went to a nearby catering college to get the students to provide it. A lot of it was teething troubles and miscommunication, but the doubt that I had done the right thing in coming here was growing. I felt as if I was swimming upstream.

I was referring things to Alastair Saverimutto but it soon became clear that Fariz was actually running the club. All his men were around, observing all the time. It was tricky because the VP's brother-in-law was the previous manager and the club was keeping him on. I made him the assessor of our opponents so that he wasn't really around, but the reports were sketchy.

I asked for a meeting with Tale and went to Baku near the end of August. Alastair and Fariz were also there. I was angry and gave it to them straight as I looked directly into Tale's eyes.

'You have put me in this region without the resources I was promised and you are expecting me to magic up a football club,' I said. 'I will stay here but you have got to tell me you are going to support me financially, both in the recruitment of players and the infrastructure of the club.'

Tale looked at me and smiled. 'No problem, Mr Adams,' he said.

I asked who I was reporting to and Tale said that Fariz was in charge of administration and budgets and Alastair's areas of responsibility were marketing and commercial. Alastair's jaw dropped while the penny dropped with me. It had never been made clear to him or me what the chain of command was. Now I knew who I had to work with, even if Fariz didn't speak English.

Alastair may have felt undermined but I went away more reassured, and I thought things might improve when a well-respected Azerbaijani footballing figure in Ali Yavash, who had played for and coached Galatasaray in Istanbul – the Azerbaijanis loved Turkish football and the Turks, the languages being similar – was hired to form the academy and become its director. I liked him. He had previously been in charge of scouting and scouring the regions looking for players for the age-group teams and was great at it. Now he was given licence to pull it all together under one roof.

In reality, though, nothing did change over the next couple of months and I was still trying to sort out minor problems. I even had to ask for the kitchen staff at the hotel to start wearing hats as we found hairs in the food. One day, Gary, Daryl, Fariz and I were eating spaghetti Bolognese but it was cold. When we pointed this out, the waiter simply stuck his finger in one of our plates and said that, no, he didn't think it was.

Then came a funny, ridiculous incident one night when Gary and I sat down to dinner.

The staff had a strange habit of serving both the starter and the main course at the same time, which was amusing at first but grew annoying. On this particular night, it became too much for Gary. He got up, called all the waiting and kitchen staff together and explained to them in English, them looking baffled, how to serve a starter first, then wait before serving a main course. To help them, he even mimed the actions, walking towards the kitchen and back for each course. I could only laugh. It wasn't embarrassing even though the scene was conducted in the dining room. We were the only ones in it.

Alastair had been wounded after the meeting with Tale, and any effort he made to gain more control was being thwarted. He had no direct line to Tale himself. And I needed him having more of a say if I was going to get things done. Eventually, wasted months later, I would phone the president and tell him as much. It was always best to be up front. In sobriety, that is the only way to be if I am to remain at ease with myself.

I told him that the staff were all looking to Fariz and it meant they were not agreeing to anything I might want done without going through him. I needed my point of contact to be Alastair. Tale agreed and phoned Fariz to tell him that Alastair would now be taking control. At many English clubs, it might have caused considerable friction but Fariz is a lovely man and took it well. He just wanted what was best for Mr Tony and the club, he said, and if that meant him retreating a little, so be it.

The next day, Alastair met with all the staff to tell them the new arrangements. It should have been the start of things changing for the better, but Alastair then made a serious error of judgement – he went on holiday for three weeks to Barbados when he should have been cementing his position and been at my side. It was the action of a man who didn't understand football and how it worked. In his absence, the staff started going back to Fariz for guidance.

By November of my first season, the players were still in T-shirts because winter kit hadn't arrived and I was still struggling to train the side every day, given all the problems that needed ironing out. But we were getting some results now, which meant players were beginning to listen to me.

In fact, we were comfortably in mid-table in the 12-team league, which was where Gabala had finished the previous season. We reached the winter break, which spanned a few weeks from mid-December through to early January, in reasonable shape and with things gradually improving off the field as equipment began to arrive and people got paid more regularly. It meant I could go back to England for a family Christmas in a better frame of mind.

Despite the hypnotherapy I'd had earlier in the year – and taking a sleeping pill if I really had no alternative but to do it – my anxiety about flying was never far beneath the surface. Now I had a bit of time on my hands, so thought I would take a leisurely journey overland back to England, picturing myself having some thinking and reading time, enjoying the scenery. With no train service to speak of in Azerbaijan, the idea was that I would have a club driver take me to the Georgian border, then a taxi would ferry me to Istanbul where I would get a train – or rather several – home.

It wouldn't, of course, work quite like that. In fact, it would turn out to be the most terrifying journey of my life.

The drive from Baku to the Georgian border took seven hours, where I walked through and picked up the taxi, which was an old rust bucket. And I soon discovered that the driver for this leg was somewhat of a nutter. That dawned on me outside the Georgian capital Tbilisi – where I played for England when not long sober in one of Glenn Hoddle's first games as

England manager back in 1996 – when the driver missed the turning for the direction we should have been going in, towards Gori, Stalin's birthplace.

We found ourselves on a 10-lane motorway going in the wrong direction. After a while, he decided to stop and seek help. And so, when he saw a police car on the hard shoulder, he stopped to get directions. Right in the middle of the motorway. He got out, ran across several lanes of traffic, leaving me in the back with cars whizzing past either side of me, hooting their horns. It was −10°C and snow was falling. I was frozen with cold and fear. Naturally, the police nicked him.

After that, it was another five hours to Batumi, near the Turkish border, and the hotel I had booked. We were now negotiating some narrow mountain passes in the dark, but it didn't stop the guy overtaking lorries, me covering my eyes, and at times he would only just make it back into our lane as an oncoming car flashed its lights. I asked him to slow down at times but he ignored me. I was grateful to get to the hotel in one piece at 11pm.

The nightmare continued the next day, however, beginning as soon as we hit the Turkish border. There, they already had a record of him being nicked the previous day and they were not going to let him through without paying a fine of $40. Naturally, that fell to me to sort out. Once under way, there was an episode where he cut up a van, whose driver promptly overtook us and stopped, forcing us to brake. A row and even some fisticuffs followed before it calmed down and we carried on. My anxiety levels, already high, were still rising.

We stopped for lunch but he seemed not to enjoy his. When we'd finished, he ushered me out of the place, trying not to pay. I told him I had money and when the staff followed us into the car park, I held out some cash. He just bundled me in the car, however, shouting, 'Tony Adams, Tony Adams!' to the staff and sped off. When we got to the hotel a few hours' drive outside Istanbul for that second night, I ran straight to my room.

The next morning he tried to set off with ice still on the windscreen but I stopped him and went back into the hotel to get hot water. Finally, when we reached central Istanbul, following the hair-raising 1,500 miles and 24 hours of driving time, I leapt out of the car and gave him the $2,000 fee. It seemed a lot but I had never been so happy to pay somebody and would have paid more just for him to go away. So unnerved by the experience was I that I checked into a hotel for a few days to recover my composure before getting on the train back home. I took in Galatasaray v Fenerbahce while there.

When I did make it to the station, from Istanbul it was trains to Bucharest, Budapest, Munich, Paris and London, which took five nights and grew more pleasant as the trains got better the further west I travelled.

Unfortunately, that meant that on the return journey, the trains got worse the further east I travelled. I was not in the happiest of spirits anyway, sad at having to leave the family behind in the New Year after a wonderful couple of weeks with them. This time I was heading for Antalya on the Turkish Mediterranean, where I had agreed the team could do a winter training camp, in sunshine, ahead of the resumption of the second half of the season. Instead of making the long journey across Turkey from Istanbul into Georgia and then Azerbaijan, I could get a driver – a club one this time, rather than some hired wacky racer – down from Istanbul.

The Eurostar to Paris was lovely, as ever, and I then got a good night's sleep going to Munich. From there to Budapest was not too bad either. I then had a two-hour wait at the station for the connection to Bucharest, when I suddenly began to feel uneasy and unsafe. There seemed to be a few unscrupulous characters around and I saw money and packages changing hands. I decided to stay on the move until my train was ready.

The train to Bucharest was shocking, a real 1930s rattler, and I just couldn't get any sleep. Near Sofia in Bulgaria, the engine blew up and we were stuck there for six or seven hours. We had been due at the Turkish border at around 2am but we were going to be very late. And I struggled to sleep yet again, finally drifting off at around 6am after 36 hours without any kip.

Suddenly, I was rudely awakened by the sound of hammering at the door of my cabin and loud voices shouting at me. I got out of the bunk bleary-eyed and opened the door, scared stiff, wondering what the hell was going on and what I'd done. I was confronted by a group of armed soldiers shouting and I just raised my hands in the air. One of the soldiers looked me up and down and began to speak more slowly and softly.

'You are Tony Adams?' he said.

'Yes,' I replied, respectfully but worried.

'Tony Adams. Yes,' he said. 'Galatasaray. We beat you Arsenal, UEFA Cup final. Thierry Henry missed penalty. Thank you. Thank you. Thank you.'

Never had I minded less being recognised. And it was the only time in my life I was grateful that I had lost a football match.

He apologised for knocking so loudly on the door but I had not answered at first, so deeply asleep was I. He explained politely that we were at the Turkish border and I had to get off the train, pay US$20 for a visa then get back on the train. I was only too happy to do so and obediently followed instructions.

Back in Gabala after a pleasant training camp, the team began to improve in tandem with the solving of problems off the field. It was good also to have Poppy and the kids with me for the February half-term holiday. I had now moved into another hotel, separate from the players, as I felt I needed some distance from them. It wasn't a problem. New hotels were going up almost by the week in Gabala now.

The way the league was structured meant that after 22 games, at the end of February when everyone had played each other twice, the teams were split into two groups, the top six and the bottom six. All in each group then played each other twice to decide the champions and the two relegation places.

I sensed the mutterings when we finished seventh, two points adrift of the top group, but personally I was not unhappy. It meant that we would have a good chance of winning the second group – we were never going to be relegated as points were carried over – and also that expectations would not be too high for the following season. The disappointment for the club, I think, was that they had recruited Tony Adams and thought they had sent out a message to the rest of the league. They were clearly expecting more. But then they hadn't taken into account the starting point of the club the previous summer.

Money had gone into the club, yes, but it was on the infrastructure rather than the team, with us filling the squad with younger players. I wrote to the president explaining as much and he accepted it. It was easier for him to do so as he rarely came to games and could be more dispassionate.

In the end, we did win the second group, establishing a league record of 11 clean sheets in a row and 19 in all that season. And so I reckoned we could all be pleased with a first season that had seen the club overcome all sorts of obstacles and take huge strides forward. Crowds had doubled to around 400 and we now had some temporary stands to seat them in.

I made another list – this time of things we had done well and made better. We had improved both the first-team and reserve squads, increasing the number of professionals, and had a proper academy set-up. We also had a marvellous new groundsman in Phil Sharples, who had been with Watford and was going to expand our operation, turning the space from two pitches into six. He was an expert in turf management who had advised a whole host of clubs and tournaments around the world.

We were now one club, instead of a group of teams, and I had implemented many things I'd learned from the Arsenal and from my embryonic coaching and management career. We had a scientific approach to fitness and conditioning, and I had established a gym in the hangar. We had a professional medical department with rehab programmes, scans and physiological analysis of players. We had new kitchens and better food, which meant an improved diet and thus better-conditioned players. I had also introduced a scouting system and the scouting of opposition.

I had managed to get all the players into the main Gilan hotel in the town and we had a proper wage bill and bonus structure. Everyone was being paid on time now. We also had a decent coaches' room. It sounds like a simple thing but it was hard-won, as with everything from getting the club website sorted to sourcing goalposts, floodlights and mannequins, often from outside the country. Patience and perseverance had paid off.

I was basically trying to turn an amateur club into one with a professional future. I wanted to engender an atmosphere of honesty and respect, of all being in it together. As well as the fans' forums, I sent the players out into schools and the community to build relationships, and hopefully support, and thus increase attendances.

Above all, I hoped I was building a club based on my own beliefs and what I had learned, both in football and in recovery from my alcoholism, a club that a region could be proud of. There were also nods to the Arsenal amid it all. As well as having the pitch made the same size as Highbury, I had a club rule book based on the one I was handed as a kid when I first became a Gunner. At its heart was the old club mantra that has always stayed with me: 'Remember who you are, what you are, and who you represent.'

After seven or eight months of frustration and now three or so of thinking I was getting somewhere, I felt I could go home and enjoy my month off before a new pre-season. Naturally, that month went quickly and soon, in the July, I was bringing the Gabala squad over to England for a training camp and some friendlies, staying at a hotel in Elstree. We played matches against Luton Town, St Albans City – as a favour to my co-writer Ian Ridley, who was then chairman there – and Barnet, whose new training ground, the Hive, we also used. It was a great experience for my boys, playing at decent grounds and in front of good crowds.

I was optimistic about the new season when we got back to Gabala – and this time I flew. After that journey from hell with the mad driver, I resolved that I could not go through that again and had gone on a fear of flying course run by Virgin Airways at East Midlands airport. There had also been an episode with the family when I was ashamed of myself and so had resolved to do something about it.

We were going on a skiing holiday and ran into some turbulence. Poppy was sitting with three young children and I was alone on the other side, shaking. She was trying to comfort me.

'Don't you feel better at least that we're all together?' she asked.

'I don't give a fuck what happens to you lot as long as I live,' I replied. Poppy recalls that I wasn't even semi-joking.

Later, I would come to love it when we were all together and would take comfort from it. That morning on the Virgin course, I learned how and why planes stayed in the air, followed by afternoon talks on how to manage anxiety before the course culminated with a 30-minute flight with fellow nervous flyers.

It helped me no end and would stand me in good stead for the future.

Now I was looking forward to Poppy and the kids moving permanently out to Baku, where there was an English-speaking school. I was aware, however, that while I had been happy with the way the previous season had ended – as had Tale Heydarov – some around the club were not. They still thought that seventh was a bad finish and failed to understand that, at this stage of the club's development, I was less focused on results than building a club for the long term. And I considered there had been a remarkable transformation.

It didn't stop a feeling growing around the place that we would surely be champions in my second season. In fact, the VP Fariz said as much publicly. The wrong messages were being sent out. I was still spending most of my time on the infrastructure, still encountering problems to be solved. I had realised after a month that this was not really a coaching job but a project manager's job.

We didn't start well and lost a few matches early on. It led to Tale, possibly receiving input from others around the club, sending me an email saying that he expected better results. I was unhappy with that and wrote to him explaining the situation. The club, the country, was not ready yet for bigger and better players. We needed to sort the stadium and the structure of the club before they would come. It would be a waste of money, anyway. We were still learning to walk but many were impatient to run. I began to think that Alastair may have told them I would be getting them into the Champions League.

The feeling out there seemed to be that we had the biggest budget in the league, but I knew we didn't. Qarabag, Neftchi Baku, Inter Baku and Lankaran were all paying more. And the place was still a building site. Despite all my work and my explanations, I was concerned the president and the region were losing faith in me. It deepened after an October defeat by a club lower than us in the league.

I asked for a meeting with Tale. The VP and CEO, Fariz and Alastair, were still marking their territories, and I was still unsure of who was in charge and had no clear guidelines. Things had slipped back to how it was after that meeting to clear the air. It didn't help that Alastair was out of the country so regularly on various commercial missions to do with the club.

Having the family there was a blessing but there were also issues around that. The schooling wasn't as good in Baku as back home and I was making a seven- or eight-hour round trip between the capital and Gabala twice a week. Coaching the team, the thing I really wanted to do, was taking second place to building the club and being on the road.

I said all this in my meeting with Tale, who in my 18 months in the job had probably been to one game. I said that I wasn't aware I had been hired to win the league but to build a club, and that I'd not been overly concerned with results. I couldn't be. It still seemed to be a lot about balls, bibs and cones.

The club, I said, needed a new coach who I would help find. Perhaps, then, I could become a director of football, who could oversee recruitment and infrastructure. Let me do that, I said to Tale, and I will finish the job I came here to do, which was to establish a proper professional football club, not just a competitive team for a season or two.

In Azerbaijan, the coach is king. They didn't understand the concept of director of football and they didn't want another man in the mix. But Tale didn't want me to quit Gabala entirely. We shared a vision of creating a club that would be a flagship for him and the region, be competitive in the country's Premier League in the medium term and perhaps even Europe in the longer term. I think he was also keen to retain my profile, certainly in England. In addition, the Azerbaijanis do not like people resigning on them. It is a matter of pride.

And so I suggested another role: I would help him put in the next coach, and become Tale and the club's adviser on all matters on and off the field as the next phase of making FK Gabala a footballing force. He agreed. I had been a player, a manager, a coach and now I was to be an adviser. It would be another interesting role and challenge for a kid from Essex.

14

Farewell to Peter

The idea that somehow, someday
he will control and enjoy his drinking is the
great obsession of every abnormal drinker.
The persistence of this illusion is astonishing.
Many pursue it into the gates
of insanity or death.

ALCOHOLICS ANONYMOUS, *page 30*

Another Cotswolds Christmas – and the unpacking of the boxes that had also been packed in Gloucestershire but never opened. For no sooner had Poppy and the kids settled into the apartment in Baku than I had stepped down as coach of Gabala and the crates were sent back to England. They had enjoyed their little adventure but it was over almost before it had begun. The holidays done, spent enjoyably, and the New Year here, it was then time to adapt to my new role, based at home but with an eye always on Azerbaijan.

The club – that is the president and vice president – chose as my replacement Fatih Kavlak, the coach I had brought in to oversee the academy. He was a good guy and quite capable of taking over the team. It upset Gary Stevens, who wanted a crack at the job himself and they eventually paid him up.

It had still been a good move for him as it furthered his coaching career. A good man and a good manager, Gary would go to Thailand to coach then do some media work on the Premier League in the Far East. It was, though, a difficult situation for me because I had brought in both Gary and Fatih. Two other staff I recruited – Daryl Willard and Faraz Sethi, development coach and physio – also left over the next six months as Fatih brought in his own people.

My first task was to establish a more regular relationship with Tale and we met more often now, with him often in London on other business for Gilan Industries. He was active in The European Azerbaijan Society, the organisation based in those offices in Queen Anne's Gate and established to promote the image and interests of the country. TEAS also lobbied MPs about the plight of IDPs – internally displaced persons – moved out of Nagorno-Karabakh, the territory disputed, and subject of a war in the 1990s, between Armenia and Azerbaijan.

I would go up to London every month or two, and Tale and I were in regular contact by email. The more we spoke, the more he understood just what was involved in setting up a club to compete at a high level. It wasn't that he hadn't taken an interest before; he was just busy with all his other commercial and political concerns. And, of course, I had been busy in another part of Azerbaijan trying to get things done.

It is why face to face works best in football, why owners or presidents and chairmen need to be close to managers, rather than too far removed, for things to work well. Often you see that they don't when an owner is based abroad, and it is especially apparent in the Premier League these days. In my case, I had a vice president who didn't particularly understand football, and the president was getting information from him rather than from my man, Alastair Saverimutto.

Meeting Tale regularly made me realise that I had more power and control as an adviser than as a head coach. I let go of playing matters, knowing that nobody was really going to succeed unless the structure and infrastructure of the club were properly established. Fatih Kavlak did well enough, the team finishing sixth when the cut-off for top and bottom six came in February, then fifth in the final standings.

At season's end, Alastair slipped away, his contract not renewed. He went to work for the Sri Lanka Rugby Association then the International Amateur Boxing Association in Lausanne, next to the International Olympic Committee's headquarters. He always was good at selling himself, even if it was a struggle for him, as an outsider, to secure sponsorship deals for the club.

Come the start of the following season, Fatih did not start well and by September he was gone, to be replaced by Ramiz Mammadov, the vice president's brother-in-law and the man I had replaced, who had apparently been attending every game of Fatih's tenure. Ramiz didn't fare much better, finishing fifth before the cut-off then sixth at season's end.

It meant that they wanted another change of manager for the start of the 2013/14 season and I advised the club on potential candidates, not wishing to interfere but wanting to earn my money. In from Dynamo Kiev came Yuri Semin, something of a legend in the Russian game having been manager and president of Lokomotiv Moscow.

Things were moving behind the scenes, with Phil Sharples sorting out the pitches and the indoor centre now in place. FK Gabala was finally looking like a football club with a stadium springing up – though it would also have its crises during the construction – and the academy was developing all the time. I kept the VP in the loop with what I was doing as well and I think he could see, and began to appreciate, that things were taking shape.

In the background, I was doing some extracurricular work for Tale in the form of helping to organise, along with TEAS, a charity football match at Barnet's old Underhill ground between an Arsenal Legends XI and an international team. The idea was to draw attention, on International Refugee Day at the end of June, to all those IDPs who had been forced from their homeland by that Nagorno-Karabakh conflict. Many of them were now housed in new settlements that had sprung up on the outskirts of Baku. There was also a block of flats for some of the refugees in Gabala.

More than 3,000 people turned up at Underhill to see the distinctly lean Mo Farah, double Olympic champion at London the previous summer, turn out in his beloved Arsenal's colours, and the distinctly portly Tony Adams, who was prompted to lose some weight by the event. I didn't mind showing myself up too much this time, unlike with that Soccer Aid game at Old Trafford, as I was now 10 years on from retirement and people weren't going to expect me to be the figure of my pomp that they would have assumed back then.

After that I became friends with Mo – who everyone was desperately worried would get injured in a tackle – and he was a lovely guy. After he won his 10,000 metres gold in Rio in 2016, I texted him to say he still had to win the 5,000 metres if he wanted to be a double double winner, like me. When he did, he rang me on FaceTime the following morning. 'Yay,' he said. 'I'm a Tony Adams now.'

A year after the Barnet match, we would also stage a charity boxing event for the Mo Farah Foundation and TEAS at York Hall in Bethnal Green, where stars such as Frank Bruno turned out. Gabala had a strong boxing club too and I was manager for the night as they took on Repton of east London, managed by one of their former alumni, Darren Barker, a world middle-weight champion.

That summer of 2013, though, I was busy recruiting a new academy director for Gabala, sifting CVs, talking to contacts. In the end, I narrowed it down to three people and they were invited to meet me, the president and a young Azerbaijani, Zaur Azizov, who had stepped up from club secretary to general manager now that Alastair had gone, for interviews in Brussels. To be fair, though he didn't know how good Zaur was, Alastair had looked after the club staff, getting them all pay rises.

Zaur was an interesting young man. Alastair had sent him to Everton and Sheffield United to see how they ran their clubs and Zaur, who spoke good English, had learned quickly. I began to see how smart he was, a great guy, and he quickly adapted to being the main administrator of the club.

I wanted him in Brussels so that he could develop his role and confidence, and so that he could have some time with the president, which was at a premium. It was really the first time he had spoken in any depth with Tale. Zaur was very grateful to me and he became an ally.

What we were looking for in an academy director was some-one to set the style of play throughout the club and give us a long-term playing vision. I showed Tale videos of various teams and asked him what he would like to see, then gave him my recommendations. Naturally, he wanted Barcelona. Which club president doesn't?

I had a man in mind, one of the three, and who would inter-view well. I had got to know Stanley Brard through my old journalist friend Marcel van der Kraan. He told me that his fellow Dutchman was doing a fine job in the Feyenoord acad-emy and that stacked up when I checked him out with some old contacts at the club. Stan had been a player for the club in the 1980s, playing in the same side as Johan Cruyff, the founder of the modern Barcelona. He had been a youth coach and also a head coach at Den Haag.

An old contact I respected, Albert Capellas, a Spaniard who had been a coach at Barcelona and was now assistant manager at Vitesse Arnhem, told me that the Feyenoord academy in which Stan was now working was the best in Holland. They played 4–3–3 possession football out from the back through the age groups and had 60 per cent of their players in all the national youth teams.

Thus was Stan ideal for the job, particularly as he had the sort of even temperament that would serve him well in a country that was always fascinating but could be frustrating at times. Tale accepted my recommendation. Being an excellent linguist, like many Dutch, Stan would become pretty fluent in Azeri in six months. I only ever really learned enough words and phrases to get me by.

I also went out to Azerbaijan to meet with contractors and architects as the new stadium at the centre of the complex gradually became a reality. The initial plans for a 25,000-seater stadium were ambitious and would gradually be scaled down to a 10,000-seater, good enough for European football and more manageable in terms of maintenance. There were, naturally, a lot of logistical problems to be overcome and the project would take three times longer and cost three times more than expected.

It all kept me busy enough, but being based in England also meant that I had time to be hands-on again with Sporting Chance and it was just as well. Things were not right. Poor Peter Kay, the chief executive of our charity, was not right. Indeed, issues that had emerged gradually over the previous 12 months would tragically come to a head that summer and early autumn of 2013.

As I had stepped back from the running of the charity over the years, and because I had become more consumed with work and been abroad, Peter had become the face of Sporting Chance, through such high-profile cases as Adrian Mutu and Joey Barton, very public figures who had come to us for help. Peter was often the point of contact for those seeking help as well as for the media.

In many ways, he enjoyed that. He was energetic, charismatic and charming, brilliant at leading educational seminars. He was very popular at the PFA – without whose support we would have folded – and his relationship with them was one reason why the charity had survived so long, beyond the natural course of many small charities.

Peter's lead role, however, often meant that boundaries became blurred, that he became almost a therapist when he didn't have the same high level of training as James, our head of treatment. Sometimes, Peter would take on cases when they should have been passed on.

In addition, it would turn out that the finances were not in the sort of shape we would have hoped. I was as guilty as anyone of not monitoring them as closely as I should have. But then Peter would come to the board of trustees to say we were pretty much breaking even, and looking at the annual accounts it did look that way. We would, for example, bring in £300,000 and maybe spend £310,000.

What's more, because we were helping people and the situation was far from the worrying times of the early days, as the PFA and FA were now contributing good amounts, we were not overly concerned. We let Peter get on with it. He was such a lovely man, so willing to help everyone. He had such a good heart.

But what did worry me, and the board, was Peter's health. I think he was trying to keep any financial and cash-flow issues of the charity away from me, knowing I had other things to preoccupy me. He also wanted to keep costs down by being a one-man band. I think, however, his ego got the better of him. He loved the attention and the control and just would not delegate. The football world and its spotlight can be seductive.

That, though, is dangerous for an addict, as Peter was. As is the stress of keeping it all together and not asking for help.

One of our trustees, Charlie Lesser, who was also a close friend of Peter, sensed something was wrong after having some conversations with him and went down to our facility at Liphook to see Peter one day. Peter was not there, however, and had not been for a while, according to James, who thought he had been on the road at a lot of meetings.

Charlie reported back to me and also confided that he thought Peter might have relapsed, into gambling. That was not Peter's preferred mood-changer – he was an alcoholic and drug addict, having been a cocaine user – but that can be the nature of the illness. People swap one flavour or behaviour pattern for another just to try to feel differently, to feel better, hoping against hope that this might work for them. An addict is an addict, however, and always will be. Once someone starts using again, any control soon goes.

We had certainly discovered that at the charity over the years and the nature of players' addictions was changing. Once, you could say that seven out of 10 referrals were for drink and/or drugs with maybe a couple for gambling and the other for another addiction, such as sex or food. Now, that had turned round, with these days around seven out of 10 presenting with gambling addiction. They knew the papers would turn them over if they were out boozing and they would lose their place in the team, or would fail a drugs test if they used. Gambling was the silent, private addiction that could be indulged on the internet, and thus more easily kept a secret, as well as being not so immediately obvious. Plus it was everywhere – adverts on television, clubs having betting partners and being sponsored by them.

It meant when players came into treatment, we would have to take their phones off them and just give them back for personal calls at specific times. Then, they would find messages on them offering free bets or an extension of credit if their accounts had not been used of late. They might owe fortunes but they would be offered another £10,000 worth. We had one player who left treatment to find that because his account hadn't been used for a few weeks, and he had been such a 'good' customer, £1,000 had been deposited in it.

There was also the issue of free bets, which I think will become one of the scandals of the age when all the social effects of the growing gambling culture really kick in. I have met with Andy Burnham MP and Lord Howard of Rising, who are both as worried about this as I am, in an effort to put in place some legislation to prevent free bets being offered as inducements. Andy had other pressing business with the Hillsborough inquiry, but Sporting Chance would continue its attempt to get a law against free bets introduced.

Peter, it emerged, was living beyond his means. We called him in to talk it over. He just said he had been working too hard and it certainly seemed that way. He looked 100 years old. We resolved to get him some help – at first in the office.

A few years earlier, I had been invited to be one of the guest editors of Radio 4's *Today* programme in that period between Christmas and New Year they give over to people in the public eye who they believe have stories to tell. I really put my heart and soul into it and worked with Robert Peston, then economics editor, on a piece about the finances of football, and Alan Davies, the actor, comedian and Arsenal fan, who talked about the game from a supporter's viewpoint. I also recruited the former sports minister Kate Hoey to do a slot on academies and sports politics.

I wanted to feature, too, something on addiction in prison,

given that many people around the excesses of Christmas get into trouble and/or want to stop drinking or drugging, and I met a guy called Colin Bland, who was then working for the Rehabilitation of Addicted Prisoners trust, of which I was a patron, up in Yorkshire. Now I contacted him again. Colin was a good man, an organised man, who was doing three days a week for RAPt and could do two for us.

And so we put him in the office alongside Peter. The idea was that Colin would do the admin and the books, leaving Peter to do what he did best – all the educational seminars and public appearances, which he was born for. We should have known we were merely putting off the problem, and I know both James and I would for a long while feel some guilt that we didn't see all this sooner.

When things got no better and Peter was still all over the place, I spoke to him and said that we needed to get him different help, professional help this time. We were, after all, supposed to be experts in addiction, quite apart from the fact that we had an employment process to follow and a duty of care to our staff. The help also needed to be external and independent.

Peter was reluctant but went on a 28-day programme, to a treatment centre in Florida that we arranged for him. Sadly, it did little good and we received reports that he was abusing the medication he had been put on. When he came back – and not in any sort of proper recovery – his wife Melissa asked him to leave their house, and Peter in turn evicted his two daughters from a little flat he owned in Richmond where he could shut himself away.

I met with him again, took him to an Azerbaijani restaurant in Sloane Street I used to frequent, Baku, for lunch. I asked him what we could do to help him more. Forget the charity and work, I said, we will make sure you are fine financially. What is it we can do to get you healthy again? He was more than my friend. We were comrades, allies. We shared loyalty. We went back a long way – 17 years of sobriety together, at that time. I wanted to do what I could to get him well, without indulging his active-again addiction.

I outlined a plan of recovery for him, getting back to AA meetings – as by now he was also drinking – and, when he had some sober time, maybe just doing the work he enjoyed rather than the stressful stuff of actually keeping the charity together. He loved the fun of the educational seminars, was a great communicator. Just do that, I said. By now Colin Bland was doing well in the office, keeping it going, to Peter's resentment. Peter even engaged lawyers.

After the lunch, in the middle of me talking, Peter suddenly asked me if he could leave now. Of course, I said, he was only meeting an old buddy. It was all very informal and I wasn't going to keep him there against his will. It had all gone in one ear and out the other. When I looked at him, his face was blank.

A month later, on 16 September 2013, Peter was found dead in his flat by his sister Naomi. Charlie had tried to stay near to him, and Joey Barton, to whom Peter had become very close, did his best for him, but Peter ultimately proved beyond all of our help. He was just 52. The death certificate would say that he had had a heart attack, but I know that he, as many alcoholics and addicts do without it being the formal cause, died of the disease of addiction.

It was heartbreaking. But then, active alcoholism is. I wished I could have done more, as did others around Peter, but, in the end, there is little you can do if the addict is bent on his own path. As they say in Al-Anon, the fellowship for the partners and family of addicts, there are three Cs to remember when you are in close contact with the addict: you didn't cause it, you can't control it and you can't cure it.

The funeral, at a church in Richmond, was part sombre and part joyous, mingling the sadness of Peter's premature death with the sheer joie de vivre that he showed when in recovery for so many years. Joey spoke well of his friend, a man he called 'The Chef' because of Peter's successful earlier career.

Peter's death shook me to the bone and made me contemplate the very nature of sobriety. I loved him deeply and I miss him to this day. I know he loved me too and would have done anything for me. 'Hello, lovely man,' was always his greeting. He was godfather to my son Hector and came to the christening with a first edition of a book of the children's TV series *Hector's House* that he had bought.

I particularly miss our relationship from the early days when we were those two drifters off to see the world, setting out on the path of sobriety and discovering its fun parts. Our relationship changed down the years as he became an employee of the charity, me his boss, but we were still bosom buddies. I felt clean at the end, having tried to show him the tough love that might get him back on track, but it didn't stop the pain of it.

It also hit home to me just how dangerous this illness can be once activated again. I had seen it around that time with two other people I knew, one with 22 years of sobriety, the other 28, who went back out drinking. And it didn't end well. If you stop going go AA meetings, don't keep your work, health and relationships in balance, you will forever remain vulnerable. I know after Peter died, I went to more meetings and shared a lot.

Peter's legacy was – and still is – the ethos of Sporting Chance. He was a remarkable man, an influential figure in the development of the charity. He was who we needed in those days, and I hope we in return offered him a chance to fulfil his potential and achieve something really worthwhile in his life.

Colin would take over as chief executive full time and bring an altogether different approach and mindset; again, the right person for the charity in a new chapter. With his diligence and attention to detail, Colin has ensured that Sporting Chance is financially viable and extremely professional.

In recent years, we have extended our facility to take more sportspeople into residential care and have also established, in conjunction with the PFA, a remarkable nationwide network of counsellors who can be called upon at any time, day or night.

Sad as things were in the aftermath of Peter's death, gradually Sporting Chance settled into its new era. Colin brought in the Rugby Football League as a client and much good work was, and continues to be, done with their players. When the scandal of sexual abuse involving young players in football emerged, it was to us the FA turned to help victims coming forward, and we established a new department to get them access to the relevant, qualified people who could help them.

Colin is remarkable in his ability to run the business, alongside our company secretary Shellie Heather, while referring clients to the professional experts on James's team, who include Julian Keeling and Andrew Jordan. I have always been proud of the charity and Peter Kay could be too. These days, I am prouder than ever and proud, too, that I knew him as my friend.

15

Heart and Soul

*We haven't been saved from the sea
to be kicked to death on the beach.*

Saying in AA

I was becoming restless and growing a little bored at home. I was not really an office person and, after sending some emails in the morning and checking up on things in Azerbaijan, maybe catching up with tracking players we were interested in, I would want to be playing with the kids by lunchtime.

People were suggesting I had the life of Riley, working from home, being based in England. Indeed, all was good and the list of my blessings lengthened in October 2013 when I became a step-grandad. Clare, now 28, gave birth to a son she and her partner Saam named Jedi. It started as a joke when they called him their little Jedi warrior and the name stuck.

Working as an adviser to Tale Heydarov and Gabala was also a great job, sure, but by the turn of the year, I was getting itchy for a more direct involvement with a club. It led to me joining a group of people who were trying to buy Aston Villa from

Randy Lerner, headed up by the former Chelsea chief executive Paul Smith. We even sounded out Tale about coming on board, though he made it clear his priorities were in Azerbaijan. My involvement would have been to sit on the board as a sporting director responsible for hiring the head coach and recruiting players. Paul met with Randy several times, in England and in the United States, and for a while it looked promising but, in the end, the deal could just not be struck.

Things at Gabala had taken a more unsettled turn after a good period following the appointment of Yuri Semin as head coach. With the back-up and infrastructure of the club having improved, Yuri had had a good season, finishing third in the league, to get the team into the 2014/15 Europa League qualifying stages for the first time in its mere 10-year existence. His team also reached the cup final in Baku, for which I flew out, and it was a wonderful occasion for the club with 10,000 people there, even though we lost on penalties to Neftchi.

I stayed out for an excellent under-15 tournament that Gabala were now able to organise given their increased, improved pitches and facilities. A 2-2 draw with Liverpool showed the progress the club had made in producing young players, and Gabala lost just one match, to the eventual winners Anderlecht.

When it came to the first team, Yuri was only on a one-year contract and, having done so well, it was inevitable he was going to get a better offer. It came from a Russian second division side, Mordovia Saransk. I warned the club that an approach was coming and Yuri would be going, and suggested that they put the academy head, Stanley Brard, in charge of preparation for the Europa League qualifying match against Siroki Brijeg of Bosnia in mid-June. I gave them a list of potential new head coaches for the coming league season.

Instead, the vice president appointed a Romanian, Dorinel Munteanu. Dorinel had had a great playing career, his 134 caps a record for Romania, but his managerial record had been patchy and he tended not to stay anywhere for long. He came to us from the Russian club Kuban Krasnodar, where he had lasted just a few months the previous year.

We were beaten 5-0 on aggregate by Siroki in the Europa League and, while it was a great achievement for a young club to have reached even the qualifying stage, we should have put on a better show. Then, when Gabala lost 5-0 in their first league match to Inter Baku, alarm bells began to ring. We had a decent wage bill by this time, with the football operation's budget being US$15 million, of which $5 million was going on playing staff – five times what I'd started with. This wasn't good enough.

I was still mainly concentrating on off-field matters and did not really wish to interfere, although I would give my opinion if ever it was sought. I, for one, wanted to give the manager time to turn things around. Come November, though, with Dorinel having won only four of 16 games and the first team struggling near the foot of the table, I emailed the president with my concerns, seeing it as part of my job and my duty. He asked me to meet him in London in early December.

'I know,' I said, 'that you want stability and I know if you do let Dorinel go the next man will be the fifth head coach since I left two years ago, but I really do think this has been the wrong appointment.'

I asked Tale to trust my judgement and pointed out what had been working. I had appointed Stanley, who had been really successful and was bringing a great style of play to the age-group teams. Phil the groundsman was another tick for me, with the complex now looking fabulous. Tale listened respectfully and nodded. Perhaps he was thinking that maybe Mr Adams was right.

Tale said that, yes, they should consider a change and that

Fariz would be asked to implement it. The vice president had suggested as a replacement a man called Roman Hryhorchuk, although Robert Prosinecki, the Croatian who had played for Portsmouth and had been managing in Turkey, was also on the list. What did I think?

I liked the idea of Roman and knew a bit about him. A Ukrainian, he had got Chornomorets Odessa into the country's Premier League then the Europa League on a low budget. He had a good, attacking style of play. He got my thumbs-up. Robert Prosinecki, meanwhile, would soon become the manager of the Azerbaijan national team.

I had also suggested to Tale in my November email – from my position of restlessness and boredom – that maybe I should go back out to Gabala and take a more hands-on approach. The club had moved on in the last couple of years, I said, and was probably now ready for a director of football. We had the infrastructure, after all. It was time to concentrate on the first team and to get them back towards the top of the league.

Tale agreed and so, my Virgin 'Flying Without Fear' course still working, I flew out in the December and took in the last match before the winter break, meeting with the new head coach Roman Hryhorchuk to discuss my role in the scheme of things.

I did not want to interfere, I said, but I was there if he wanted to consult with me on anything. I was not there to be the coach or to put pressure on him, but to support him. He could lean on me. My stock was high, with all my appointments working out around the club, and I think Roman realised that he needed to confer with me on a regular basis as the president trusted me. I liked him and enjoyed speaking with him.

At the winter training camp in early January, I was even more impressed with him as I watched every training session. He had some imaginative ideas and was clearly an offensive coach. It wasn't quite Premier League but the sessions were entertaining, fun and directive. He communicated well, speaking Russian to them.

Once back in Baku, I realised I needed to reconnect with my AA programme, and in the list of contacts for the country that was now available was a guy called Jan, a Norwegian. I got in touch with him and soon we were setting up a meeting that would take place at his flat. As word got around more people would come, such as Scott, a Scotsman working in the oil industry, and a young Azerbaijani girl – the first native member – who kept relapsing into drink but who kept coming back and trying. The most we had was eight people, who came during the European Games held in Baku in the summer of 2015.

Over that spring and early summer, Roman rebuilt the team and the squad, with me working alongside him. Dorinel Munteanu had brought in five poor players who were no better than the Azerbaijanis on the books. If you are going to bring in foreign players, they have to be better than domestic ones. We also had a proper academy now with young players needing to come through.

Roman brought in a host of his own, mostly ones he was familiar with, and to his credit they were decent players. I also suggested some. He wanted a pacy winger, but I pointed out we had a good Brazilian at the club already in Dodo, who would eventually be the subject of a US$1 million bid by a Chinese club. Roman was also after a left back and Zaur recommended one that we duly recruited, a Brazilian who had played in the Champions League with Malmo, by the name of Ricardo.

For a while Roman didn't play him, however, as he had trouble balancing the number of Azerbaijanis in the team with the foreign players and getting them in the right positions. I said this was a player worth getting in at the expense of even one of the best local lads as it would improve the balance of the team.

Roman duly did and it worked. We won eight games in a row at the end of the season and finished in third place, good enough for another crack at Europa League qualification the next season. It had been a good six months' work and would be an even better one over the summer.

Amazingly, Gabala went on to win through four qualifying rounds of the Europa League, though very nearly exited the competition at the first stage. That was against Dinamo Tbilisi and we lost 2-1 in Georgia. We levelled at 2-2 in the 88th minute of the home leg but it seemed we would go out on away goals – until three minutes into added time when the Ukrainian Oleksiy Antonov grabbed a winner to send a remarkable home crowd – for us – of 4,400 into raptures. I too went wild and in my celebrations contrived to punch the mayor of Gabala in the stomach – not long after he had had a heart attack.

Every game after that became an epic tale. We lost 1-0 to the Serbian side Cukaricki in Belgrade in the second qualifying round but won 2-0 at home, or at least in the Bakcell Arena in Baku where we now played the European games. UEFA had decided that we should switch due to the crowd scenes after beating Tbilisi, but with 8,500 watching anyway, we would have had to move the games due to the interest.

After that came a 1-1 draw in Limassol followed by a 1-0 win in Baku – and then a terrific two-legged win on away goals over Panathinaikos. We drew 0-0 at home and I thought that going to Greece might be a challenge too far for us but we drew 2-2, thanks to two goals by Dodo – to show we were far from as dead as one. Little Gabala had reached the group stages of the Europa League.

In those, we were drawn against Borussia Dortmund, Krasnodar of Russia, and PAOK of Greece. I told Tale that if we got a point, we would have done well. In the end we got two, draws home and away against the Greek team, which was quite an achievement. Even if the team was struggling in the league – going 11 games without a win that autumn as the coach wrestled with having to rotate foreign and Azerbaijani players, the quota rule only applying domestically and not in European competition – Gabala were on the map.

I would, however, miss a good deal of the campaigns, both on the domestic and European fronts, due to something that seemed like nothing at the time.

It began in the run-up to the Dortmund game at home in October 2015. I had played a long game of tennis and started to feel pain around my right shoulder. I thought it was muscular, even when I began getting chest pains when out for my daily run and having to stop after a mile or so.

Otherwise, when not doing any activity, I felt fine. I went out for lunch with the Dortmund president and officials on match day and was impressed by the way they conducted themselves and ran their club. I also enjoyed the game. Even though Gabala lost 3-1 to a very good side – hot property Pierre-Emerick Aubameyang scoring a hat-trick – we gave a decent account of ourselves. I was sure any physical discomfort I was feeling would be resolved when I got back to England for a visit I was planning to make in a couple of weeks' time and could see my doctor there, maybe get some physio on the shoulder.

As the old saying goes, though, life is what happens when you're busy making plans.

I was in Gabala the following Sunday for a league game and felt really unwell that night. The next morning, I went to see the club doctor, a Ukrainian named Roman Zhoolobaylyuk, who informed me that my blood pressure was going through the roof. From there, I was bundled off to the small hospital in Gabala, where I was given a stress test on a treadmill simulating walking uphill.

My heart rate was increasing and I was getting chest pains.

The doctor told me to stop. I needed to go to Baku for some tests, he said, but there was no need to panic. That panicked me. I phoned Poppy. I was due to stay on in Gabala for a mid-week game but she told me to get myself to Baku, ready for tests first thing the next morning at the Medical Plaza Hospital, where I had been booked in.

After an anxious three-hour drive back to the capital, I spent a long night in my hotel room worrying about the following day. I phoned my GP in the UK, Dr Anton Borg, and I asked him if I had time to get home to England. He thought it best I stay where I was. I still thought it might be muscular, that maybe I had been overdoing the weights and press-ups. Or that I wasn't fit enough. Maybe I just wanted to believe that, such was my state of mind.

When the morning came, I was keen to find out now what was wrong. After some blood tests, I was given an angiogram at 11am. I was tense and confused, but holding it together. Any instruction to keep calm, though, by the Azerbaijani doctor – Dr Uzeyir Rahimov, who had been trained in Turkey and was recommended to me by Samed Nasibov, the Gabala commercial director – had the opposite effect on me.

Soon, the doctor told me I would be going down to theatre and I grew frightened. Very frightened. He gave me a sedative tablet and I was taken down in a wheelchair. Once there, I was laid on a slab and a camera was pulled above my head and a cannula inserted into my wrist for a drip. Then the camera was inserted through my arm and I could see pictures of it going across the chest. There were two red blotches with a white line, looking like cotton wool, linking the two. I was wondering, in my sedated condition, what the hell was going on. In fact, I was getting tearful.

Dr Rahimov said he had to leave the room to consult with a colleague. When he came back, he didn't pull any punches.

'Mr Adams,' he said in a serious tone. '*B-e-e-e-e-g* problem.'

'Big problem? Oh my God,' I thought.

'You are a very lucky man,' he added.

I didn't feel that way.

I can't remember giving the guy permission, but I must have done, because within minutes, through the same cannula, he was passing in two stents – small mesh tubes that are inflated to open up blocked arteries. That, I now discovered, was the problem: I was getting chest pains because my heart was not getting the blood through that it should have been pumping. In fact, I would find out later, two of the arteries were blocked, one a dangerous 99 per cent and one a barely less dangerous 70 per cent.

As I would realise when I came round properly and in speaking to people in the coming weeks, I had indeed been a very lucky man.

The procedure took somewhere between 10 and 20 minutes and I was part-amazed, part-relieved and part-emotional as I watched the screen on which the camera was recording it all. I did what my AA programme taught me to do: I surrendered, said the Serenity Prayer – *God grant me the serenity to accept the things I cannot change, the courage to change the things I can, and the wisdom to know the difference* – and a massive acceptance came over me. I was teary again, but knew now that my fear that I might die was not going to be a reality today.

Soon, the red blotches had gone and the white area that resembled cotton wool was a red line, which meant that the blood was flowing properly again. And then I was back in a wheelchair being returned to my room, waving the cardiologist goodbye and thanking him.

As I lay there that evening, being monitored overnight, there came the welcome sight of Poppy appearing through the door. She had taken the 10am flight from Heathrow and looked as if she had been crying the whole way, which she said she had. She, too, was relieved and left me to get some sleep. She needed some herself, now that she knew what was going on.

In the morning, she was back, helping me to fix up a flight home for the following day, the doctor having given me the go-ahead, along with bottle of tablets. There was no fear of flying any more, just a feeling of gratitude that I could get on that plane and return to my safe Cotswold haven.

Over the coming weeks, however, something strange would happen to me.

Everything was fixed, Dr Rahimov told me, and I thanked him profusely. I had nothing to worry about physically. I just needed to sort out a fitness and physio programme with the doctors back home. It might, though, take me a while to get over it psychologically, he added. He would be right.

Not longer after I got back, Tale Heydarov called me to see how I was. Dr Rahimov had been to see him and shown him a DVD of the procedure.

'The doctor has saved your life, Tony,' he said. 'He got to you just in time. He said that if it had been left any longer, you would not be alive.' I felt grateful, certainly, but was also only too aware of how serious this health scare had been.

Feeling both thankful and well, I arranged a party two weeks later to celebrate my 49th birthday which had just passed. It was in the Whiteleys shopping centre, in west London, where they had a film theatre that you could hire privately and I did so for 20 of my best mates. It was for the James Bond film that had just come out, *Spectre*.

David Seaman, Lee Dixon and Ian Wright were all there and they started asking me about what had just happened to me in Azerbaijan, as it had been in the papers. As I went through the story with them, I suddenly began to feel very emotional, almost overcome. I went to the toilet and there I had a full-scale panic attack. Actually, I thought it was a heart attack, but I calmed down eventually.

I sat down to watch the film but couldn't, in my agitation, and so asked Poppy to take me back to the hotel we had booked round the corner. There, I grew anxious again, thinking I was having a heart attack, and at 1am, Poppy by my side, I decided I just had to go to the nearby A&E at St Mary's, Paddington. There must have been 400 people there. It was not like a private hospital in Baku.

When I was seen, I was given an electrocardiogram, which showed nothing untoward. My heart rate was raised, along with my blood pressure, but that could have been tension, they said. I could wait to see a doctor, but it might be three or four hours. We resolved to go back to the hotel. If I had a heart attack, I figured, I could do it in comfort and then jump the queue.

I had no sleep and we drove back to Gloucestershire in the morning. By midday, I was still feeling panicky so Poppy drove me to the A&E at Cirencester. Again, they told me nothing was wrong but it just didn't feel like it. I rang Dr William McCrea, the cardiologist at the Great Western Hospital in Swindon I had been assigned after coming back from Azerbaijan. He couldn't see me until 7pm, he said.

I just wanted to get over there straight away. The paramedics at Cirencester were great and offered to take me over in an ambulance but we didn't need it. Poppy drove me instead and we were there by 5pm. While, ever supportive, she waited in the car park, I just sat outside his office. I was a mess psychologically and just felt safer there. At 7.30pm he emerged to say he would see me now.

Dr McCrea is a big Irish guy, who loves his football. He liked to talk about potential candidates for heart attacks among managers. Alex Ferguson was unlikely to have one, he reckoned, because he gets his anger out. Arsène Wenger was more of a possibility as he bottled things up. One of Dr McCrea's ideas was that red wine helped prevent heart attacks but, since I'd told him my history, he knew better than to suggest that with me.

Basically, he gave me my marching orders. He told me that the stents had been a success and a straightforward procedure that he himself did 10 times a day. Any heart palpitations were to do with the psychological rather than the physical. Two weeks ago, the danger level for me was nine out of 10; now it was 0.000001. He added that it was time to look after Poppy and the kids and to get on with my life.

The hospital gave me a physical rehab programme and over the next few weeks I became more confident. I started putting strain on my heart again, running and playing tennis, and felt fine. The palpitations and anxiety attacks had been manifestations of self-imposed stress. My mum and dad had been worriers and here I was, following in their footsteps.

There were still wobbles now and then, still times when I imagined numbness in my fingers and toes and had to talk myself down from any anxiety, but I largely managed to get on with things and enjoy Christmas at home. Just before then, I went to see Tale, to tell him I was ready to go back out to Gabala.

Once there in mid-January after the winter break, I worked with Roman to vet and recruit new players. Results were not great, after the excitement of the autumn Europa League campaign, and there was a thrashing by Qarabag. It was a little frustrating for me as I watched a good defender I had recommended, a Ukrainian by the name of Vitaliy Vernydub, being in and out of the side.

In the end, the team finished a reasonable third on a budget that had been halved from $5 million to $2.5 million – still double my first couple of seasons. There had been a downturn in the country due to the oil price falling.

I sensed my time at Gabala had passed. I hosted around 20 friends in the early spring knowing that this would be my final period in the country, taking them on the 'Tony tour' of Baku – the Croisette, the old city, the remarkable buildings like the Flames, symbolic of the burning gas the country produced, the streets where the first Azerbaijan Formula One race would take place that summer – and then to Gabala, where the new ski resort was now fully operational and had the wonderful bonus of being quiet so you could ski to your heart's content.

I had done what I set out to achieve. I had built a team from nothing and a club from scratch. It had a wonderful training facility now with a decent stadium at its heart. It had reached the group stages of the Europa League and would be having another shot at it the following season.

I went to see Tale to tell him that it was time for me to move on and he understood. He told me that I could always remain as an adviser to him and Gabala if I wanted and it was a generous offer. His friendship and five years of a remarkable odyssey would not be forgotten that easily, but it was time now to see what else the footballing world held for me.

16

Leadership – 2

One of the main things I discovered in getting sober was that I like people and enjoy working with them to improve both them, hopefully as professionals and people, and myself through our interaction. It has stood me in good stead through 15 years of coaching, management and being a sporting/technical director.

There are clearly differences between leading men on a football field and creating the environment off it in which they can thrive. For me, leadership on the field of play was all about being focused on one job without distraction. You could be single-minded, without the need to see the bigger picture of what went on around the club. You could also directly influence the outcome of what everyone worked all week for – winning a match.

As a leader off the field, you have many factors to consider in picking a team and gelling them together, making decisions they may not understand from their own narrow playing perspective. You have to take into account how players complement each other, both in playing ability and temperament, as well as what type of formation will suit them and best counter the opposition at hand and how they set themselves up.

For that, you also need people in your coaching and technical staff whom you respect for their talent and trust for their support and discretion. The selection and appointment of them is crucial. You don't just want yes-men. You need people who will be brave enough to challenge your ideas, have input into team matters. After that, they need to support, rather than sulk, if you do not always take their advice. Because you disagree on odd subjects, it doesn't mean that admiration and cooperation can't flourish.

The Arsenal club motto of *Victoria Concordia Crescit* may also have been a code by which I have lived my footballing life, but my interpretation is slightly different from the usual translation. Rather than Victory Through Harmony, I prefer Victory Through Togetherness. Rather than the ideal, the reality is that things are not always going to be harmonious in football clubs, nor should they be if shades of opinion are to be encouraged and embraced, but after any disagreements must come unity.

Behind all team matters come the elements that fans do not see; the huge underwater part of the iceberg. You have finances to deal with as well as the internal politics and personalities at clubs. You have the demands of owners, shareholders and supporters. And, of course, once players step over that white line, you are powerless. The AA programme is certainly good for showing you that you are simply not in control of events sometimes, and that you can only do your best to prepare for situations and then leave outcomes to play out in the way they are supposed to.

Of course, there are also similarities between leading on the field and off, and they boil down to whether you have the honesty, character and charisma to win people's trust and get them to follow you and implement the plan that in your experience will bring results. It is true that people don't necessarily have to like you, either as a team-mate or a coach, but they do have to respect you. And that respect is earned through you knowing your own job and being good at it, and people working with and for you as a result of seeing that.

There is a lot of nonsense talked about motivation. Many football fans seem to need to see managers or coaches shouting and screaming as a sign that they are motivating players. There are times when such reactions are understandable, even necessary, but it won't achieve anything unless the players have been coached properly and understand their jobs.

There has to be an element of self-motivation in players, as I had when I was a player. You can't always instil it in people. Finding the right characters is part of the recruiting process for a leader in football. You have to do your homework to discern whether a player has the right mentality to go with his ability.

To get players really fulfilling their potential is more about giving them the tools to do the job. Good practice makes perfect but bad practice can make permanent, as Terry Venables once said. You are looking to rehearse players through enjoyable repetition so that they repeat the right things as a matter of routine when under pressure. From that, confidence comes. And from that comes success – which is the greatest motivator of all.

Everybody wants to experience that sweet feeling and will do their utmost to achieve it. It is addictive. Fortunately for a character like me, it is a natural high.

I like to think that I have become a good judge of character and can tell if people are being honest with me or not. I certainly get a gut feeling with people and, with players for example, whether they are in it for the money – or the location of the club – and acting out of self-interest, or whether they are going to buy into what you are looking to achieve together.

The story of two bricklayers at work appeals to me . . .

A man asks the first what he is doing.

'I'm laying bricks,' says the first, bemused by what sounds like a stupid question.

The man asks the second bricklayer what he is doing.

'I'm building a house,' he replies.

I have always wanted people who see what they are doing as building a house. Your job as the site manager is to create the right environment so that they feel that too.

It echoes the wisdom of Sir Clive Woodward, the man who coached England to winning the Rugby Union World Cup: you have to get the right characters on the bus with you, he said.

My spell at Brunel University gave me a feel for the wider elements of the game, including economics and sociology, and I have carried that into my life in football off the pitch. I also feel I learned a lot in my early days of coaching and management about compromise and mediation. Despite what people think, with a manager's word being the final one, sometimes those are qualities required in dealings inside clubs.

At Wycombe, for example, we had a new money man come in who eventually became the owner. There was no point resenting his presence and worrying if things might change; you had to work with him to do what was right for the club.

Then at Portsmouth, I was often the mediator between Harry Redknapp and Joe Jordan. Again, it was a case of working out what was the right thing for the group of players and the club. I think I also learned a lesson then from Harry in knowing when to accept the advice and suggestions of staff, as he did when listening to my input about the FA Cup final team.

You are basically looking to enable and empower the people who are, when you get down to basics, going to win you football matches, from which everything stems – the enjoyment of staff and supporters and all the revenue streams that keep the club prosperous. Good results equal bigger crowds and sponsorship. And the more revenue generated, the more you have to spend on the team. It is a virtuous circle, simple in concept but difficult to keep repeating.

As a leader, you have to be sure that you are able to shoulder the burden of being responsible for the wellbeing of those under you. It often means listening to them, hearing their problems and being their support. Patience is vital. Leaders also need support of their own and I guess I have been fortunate in receiving it from AA and my therapist James West, as well as from my network of AA friends. I have also learned much about dignity and respect, and quiet leadership, from James.

When you are able to do that well, to empathise with people, it helps you get the best from them. I would cite an example of a player we had in Gabala during my time as sporting director.

The player concerned found himself out of the team when the coach brought in a new player. Naturally, he resented it, and his reaction was to begin drinking heavily. The feeling grew on his and the coach's part that the club would just release him when convenient.

After a while of watching him go further downhill, I sat him down and talked to him. First, I had to listen, to find out what was going on with him. It emerged that he thought he was making a statement, a protest, by drinking and not trying in training.

I told him that he had to sort himself out and knuckle down, not for the team or the club, but for his own sake. Any protest was going unheard and it was him who was suffering. He might well want to leave the club when his contract was up but, football being a gossipy game, word would get round about him and nobody would want him.

He seemed to appreciate the talk, quit drinking and worked his way back into the team. When it was right for player and club, we found him another club where he might play more regularly.

I know I can manage, and manage well, but ideally I will be looking in the future for a job with an element of coaching involved.

Being a sporting director feels easy to me – working with a coach, getting rid of bad players and recruiting good ones, creating the right environment. Managing a club can be frustrating, with the way so many things can be beyond your control and your fate is in the hands of others.

It is, I believe, in coaching where I excel. There, you can teach and develop, talk and suggest. Encourage and empower. The rewards come when, years later, players acknowledge that you made a difference to their careers and lives.

There have been leaders I have admired down the years outside football, chief among them Winston Churchill for the way he united the nation during World War Two and for his inspiring oratory. Football is not war, but it is a battle. The British used to be good at strategy and organisation. We need to rediscover that.

Indeed, I have often observed politicians and how they speak and conduct themselves. To learn more, I tend to read their autobiographies, and those of business leaders, rather than fiction these days.

I did meet Margaret Thatcher, and was struck by the powerful – and scary – aura she gave off. Whether you agreed with her or not, she had conviction. 'You came through YTS [Youth Training Scheme]?' she asked. I said yes. 'My idea,' she said, turning to the gathering. I liked John Major for his understanding of sport, shown in his setting up of the National Lottery, funding from which has helped Great Britain to be so successful at the Olympic Games. I also admired Tony Blair for securing the Olympics for London in 2012.

Mind you, I don't think people should be getting knighthoods and being made dames for running round an athletics track, as I joked to Mo Farah. They should be for people who transcend their sport and contribute more widely to our society.

I like to read books that aid the process of leadership such as *Moneyball*, about how finances impact sport, by Michael Lewis, along with Simon Kuper and Stefan Szymanski's book *Soccernomics*. I also enjoyed their book, *Why England Lose*, and Michael Calvin's *Living on the Volcano*, about football management. It gave great insight into the pressures and difficulties managers face.

In leading a football club, you need to create leaders around you as well, particularly among players. I agree with Brian Clough, who once said that if you've got fewer than four leaders in your team going to an away game, then you might as well not bother getting on the coach.

It was another reason why I admired Terry Venables' way of doing things. He made a big call in taking the England captaincy away from David Platt and giving it to me. As well as not being certain he would be starting David, Terry wanted a lot of leaders in his side – Paul Ince, Stuart Pearce, Alan Shearer – and thought that I could best mediate and control them. You need to be a secure enough figure, as Terry was, to have so many strong characters in a group.

The people you are looking for are those who get into training first, who will set standards, morals and morale. They will spot situations, such as unhappy players, and lift them. Like Terry, Sir Alex Ferguson was superb at developing such figures.

And inside the club I have had a lifelong love affair with, I was fortunate to have role models, right from the understated but brilliant Terry Burton in the youth team, through the inspirational George Graham to one of the most intelligent men in the game, the man himself, Arsène Wenger.

17

Good Old Arsenal

*As a club, we have an educational purpose:
to give back to those people who love
Arsenal so that they learn moral values
from our game and how we behave.*

ARSÈNE WENGER, 1998

Another big reason for leaving Gabala was that I had the urge to get the grass beneath my feet again. I wanted to coach, wanted my own team to shape and improve, and at a reasonably good level. It was unlikely to be in England, however. I confess that after my Wycombe Wanderers and Portsmouth experiences in English football, I was probably still seen by many club owners, chairmen and chief executives as damaged goods. Not that it seemed to stop some other damaged-goods managers from getting jobs time after time.

I was sad about that but guess I understood a little, given my record and the fact that many chose to take it at face value rather than look into the circumstances behind it. Fortunately, I had more respect abroad. My coaching in Holland still counted for something and my role in the development of Gabala would be noted more on the wider European stage, where more attention was paid to these things than in the sometimes insular English game.

I received a call from Benny Nielsen, who had been a player for Anderlecht and was now a scout for Chelsea in his native Denmark. He had sent me Danish players to look at when I was at Wycombe. He told me that Brondby, the well-respected Copenhagen club, were interested in me as a head coach, as they were in the market for a new one after a bizarre row.

It seemed that the club president, Jan Bech Andersen, had been exposed for having gone anonymously on to a supporters' message board to criticise the coach, Thomas Frank, who had quit amid the row. Mr Andersen also resigned as president but would remain pulling the strings as he was a co-owner and major investor.

I had talks with Mr Andersen, which seemed to go well, and he sent me a contract with terms and conditions in it. The money was going to be less than at Gabala but I was willing to take it. Things then went quiet, until I heard that they had appointed a German coach and that was that. I just emailed Mr Andersen to wish him and Brondby well.

There was also a possibility of going to Grampus 8 of Nagoya in Japan, who were thought to be making a change, and with Stanley Brard, my old academy director at Gabala, already there, it had potential. It was interesting that Grampus had been Arsène Wenger's club before he came to Arsenal. As it was, nothing came from the Japan interest – though I did get some from Arsenal.

In the May of 2016, the European Under-17 Championships were held in Azerbaijan and I took them in to further my education. The quality of football was very high and I used the tournament as the basis for a future research paper.

While watching, I noticed that Arsenal did not seem to have any representatives there and so I contacted Steve Rowley, the chief scout, to ask if he would like analyses of the performances of the four young Gunners who were taking part, two English, one French and one Dutch. Steve liked the idea and so I emailed him reports.

He emailed me back to thank me, adding: 'By the way, Tony, there's a vacancy for an under-18 coach in the Arsenal academy.' I thought about it. Having watched elite players at the tournament, I thought it would be nice. I hadn't coached for three and a half years and it appealed to me. I suddenly felt stirred. This is what I had been missing.

I contacted Andries Jonker, the Dutchman who had taken over from Liam Brady as the head of the academy in 2014, as Steve suggested I do. Andries said he would get back to me and soon he did. It seemed he had had the thumbs-up from Arsène and he asked me to a meeting at Hale End, the Walthamstow home of the academy.

My relationship with Arsène had been warm over the previous six months following my heart scare. He had texted me saying: 'I admire your strength. Respect and love.' It prompted a bit of a text love-in, and I think he appreciated me doing an article in the press defending him when he came under pressure from supporters again over the winter as Arsenal slipped out of the title race.

I also texted him about the under-18 job and he just replied: 'Good luck Tony.' The papers were reporting that he wanted Thierry Henry for the post, but I don't think Arsène ever really considered it as Thierry had lucrative punditry work for Sky and Arsène did not believe the two could or should be combined. I got word back that Ivan Gazidis, the Arsenal chief executive, also approved of me taking the job.

And so I drove the two hours from my home to Walthamstow

on a Saturday morning to meet with Andries at Hale End. He outlined the job: I would be working alongside the existing coach Kwame Ampadu initially, with a view to being the lead coach, but that this was the extent of the job – there was to be no pathway to the reserves or the first team. The salary would be £45,000 gross.

'What, a week?' I asked, and Andries laughed.

I said I needed to go home and talk it over with Poppy to see if I could make it work logistically and financially. The commitment was going to be considerable, after all – five days a week, to include one evening, plus a Saturday morning match.

But it was appealing. And it was the Arsenal. After speaking to Poppy, who simply wanted me to do what would fulfil me, I agreed an arrangement with Andries. I would give it a month, starting at the end of June, to see how it worked for both parties and then Arsenal would make the decision about whether I was to be the lead coach for the under-18s.

It was, finally, a chance to get back into my spiritual home and, goodness knows, I had made some attempts down the years . . .

The first time it looked as if there might be a route back to the club came during the time I was working for Tale Heydarov at Gabala and there was a power struggle going on for Arsenal between two potential owners – the American Stan Kroenke and the Russian Alisher Usmanov. Several of the major shareholders were considering selling their stakes, as David Dein had done in 2007 when he sold his 14.5 per cent to Usmanov for a reported £75 million.

I went to see Blackstone, an American organisation with offices in Berkeley Square, who were then selling the 15 per cent shareholding of another Arsenal board member, Lady Nina Bracewell-Smith. She wanted £100 million for them. I also had lunch with the great Danny Fiszman, Arsenal through and through, who owned 16 per cent. Danny was worried about who might take over the club and I thought that possibly we could all link up if perhaps Tale was interested in buying Lady Nina's stake. That would give the two of us more than 30 per cent, compared to Kroenke and Usmanov who then had around 25 per cent between them.

Danny was receptive but said that I should come through the front door and talk to the chairman, Peter Hill-Wood, who had a smaller shareholding. The board had fallen out with David Dein because they felt he'd sold his shares behind their backs and did not want any more of that kind of thing. I was interested, I told him, in being the board's adviser on footballing matters.

In the event, as with that initial interest in Aston Villa some time later, Tale's involvement waned as he needed to concentrate on events in Azerbaijan. Lady Nina also sold her stake to Kroenke for £120 million, Stan having his hand forced when he thought there was another player in the equation. Lady Nina had also fallen out with the board and sent me an email complaining about the state of the club.

Then Danny grew ill and would die of cancer, which saddened all who loved the club. He had been such a central figure, a force for good, for so long. Just before he died, Danny made arrangements to ensure that Usmanov, whom he did not warm to, would not get his shares and they ended up being sold to Stan for £110 million. Danny's wife Sally still goes to the Emirates, and the Diamond Lounge created in honour of Danny's business is still there. Stan now had full control of Arsenal, but he retained Peter Hill-Wood as chairman to maintain the link with the old club and its culture and principles.

Peter did an article with a newspaper in which he questioned – in light of all the new executive directors in the game receiving considerable payment at Premier League clubs – where all the people, like him, who gave their time and expertise and ran football clubs for free, out of love, had gone. He was in his seventies, he added; where are the younger people?

I wrote to him. I am in my forties, I said, and I don't need paying. I will come and advise about playing matters and the future, perhaps Arsène's long-term successor. The board needed someone like me, I reckoned, on footballing matters. In the end, Peter became unwell and I never got a reply. A year later Peter would step down, with Sir Chips Keswick taking over as chairman.

Before that episode, and after the initial sounding-out about buying a stake in the club on behalf of Tale, I heard in early 2012 that Pat Rice was retiring as Arsène's assistant. I hadn't wanted to be an assistant again; I had wanted to be a number one. But this was Arsenal.

As it had been rumoured the year before that he would be going and it didn't happen, I went to see Pat to get it from the horse's mouth. He confirmed to me that he would definitely be going in the May and that he had bought a house in Spain. I said that I wouldn't want to do anything behind anyone's back, so would he be OK with it if I went to see Arsène? Pat was fine with that.

Arsène was happy to see me and so I went to London Colney. We talked for an hour, a lovely conversation about the good old days and now ...

You always could talk to him. Sometimes as a player, I would go into his office angry about something and then leave, disarmed, in a better frame of mind. I remember once having a discussion with him about God or a Higher Power, and he said he liked to believe in something, that it would be miserable to think we would go to the grave and that would be the end of it.

On this day, I told him he wouldn't win the Premier League with full-backs playing like wingers. 'Yes, I know,' he said. I asked him if he was going to do anything about it and he simply smiled.

Then he asked me why I was there.

'Well, Pat is retiring . . .' I said.

'Oh no,' said Arsène. 'He won't retire. He said that last year.'

I told him I had spoken to Pat and that he'd said he was going. Arsène then said he would be convincing Pat to stay, as he had done 12 months ago. 'Fair enough,' I said and shook his hand.

Then came Pat's leaving-do at the Arsenal, which Arsène did not attend. I texted him again and asked if I could come and see him.

I went back to London Colney and we had a lovely conversation about the good old days and now . . .

I recall asking him about the differences between then and now.

'Well,' he said. 'From Monday to Friday it was difficult. You players did what you wanted to do. But on Saturday, you were brilliant and I could relax. Now, it is great from Monday to Friday but on Saturday I tear my hair out.'

I thought back to that time when Manu Petit was late on to the training pitch and I went ballistic and threw the plastic cup. I wondered again who in the current set-up would be pulling people up now.

Then he asked me why I was there.

'I went to Pat's leaving-do and I understand there is a job going,' I said.

'Oh no,' said Arsène. 'I am moving Steve Bould and Neil Banfield up from the academy.'

'Oh, OK,' I said. 'Good luck to them and you.' I thanked him for his time and left.

I then texted Steve to congratulate him. He texted back to say he knew nothing about it. He had been offered it last year, he added, when Arsène thought Pat might be going then, but had heard nothing this time. He wasn't sure he would take it anyway, he said.

Two days later Arsenal made the announcement about Steve and Neil stepping up. The next day I texted Arsène to ask if I could come and see him. This was three times in just over a month.

Back to London Colney. And we had a lovely conversation about the good old days and now. We also discussed how unlucky Arsenal had been this year.

Then he asked me why I was there.

'Well,' I said. 'With Steve and Neil moving up, you have two jobs vacant now in the academy.'

'Would you be interested?' Arsène asked, surprised that I would work lower down in the club.

'Maybe not at another club but it is the Arsenal,' I said. 'I do have the connection and even if it's the youth team, the development squad or the EPPP [Elite Player Performance Plan] squad, I'd like to give something back.'

'OK,' he said. 'I am going to the European Championships soon but leave it with me and I will call you.'

Euro 2012 in Poland and Ukraine began and I had heard nothing. I texted Arsène to ask if anything was happening. He replied that I should talk to Ivan Gazidis and Liam Brady, then head of the academy, as they were choosing the candidates. I rang Liam, who was in Ireland working for the media on the Euros. He would talk to me when he got back, he said. He had influence with Arsène, he added, but it would be the manager's decision.

I emailed Ivan, who was in China working on a commercial project. He replied to say that it was Arsène and Liam who were deciding this. I texted Arsène. He texted back that it was ridiculous, that he would talk to Ivan straight away.

Then Liam rang me, to ask me to come and see him.

At our meeting, he told me that I was overqualified and they wanted somebody younger who they could train up, as they had with Steve Bould. I was just pleased that someone had given me an answer.

That still left the reserves and the development squad for which Arsène could appoint, and so I texted him again to relay what Liam had said, that the youth was not available. He said to leave it with him and he would sort it when he was back. This was the Friday towards the end of the European Championships, and the players not involved were due back in training on the Monday.

Then I got a phone call from Terry Burton, my old youth-team coach and a great man revered in the profession, whom I had tried to recruit for Portsmouth. He said he had just had lunch with Arsène and been offered a job but he wasn't quite sure yet what it was. He had been told just to turn up for work on the Monday and they would sort a contract and his role. He said he didn't think he could combine reserves and development and that he would recommend me for the reserves. I said I would be up for that. Two days later, the club announced that Terry was to be reserve-team and development-squad coach.

I was not going to let this go by now, having been messed about so much. I texted Arsène to congratulate him on Terry's appointment, saying what a great guy he had taken on. A while later I noticed a missed call from Arsène and rang him back. He asked me if I had received a voicemail and I said no, then asked him what it was about.

'I see big things for you,' he said. 'You are a great coach and you will be the next manager of Arsenal.'

'Arsène, Arsène, Arsène,' I said, proud of myself that I did not raise my voice or lose my temper. 'I have too much respect for you to fall out. It would have been better if you had just told me you didn't want me.'

'No, it is not like that,' he replied. 'You have got the wrong end of it.'

'Arsène, let's forget it,' I said. 'Have a wonderful season and good luck for it.'

And that was that. I saw him a few months later at a League Cup tie at Reading, which Arsenal crazily won 7-4 after extra time, and he was pleasant but cool.

It was only when I discovered that my phone was being hacked by the *Daily Mirror,* a long time after settling with the *News of the World* after being hacked by them, did it occur to me that Arsène may have indeed left me a voicemail that I never received, just as happened that time with Peter Taylor all those years ago when he told me he had left a message to say he would not be including me in his England squad. I remembered that when a message is hacked, it can be lost.

The next instalment of the saga came around 18 months later. I was still advising Tale Heydarov and Gabala, but by now was getting twitchy about wanting to coach again and so rang Terry Burton. I asked him if he would be interested in me coming to work with the academy players a couple of days a week, just for expenses, though I wasn't even bothered about getting any money at all.

Terry was great, thanked me profusely and offered Monday and Wednesday afternoons and Thursday all day working with the 11 living in the academy. I knew they had a couple of decent defenders I could help. He said he would just clear it with Arsène, Liam and Ivan.

When Terry phoned me back a couple of days later, he was very embarrassed. It had not gone down well at all, he said. Liam was retiring at the end of the year and didn't want to take it to Ivan so Terry had done so himself. Ivan had said that if Liam didn't want to make a decision then he didn't either.

'Then I was told that a message had come down from the

boss,' said Terry. 'I don't know what it was but it looks like you can't come in.'

I told Terry not to worry. It wasn't his fault. It was just internal politics and had been handled badly. I mentioned it sometime later to Ivan when I saw him. 'Well, you know Arsène better than me . . .' he said.

So that was four attempts to come back to Arsenal – one to get on to the board, one to become Arsène's assistant, one to do the reserves, then the offer of a freebie. But I wasn't done yet. My next action was partly tongue-in-cheek, partly to make a point.

By now, Arsenal had an HR department and they were advertising for a youth coach to take the under-14s. I thought: 'Fuck it. I'm going for it,' and I stuck in my CV. I remember being at a football conference at Canary Wharf with Damien Comolli, who had been at Arsenal as a European scout in the nineties and then director of football at Tottenham and Liverpool, when I got a call from the Arsenal HR.

They wanted to know if I was serious, pointing out the modest salary of £15,000 a year and that it involved five nights a week in north London and a Sunday game. I said that on reflection it wasn't for me, though had I lived nearer I would certainly have thought about it. It was the Arsenal, after all.

It was actually the way Arsène dealt with it all, rather than not getting a job, that saddened and annoyed me. I wasn't really hurt as such, as it wasn't as if I wasn't good enough for the various jobs, though I might have been more upset had someone other than Terry Burton got the positions. Looking back, I believe there were a couple of major reasons why Arsène didn't want me back at the club at the time.

First, the club had put up the statue of me, made by the London art and design company MDM, outside the Emirates in December 2011. It was a fantastic honour. I had known about it for a while prior to that as I had received an email from dear, loyal Ken Friar, now a director, while I was in Azerbaijan, saying they wanted to do it and needed all my measurements. I put Ken on to a guy called Geoffrey Klass, a tailor with Pal Zileri in New Bond St, who had done Arsenal cup final suits in the past, my first for the Littlewoods Cup final in 1987. The statue was to be three times life size, so they needed them tripled.

Because I had loose ends to tie up in Gabala, I was unable to make it over for the official unveiling, but Arsène and Ken said some kind words about me and I got to see it for myself a couple of weeks later at a game against Queens Park Rangers when I was home from Azerbaijan for Christmas. I was really proud taking my kids to see it before the game and having my picture taken. First, though, we had to wait for three Chinese kids who were having their own picture taken on it.

I noticed that my playing dates were inscribed on the base and said to the current club secretary David Miles that it was like I had died. I asked him what they would do if I came back and managed the club successfully. He replied they would put another one up of me in a suit – and that they would take it down if I was a failure.

Given all that, and with the career I'd had, it might have been difficult for Arsène to bring me in around that time. He was coming under pressure, then not having won a major trophy since 2005, and to have me around as a successful old captain who had lifted a host of trophies might have been to highlight the underachievement, and my presence could have been something he didn't need. There may, too, have been an element of what Patrick Vieira once suggested to me: that Arsène does not like big characters and personalities, especially ones from Arsenal's history, around him.

If Arsène had been up front and given me reasons like that,

I would have understood and respected his decision, even taken it as a compliment. Instead, I was not told anything, except by Terry Burton, and I didn't know what Arsène was thinking or what I was supposed to make of it.

Perhaps Arsène thought I might be too challenging for him. He seemed to like an assistant such as Pat or Steve, both great club men but who were not going to ruffle feathers. Arsène is so dominant that he was probably not going to like it if I said: 'Look Arsène, we are conceding bad goals. I'm going to take the back four today and organise them.'

Because Arsène is essentially not a coach – and in that was the second reason why for so many seasons I believe he didn't want me.

Back in the day, I gave an interview to British Midland Airways magazine *Voyager* and said that I sometimes got upset that George Graham wasn't given the same credit as Arsène Wenger for what he also achieved with Arsenal, and that George was better at working with players. Arsène's strengths were in physiology and psychology, I said.

'Don't get me wrong, I'm not having a go at Arsène Wenger,' I added. 'One of the gifts he's got is that he's a lovely human being and I respect him a great deal. But I've got to get it real, coaching isn't his strong point.'

Actually, in the original draft I had said that he couldn't coach his way out of a paper bag but I had copy approval and, when I realised I had gone over the top, I asked the writer to modify it for print.

'I love him dearly,' I continued. 'He's a fantastic physiologist but he's not a great motivator. I'd just laugh at his attempts to gee us up, but I come from a different place, time and culture. But he got me in the best condition I could possibly get in to do my job, and for that I love him and have so much respect for him.'

Despite it being what I thought was a rounded piece, it didn't go down well. The journalist John Cross, in his biography *Arsène Wenger: The Inside Story of Arsenal Under Wenger*, wrote that Arsène was spotted reading it on a plane and was apparently not happy.

The piece, it seems, came over as just another cx-player having a dig, as they seem to do a lot at Liverpool and Manchester United, when it was supposed to be an honest and balanced appraisal. I am always going to be truthful if I am asked an opinion. George taught us to defend in ways I didn't see Arsène doing – such as, for example, one defender running the line of the post to the byline to stop the cut-back while the other drops off if the cross does come in. They were just basic things that Arsenal don't routinely do because they are technical points that they haven't learned.

It all left me feeling for a long time that I would never get a chance in any capacity at Arsenal while Arsène was at the club. Much as I admired and respected him for his long and successful tenure, my reputation and my occasional willingness to pass comment on him and the team when asked probably counted against me.

But I have always wanted to be fair when it comes to Arsenal and Arsène; like a critical best friend. One who will love you no matter what but also tell you the truth.

Arsène was absolutely the best man for Arsenal when he had his English defence and more exotic overseas attacking talents, as the trophies testify. He was also the perfect manager to keep Arsenal competitive with the big-money clubs of Chelsea, Manchester United and Manchester City during the transition from Highbury to the Emirates Stadium, with all the costs and disruption that involved. As well as being a great sports scientist, he had a sound grasp of football's economics too.

I do believe, though, after 2006 and the departures of Ashley Cole and Sol Campbell – with whom Lauren and I formed a pretty good back four in my last season – a lot was lost that has never been recaptured. The replacements and other defenders recruited have simply, by and large, not been up to the standard of what came before. It is because they have not been taught the art of defending properly, and while they may be individually decent players, they have not blended as a back four with all the discipline necessary in that.

Now, that old back four of Dixon, Bould, Adams and Winterburn is revered, to the point even of being immortalised in the film *The Full Monty* which used us as an example of what a proper formation should look like. Individually, though, I played with better – Viv Anderson at right back, David O'Leary alongside me, Kenny Sansom on the left. Put Lee, Steve, me and Nigel together, however, and we gelled and complemented each other.

A lot of that was down to hard work and self-improvement, facilitated by George Graham, even if we did curse him sometimes. The old training trick of binding us together with a long rope so that we moved up, down and across the pitch together in harmony worked wonders.

Sadly, I saw defenders coming into Arsenal and not improving, players like Gael Clichy and Hector Bellerin. Kieran Gibbs was a good young English left back who has not progressed as he might have. And while Laurent Koscielny is a good marker, Per Mertesacker is a zonal defender who unfortunately gets exposed because of a lack of protection in front of him.

I have watched Arsène's training and it is fantastic – pace, combination play, tight passing play around mannequins. You come away thinking what a great team they are. And in many ways they are. It is just, in my view, that the balance between defence and attack has not been right for a good while now. It will open up opponents and win you games at home, even ones away against lesser opposition. But it is not going to win you often enough the big games against the bigger clubs, with their top attacking talent which exposes undercooked defenders.

The emphasis on attack is understandable in some ways. I am being picky here but then such are the fine margins at the elite level. And, I have to say, the lack of work on defence is often a trait of coaches who have not played the game at the top, Jose Mourinho being the exception. We all use our strengths and Arsène's is in attacking play. You can't argue with the trophies, the building of the club and the stadium and his part in how well run financially the club is. It is simply that – judging by the highest standards – the Premier League titles have been receding into the distance and, while the constant qualification for the Champions League is admirable, it does also mean by the same token a lot of opportunities not taken to win it.

Amid all the debate that went on, some of it very disrespectful, what I would say is that Arsène, having passed his own 20-year milestone, certainly earned the right to say when he would go, just as Sir Alex Ferguson did at Manchester United.

Now, in this summer of 2016, all my views and constructive criticism seemed no longer to count against me and, after my heart trouble and my subsequent contact with Arsène, I had the chance to come back to the club and see, in this one-month trial, whether they liked me and I liked them.

Returning to London Colney felt like going home to my first love, *the* Arsenal – except the home had gained a few extensions now, after 14 years away. They were needed to house all the new staff. When I left in 2002, there were 77 people working there. Now there were 157 off-the-field support staff, working in education and welfare, sports science and conditioning, catering and administration. And that was just at the training ground. In all, Arsenal now employed around 550 people.

There were also new little touches, such as the door handles being treated with antibacterial gel. These days players and coaches, particularly the French, like to shake hands before and after training, as well as around the facility all the time. It can lead to the spread of colds and infections. The antibacterial gel was supposed to minimise the risks.

Working with the 16- and 17-year-olds was hard, but great fun. I would drive up on the Monday morning from Gloucestershire, work with them during the day, then stay at the Premier Inn at South Mimms services for the week. Glamorous life, football. I would then go home after the Saturday morning game. There were no expenses, for petrol or accommodation, so it was costing me, but I was happy enough for now.

It was summer in England and I was enjoying being back home, though, like the rest of the country, I was enjoying less watching our national team's latest attempt, 20 years on from Euro 96, to impress at a European Championships finals.

18

Our England

*Insanity is doing the same thing over and over
again and expecting a different result.*

ANON

The quotation above is often attributed to Albert Einstein,
though he once stated he could never remember saying it. It
is certainly well used in Alcoholics Anonymous as an example
of how addicts behave before they get sober, and it went
through my head a lot as I watched Euro 2016 in France and
contemplated how we had squandered the promising position
our football was in 20 years earlier. You don't have to be
Einstein to see that England were products of years of problems with the national team and of another similar pearl of
wisdom: if you do what you always did, you get what you
always got.

The shortcomings of selection and formations were of course
part of it. So too defensive standards not being what they were.
But it went much deeper than that, to the structure of the
English game and the quality of coaching.

Before the tournament, I was asked many times for interviews to celebrate the 20th anniversary of Euro 96, when we reached the semi-finals; and then during it for my opinions on the England team's performances, which reached one of the lowest points in our modern, post-1966 footballing history with the 2-1 defeat by Iceland in the last 16.

One of the reasons we were still harking back to events 20 years ago was because we have done very little to impress in European or World Cup tournaments since. That is because we have never learned the lessons. Over and over, they are thrown in our face and always we fail to act, seeking solace in our entertaining Premier League.

I remain convinced that if the FA had just given Terry Venables the extended contract he was seeking ahead of Euro 96 we could have won the 1998 World Cup. Instead, after Kevin Keegan replaced Glenn Hoddle, we had that mess at Euro 2000 similar to the one that unfolded in 2016. So what did we do back in 2000? We hired expensive foreign coaches to be followed by Englishmen who have also floundered in a failing coaching and development system.

Roy Hodgson departed after Euro 2016, to be replaced by Sam Allardyce, who was chosen by a panel of three men – Martin Glenn, the chief executive of the FA, who admitted he was not a football expert, Dan Ashworth, the technical director, who was fairly new to international level, and David Gill, who was fortunate at Manchester United because he never had to appoint a manager as he had a brilliant one there for his 10 years as chief executive.

Then came that sad, manufactured affair with Sam – who I never really thought was a progressive appointment anyway – when he lost the England job he so wanted after 67 days and just one match, with the FA saying that his taped meeting with an agent, in which he apparently claimed the rules on third-party ownership of players could be circumvented, was worthy of dismissal. It was soul-destroying for our game, another episode that drove our standing down and illustrated the paucity of our coaching and management structure.

That brought Gareth Southgate, my team-mate from Euro 96, into the spotlight and I texted him to wish him well. I do know from conversations with him that he went into the job with his eyes wide open, knowing how seductive the role can be but also its potential for draining and damaging reputations. In discussions at Burton when I was renewing my Pro Licence and he was there with the under-21s, it was clear that we shared similar views on the state of the English team and the English game.

His statement at an early press conference was certainly telling and accords with my view in many ways: 'I have to say I'm involved in a sport that I love and an industry that at times I don't like,' he said.

I could only hope that he did not become another victim of a failing system. That would be a shame, as Gareth is one of the good guys. While it may have been structurally convenient for the FA to give him the job, I hoped he was not being set up to fail and that finally we had someone who would also take note of what was going on beneath the full national team. Given his background with the under-21s – a job I considered applying for before deciding it was not for me – and his success in winning the Toulon Tournament in 2016 with them, I am sure that would have been his inclination.

I also hoped that the FA tapped into the experience of people who knew what they were talking about, such as Sir Alex Ferguson and Arsène, though I knew neither would even think about going near the job themselves. Because they know what pretty much everyone inside the game knows and what Gareth was probably worried about: that it really didn't matter who was appointed because until we re-examine our philosophy of football, its structure and attitudes to the England team, we are condemned to repeat failure.

I had a taste of the England set-up when I worked with the excellent Noel Blakc, now sadly departed as part of Dan Ashworth's purge upon taking the job, for an under-19 game against Turkey during my time in this country when working as adviser for Gabala. It was an enjoyable experience, and being involved in the England set-up again one day remains an ambition for me.

One thing I do know about is defending, and we have got to get back to learning the basics if we are not going to be embarrassed like we were against Iceland. During that under-17 tournament in Azerbaijan that I watched, I looked closely at the England side. And I am well aware that we are decent at that age group, winning European Championship titles under John Peacock in 2010 and 2014.

It struck me that we are producing athletes who are strong, conditioned and well prepared. Technically, though, they are not as good as the Spanish and Portuguese, both of whose defences I again admired at Euro 2016. In fact, the perception abroad is often still that we are all heart and no head, not confident in playing to a blueprint for successful football that suits our qualities.

As I worked with the under-18s at Arsenal that summer, it became evident to me that we do not get the balance right between time spent in the gym and on the pitch. Academy players need to be out on the pitch working more. There's too much emphasis on sports science nowadays.

When I speak to young defenders and ask them what they want to improve, they often say: 'my heading'. It is a neglected skill because they don't get enough practice in these 'pass, pass, pass' days. That style of football may be admirable but sooner or later you are going to have to head a ball properly – as we saw in England's game against Iceland, when we also lacked leadership, I thought.

It was a failure of coaching that Wayne Rooney was caught marking – or not marking – a big centre half at a long throw that brought Iceland's equaliser, but it was also a lack of leadership in the side which meant that nobody was shouting and sorting out the mismatch.

It's an old hobby-horse of mine but I still don't understand why Roy Hodgson didn't go back to John Terry five years ago. Instead, Roy went for easier, less controversial, options. And we ended up with kids and babies out there, with only Joe Hart and Wayne Rooney in the starting line-up having more than 50 caps. Chris Smalling seemed to be seen as an experienced player, but he went into the tournament with 24 caps, when I think it takes at least 25 to feel confident as an England player.

Nor did I see any evidence of the nous needed to change things. Why, for example, do we press high up the field against a team that just wants to sit deep? So we can look busy and 'English' for the fans? Or because it is the vogue, favoured in the Premier League by some overseas coaches?

Pep Guardiola and Jurgen Klopp are fans of the high-press, but too often players in English football tire in the second half of a season because of the intensity of games that they may not have experienced in Spain and Germany, and it might count against Manchester City and Liverpool at the business ends of seasons. We played it at Arsenal for a while in the George Graham era but ran out of steam in the second half of a season. It can also be tiring in hot summer tournaments when games come in quick succession after long domestic seasons.

We should be making sure we get our shape right, to be defensively secure, dropping off to the middle third to allow teams to have the ball in their defensive third, inviting teams on to us and winning the ball further back. OK, so some teams won't want to attack us. Fine, let them have the ball. They will, trust me, eventually kick it forward to you, whether from a goal kick or in open play, due to a lack of patience. And then you are in your proper starting positions. You can work on that in training, setting out 11 cones to represent those starting positions and, when the ball is lost going forward, getting back to them quickly.

Then you have to open teams up with ingenuity or pace, if the opposition haven't recovered their own starting positions. England certainly do have pace in players such as Theo Walcott and Marcus Rashford. Opportunities will also come from set pieces, free kicks and corners, and the English have traditionally been strong in those departments.

Having quick, attacking players also gives you the option of being more direct and knocking the ball forward early. Sounds primitive? Spain and Germany don't mind doing it now and then. And no one would accuse Arsène Wenger of being primitive, but when we had Thierry Henry it made sense to drop off so that the opposition pushed forward, providing space into which to knock the ball for Thierry.

We should recognise that the English strength is as a defensively orientated counterattacking team, but there is a snobbery about defending in the modern Premier League, particularly when it comes to long throws and high balls. People don't see it as the sexy side of the game. Call me weird, but I do.

And those managers who do coach well defensively often get ridiculed in the demand for attacking football that will please a worldwide television audience. It is why I like Jose Mourinho as a coach. I share his philosophy that if you get things right defensively it gives you more space offensively.

These days – and England and most Premier League sides do it – the fashion is for full-backs to show the opposition's wide players the outside; that is, to shepherd them down the touchline towards the byline. I don't like that. I would want them shown inside, across the field. If you show wide players the outside, the back four has to drop deeper into the penalty area to cover the cross, leaving space for oncoming attackers to run into at the edge of the penalty area and its interior.

If you show the wide players the inside, however, they have to lay the ball off and the defence can hold its line along the edge of the penalty area so that attackers don't penetrate the interior. If you can force a team to shoot from distance, then you're doing your job. With 85 per cent of goals coming from inside the box, you have a better chance of maintaining clean sheets if you can keep the attacking side outside the box. Statistics, by the way, don't lie. And they tell you that, at the top level, if you score the first goal you win the game 71 per cent of the time, and don't lose it 93 per cent of the time.

I see that kind of defending with the Italians and the Germans and saw it with Spain when they were winning tournaments. For all Spain's attacking talents, it was Gerard Piqué and Sergio Ramos at their peak who were the foundation.

The Premier League has its brand, the FA needs its own vision, and somehow the twain have to meet. The basic conflict is that the Premier League has the money, the FA doesn't and so has lost much of its influence and power. It probably needs an oligarch to buy the league back and give it to the FA – and I'm only half-joking.

The Premier League may say the England team is not their responsibility, but it is an English competition and owes a debt to the country, in my view. It should also make good commercial sense – a strong national team means people feeling better about our football and thus wanting to go and watch these players play. Or buy satellite TV subscriptions.

If we are to defend England's honour, as important as the quality of the manager is the need to get things right – and the right people – at the top of the FA then sort out the coaching system. We need to produce more and better-qualified coaches to teach kids the game thoroughly from an early age, and to get better English coaches into club academies.

To do this, I would have preferred regional coaching centres rather than the St George's Park facility near Burton, but we are where we are. Sadly, this should have been done 20 years ago and we have to realise it is going to take time to catch up. We have fallen a long way behind countries such as France and Spain, who had these facilities and structures years before us.

If you look at the statistics, UEFA data shows that for every coach England produces with the B, A and Pro badges, Germany produces 12, Italy 10, Spain eight and France six. And those four nations have regularly been providing the finalists at World Cups and European Championships in the modern era, while England have not appeared in a major-tournament final since 1966.

Surely we have to make the link in a practical rather than theoretical way sooner or later? It might help if the costs were reduced. In Germany, it costs around £400 to put yourself through the system to the Pro Licence; in Spain around £1,000. England? £5,820.

The problem is twofold, with both the dwindling number of English players coming through at the highest levels as well as the lack of English coaches, and opportunities for them. It is something the FA has to do more about if England are to compete.

It is now the clubs' academies which are producing players – and that is as it should be, as they have the time and expertise on a daily basis – but even through their age-group sides you will now find more and more overseas players, and again that is likely to increase as the years go on, depending on how Brexit regulations about the movement of people are negotiated. Those English players in the academies need to be monitored properly by FA coaches, perhaps 20 of them, based at Burton. Now that we have the facility, we might as well use it properly, not just for Midlands clubs. Those coaches would actually be more like scouts, who monitor players and their progress.

The Premier League also has to allow access for the good of the England set-up. When Sir Trevor Brooking was head of development at the FA, he found it difficult, I believe, to get himself into academies, and it is another area where we need a modifying of attitudes. It might alter what I saw with Noel Blake when I worked with him on the under-19s. He's a fine coach and loved working with them to the point where he kept them out for a two-and-a-half-hour session. 'Tone,' he said. 'There's so much to do and I might not see them again for another few months.'

Producing elite English players should be a cooperative process between the FA and the clubs. After all, both surely want what's best for the player. From age five to 12, that means instilling good technique rather than tactics.

Unfortunately in England, safe spaces for kids are becoming fewer. They can't just go and play in the street like I used to. And there are not as many green spaces sometimes, either. I like what they have done in Holland with an initiative by Johan Cruyff. Cruyff Courts are fenced-off five-a-side areas and there are 80 in the Netherlands. In fact, I'm told no kid is more than an hour's cycle ride from one. Robin van Persie and Dennis Bergkamp helped get one in Islington and I'd like to see more of them in England.

From 12 to 17 it becomes more about awareness of tactics and formations. Often, a head coach will want all the age-group teams to play the same way as the first team and there might be a worry within a club about a conflict of styles when a player goes to the national team, should it be playing to more 'English' strengths.

Well, Dan Ashworth has now established the 'England DNA',

which hopefully reassures people about good habits being taught. It is, after all, about footballers not systems. Personally, I would want my players being exposed to all sorts of different ways of playing the game to give them every bit of the puzzle. I also think older kids in academies should be put through their coaching badges to give them a fuller appreciation of the game and prepare them for the future if their own playing career doesn't work out. And for many, it will not.

The other problem we have is that while the England age-group teams do have some notable successes, not enough players 'train on', in horse racing parlance, and become first-team players at the biggest clubs. It is the problem we are also having with English coaches, who are not getting chances any more at potential Champions League clubs.

There is not enough bravery in giving young English talent a go, whether that be from coaches with players or owners and chief executives with coaches. When it comes to players, Arsène Wenger, in fact, is one of the exceptions given his record in recent years of signing and playing young British players.

I have to say, though, that in my experience of the under–18s at Arsenal, there were no real outstanding talents, which surprised me. While they were fine with me, I did also detect a lack of respect towards some senior figures. I happened to overhear a couple wondering what Thierry Henry would know about coaching. The arrogance of youth aside, there seemed to be an attitude that they are Arsenal players already. If some young players in elite academies are not careful, they will soon find themselves in lower-division Football League clubs or even non-league.

English players also have to accept what it takes to become an elite footballer these days. Modern life has many advantages for kids in England, where the standard of living means that most have comfortable lives and do not go hungry, unlike many

African and South American players who come from impoverished backgrounds. Many kids, like mine, enjoy a lifestyle where they don't need to struggle, as well as having many other sporting opportunities. In England at least, players still largely come from the working classes; I certainly don't see many come from the middle classes or public schools. Of course, we want to produce nice, rounded kids, but they have to be hungry and focused too.

I was part of a group of kids who just had a ball – literally and metaphorically – and I experienced something similar watching the kids in Gabala. They didn't have phones and laptops, TVs and computer games, but they did have the four cornerstones of development: coaching, practice time, direction and facilities. After that, it comes down to the desire of the player. I am sure we will see an Azerbaijani playing at one of Europe's top clubs in the next 10 years because they are improving them tactically and technically and giving them every opportunity.

You can't even say we are giving those things to kids in England any more. More and more pitches are being dug up, with 11-a-side football declining as more play five-a-side, and even with those pitches that are still there, many are not being maintained properly because of council cutbacks. It is difficult to teach kids on mud heaps or where the grass is six inches long. Not that we are teaching kids. The number of coaches at the grass-roots level is as low as the number at elite level. We have too many unqualified ones teaching kids. Again, it is often down to the cost of acquiring qualifications but also to the lack of value attached to youth coaching.

It can still be the same at big Premier League clubs, let alone at the grass roots. Development coaches are barely paid living wages, which means they have to do it part time and have other jobs alongside. We need to value them the way they do in Holland, for example. There, I came across the under-12s coach at one club who had a salary of £35,000 plus a car and a phone. Compare that with the £15,000 on offer that time at Arsenal for the under-12s. And there are certainly not the same amounts of money in the Dutch game as in the English.

As I saw from the salary for the under-18s at Arsenal, it means that career coaches in the development area are few and far between, as often they have to look to get jobs higher up, becoming manager of a Football League side, for example, to earn a decent wage. And then they get killed when they get there. I understand Chelsea have taken steps to remedy the problem and their youth coaches are on £90,000 a year, but in many places coaches seem to be up there with MPs and journalists for respect.

That may be another reason why the lower divisions are not producing players ready to step up, by the way, like they used to. They are not attracting great coaches, given those low salaries. Jamie Vardy is probably the exception that proves the rule and why there is so much attention on him.

In England, you are always going to get, say, the top 10 elite players coming through no matter what. It is depth that England will lack, a high-quality squad of 23 for a World Cup. Unfortunately, we still have this habit, or sections of our media do, of insisting that certain English players are great talents at too early an age, or when they are not at all, because we don't look overseas enough to compare. It is also because there is a shortage and thus fewer for them to focus on.

For example, John Stones was hailed as a great new English central defender, first at Everton and then at Manchester City. I have always had my doubts about him, considered him to be average in all honesty, despite this hyping of him as a ball-using defender. I saw him as a Tony Gale, a centre back who passed the ball well, and was good enough to win a Premier League title with Blackburn Rovers, but who did not win an England cap. Such is the dearth of English ball-playing defenders, though, that Manchester City were willing to pay nearly £50 million for Stones.

Like Vardy and Harry Kane, Stones might have had to wait longer in previous eras, but because of the rarity of talent, people do make England squads sooner and caps are cheaper these days. More and more players will be coming from the lower Premier League clubs and even, if we are not careful, from the Championship.

Brexit may help in that one area, with European players having to go through more hoops to get work permits, as the non-European ones do. Thus might English clubs have to look more at native talent and developing it. Who knows, though; new rules may be implemented about free movement for footballers with the Premier League such a plus for the country now. And that might mean more relaxed rules for non-European players too. What we do need to ensure is that we get the balance right between hiring the best and giving our own players the chance to develop.

It could be the same with managers. We already know that the biggest English clubs are not really going to look at English managers in the near future, even though there are some talented ones around. About the only way to get a job in the Premier League is to take a Championship job – as precarious as that is – and try to take a club up. The problem with that is that your club is unlikely to be competitive the following season, so you are just trying to avoid relegation. If you don't, or don't even look like doing it after about 10 games, you can be out on your backside.

English managers seem to fall into two categories, neither of which is about winning the biggest prizes of a title or European trophy. There is the manager who can keep you in the Premier League, like Tony Pulis. Then there is the manager, like Eddie Howe, who will get you up. I can see Eddie being offered a bigger job than Bournemouth but a top-six club? It was going to be intriguing to see if Arsenal really did have an interest in him as Arsène's successor or whether that was just paper talk. To add to the pigeonholing, the former type of manager tends to be seen as older, the latter younger.

It was interesting to me that Chris Coleman, the Wales manager, turned down the Swansea City job even though it was a Premier League opportunity. He said he would prefer to go abroad to a club where he might have a chance to reach the Champions League.

All those factors offer reasons why I spent so long out of the country and why English football is not attractive to many who would want to work with elite players. So many times you are on a hiding to nothing. It is also much to do with a facet of football that has changed beyond recognition and is one of the subjects least taken into account in the modern game. Agents may these days get a lot of coverage but their unhealthy influence is not spoken of enough.

It has always been a badge of honour with me that I have never really tied myself to agents, though I have had informal agreements with some at certain times, and have been open if they want to contact me and I believe they are credible. I prided myself on doing my own contracts with Arsenal when I was a player, at first with my dad in the room then on my own when I felt enough of a man. After that, I would just get a solicitor to check the contract was legal.

Trusting the club probably cost me, though I was fortunate to have the luxury of long-term contracts for most of my career. While acknowledging that I did very well for the mid to late part of my career, for much of my early career I would sign a new three-year deal every year with an improved wage but with the signing-on fees I was due under the terms of the old contract being waived.

For example, I would be due a signing-on fee of £265,000, broken down into £75,000 in the first year, £90,000 in the second and £100,000 in the third. But all I would get would be the £75,000. The next contract would have a bigger wage, and a bigger first-year signing-on fee, of course, but I would never get the second- and third-year sums. I signed them anyway. It was the Arsenal.

Sometimes I would use the Jerome Anderson agency for outside deals and, in the early days, they got me a boot deal and a contract for 10 columns with the *Daily Express*. It was the usual story. The paper was nice to me when I was their columnist, but didn't spare the criticism when I wasn't. I remember one article deriding suggestions I was the new Bobby Moore by saying I was more like Dudley Moore, but taller.

I also worked on occasions with Steve Kutner, mostly for certain deals such as personal appearances, though he did help me get the Wycombe job. And I was approached by Lorenzo Paolo about the Gabala job. Otherwise, I always preferred to be my own man.

Back in the old days, there were probably about 20 agents who had a name in England. Most managers would deal with them. Sir Alex Ferguson would have had one, or ones, he trusted, as would Harry Redknapp. Gradually, the landscape changed with all the overseas players coming into the game over the last 20 years, to the point where the number of agents has exploded and managers have to deal with swarms of them. Now the game is full of greedy and unscrupulous characters.

I first saw it close up during my spell at Portsmouth with a player I was interested in signing. I would get five phone calls from different agents who would all claim he was their player. You would often be used as a bargaining tool.

For example, an agent would ask you – sometimes by text message – if you were interested in Yaya Toure. If you said yes, they would go back to Toure and say that Tony Adams at Portsmouth was interested in him. Was Yaya interested in them? If he said yes, then the agent would claim they were acting for him, even though when it actually came to doing a deal, you would be dealing with someone else altogether, maybe even a brother or a friend. Then the agent who had sent you the original text would want paying for his part in the process if you ever did sign that player, reckoning he had done the deal.

I have never, by the way, been offered a 'bung'; that is to say, an inducement to buy a player. I am sure agents would have known they were wasting their time with me as I am straight and would never take a player who couldn't do a job for me. I look at talent and age and statistics, never a pound note.

With regulations now meaning that anyone can register themselves as a 'representative' for a £500 fee, it makes for a crazy system – that is only going to get worse with the TV billions growing all the time – where money is leaking out of the game. Mind you, it can be worse in other countries, as I witnessed first-hand on a visit I made to Rwanda for an under-18 tournament.

There, I saw hundreds of agents swarming all over players. I remarked on it when I spoke with the president, Paul Kagame, and the head of the country's FA. They had some excellent players but poor facilities. Could they not own the players and deal for them abroad, rather than the agents, so that the country's football earned the revenue? Great idea, I was told, but they did not have the expertise to administer a scheme like that. And anyway, the country had other priorities.

Sometimes it is less about how good you are, as a player or manager, and more about how good an agent is. I am sure I have been down the pecking order for jobs just because I don't play the system and use somebody to get into owners, chairmen and chief executives on my behalf. I have tried on occasions to forge relationships with good and respectable CEOs myself but there are not a lot of those about, in my experience.

It got to the point where Poppy suggested to me that I should just go and see the 'super-agent' Pini Zahavi and align myself with people who knew people. But I felt uncomfortable about doing that. I thought that if I did get a job through an agent, I would then feel obligated to take some of his players. You see it now in the game, though hardly mentioned: some managers are clients of an agent whose players they then take. To me it's wrong, a conflict of interest, though it might not technically be breaking any rules.

The increasing amount of money in the game due to ever-increasing TV deals is directly responsible for the powerful force in football that agents have become, and made them a symptom of the dysfunction in the game. The system – if it can be called that – is flawed, wrong in fact. Just by the rotation of managers – and expectancy of tenure for a manager in the Championship is now apparently down to 10 months – you can see it's not working.

The other reason agents have become so powerful is because people running clubs who don't know the football business – or even their own jobs very well – have allowed them to be. Too often when a manager is sacked, owners, chief executives and boards do not have a plan in place for the next appointment and are thus too influenced by agents all putting forward their clients. Often agents will be in their ear even before managers have gone, during that period when results are bad and they are under pressure.

When Gabala played Borussia Dortmund in the Europa League, during that lunch on the day of the match with the German clubs' officials, the president, Reinhard Rauball, told me that they knew they would at some point be losing Jurgen Klopp and they were well aware of all the promising young coaches in Germany, having kept tabs and done their research on them all. He knew the game and where to look and was not going to rely on an agent with an agenda phoning him up. In the end, they chose Thomas Tuchel, then 42, who had led unfashionable Mainz to seventh in the Bundesliga the previous season.

What I concluded at Gabala, having learned so much overseas and stepped back from the madness of the Premier League in which it is sometimes difficult to gain some perspective, is that partnerships and teams within clubs are what work best.

At Manchester United you had Sir Alex Ferguson and David Gill as manager and CEO. At Arsenal it was Arsène Wenger and David Dein, the vice-chairman. You can see what happened when one or both departed: United struggled to regain their pre-eminence in the English game, while Arsenal went six years without a trophy after David Dein left.

It is why I was interested in 2015 in joining that consortium of people looking to buy Aston Villa from Randy Lerner. I had hoped to become the board member with responsibility for the football side of the business and working with a head coach whom I could appoint, along a more Dutch model. That way I would have had some say in events, rather than being a victim of them.

I also think that a team of people would work so much better. The job of running the playing side of a club is now so big that it is too much for one man, even if that person's ego can be so big these days that they think they can still manage, identify signings, negotiate contracts and transfer fees, as well as coach and pick the team, all by themselves.

It is about getting the structure right and putting the right people in place, all working together rather than having dictators, though naturally the coach has to have the final say in all playing-related matters, free from executive interference. That way, you might not see so many managerial changes all the time.

Because the English game is so rich and so revered in the world, there seems little appetite to change things, however. It is as if the dysfunction is part of the game, and what makes it what it is, and nobody wants to interfere while it is bringing in so much money. All the intrigue and the sackings, all the financial chaos, give it spice that audiences, both in stadiums and on TV, and the media, with their short attention spans and need for the new, love so much. That at least seems to be the underlying ethos of those with the money and the power who deliver this huge circus.

But too many careers are cut short and too many costly mistakes made, with coaches and managers the victims of the chaos. In other industries, the CEOs would be the ones to carry the can when a business is failing. In football, they seem to escape, sacking the manager before crowds turn on them. And so the cycle repeats itself, with the people at the top not implementing the vision, as they are supposed to, because they don't have a vision beyond the short term.

We have to come up with a new model of running clubs but no one seems to be grasping that nettle. The League Managers Association seem to see their role as simply to ensure that their members get paid up properly when they are sacked. Then they take their percentage, so are doing well for themselves and maybe don't want to see change.

The Premier League is a hugely successful entity with its own identity, but that identity is not English and it is bringing down the English game and the England team. It also has to be said that the FA's house has also not exactly been in order for some time.

We now have just one English player in three in the starting line-ups on average in the Premier League. That is probably less at the bigger clubs as well. That 33 per cent figure compares with 50 per cent German players in the Bundesliga, 58 per cent Spanish in La Liga, 56 per cent French in Le Championnat and 43 per cent Italian in Serie A.

When it comes to football, we are foreigners in our own country and it is getting worse, with the number of English players in the Premier League falling by 2 per cent a year. Sooner or later we are going to have to put a cap on it, perhaps when it gets to 25 per cent, though I saw that Greg Dyke's replacement as FA chairman, Greg Clarke, immediately ruled that out.

While the TV money keeps multiplying, we are clearly still going to get overseas players keen to come to the Premier League, as we did with Paul Pogba coming for a ridiculous £89 million, plenty of which would leak out of the game in agents' fees. Decent player though Pogba is, my problem with it is that we are not getting the real elite at the peak of their powers, like Lionel Messi and Cristiano Ronaldo. Quite simply, that is because it is not the best league in the world, although it may be the most competitive and most exciting for TV audiences.

The fact that the best of the best are still in Spain is because Barcelona and Real Madrid can negotiate their own TV deals, and thus get more than any other club, while in England the agreement is collective and the money spread around more. There have been moves in Spain to make it fairer but still the rich at the top – Barcelona and Real Madrid – get richer by earning €150 million a season in TV money, around €90 million a season more than the bottom clubs.

The English model of less of a differential between top and bottom is to me a much fairer system and also cements the policy of clubs sticking together, with 14 of the clubs needing to vote collectively for any change to be made.

Still the Spanish, and Italian, leagues look enviously at the revenues of the English game and are thus considering the possibility of a European Super League as an extension of the Champions League. That may be attractive to the big – overseas – owners in the Premier League because it means they are guaranteed to play in Europe every year, with all the money that brings. They need to be careful, though. I sense people are getting a bit fed up with seeing the same teams in the Champions League every year.

People ask me why English teams have not been faring so well in the Champions League in recent years. I am sure it is cyclical and we will see Manchester United and Chelsea back winning it, probably even Manchester City, over the next decade. Currently, you have exceptional sides in Barcelona, Real Madrid and Bayern Munich, but they will sooner or later go through the same sort of transition that befell United and Chelsea.

Add it all up and you have the contrasts of the English game: national team often a laughing stock in the world – and even engendering a growing indifference at home – but Premier League and club sides that have the admiration and envy of the world. It is brilliant in many ways but forgets the basics in others.

I still love football, love coaching it, even if, like Gareth Southgate, I don't love a lot of the nonsense that goes with the money and all the hangers-on attracted by the smell of it around the game. England has more of that than most nations given its financial status, though there is somewhere with an even greater growth potential. And it would be my next port of call.

19

China Crisis

Living one day at a time,
Enjoying one moment at a time,
Accepting hardships as the pathway to peace . . .

Verse Two, The Serenity Prayer

Euro 2016 had just started and I had not long been working with the Arsenal under-18s when my phone rang and the name of a French agent called Ivan Blum showed on the screen. Three years earlier, Ivan had been working for the new Mumbai team in the Indian Premier League and had asked me if I wanted to go out there, but it was not for me and I think in the end Peter Reid, latterly of Sunderland, got the job. Ivan and I stayed in touch, though, and now he was asking if I fancied working in China.

Maybe, I told him, but thought little more of it. These kinds of phone calls come now and then and often aren't followed up. The agent relays any interest to a club owner or chief executive and you may get on a long-list of candidates but after that it can go quiet.

Then, a couple of weeks later, I was at Birmingham New Street station on my way to a course at St George's Park to renew my UEFA Pro Licence when Ivan called again. The adviser to a team called Wuhan in China League One wanted to speak to me, Ivan said. He was Spanish, by the name of David Belenguer, and in his playing days he had turned out for Getafe in La Liga.

I spoke with Ivan for half an hour, at the end of which he asked me to send him my CV. I also did some research and sent him a report on Wuhan and how I might improve them through my style of play. In there too was a film about me in Azerbaijan that my old friend Tom Watt, Arsenal fan, former *EastEnders* actor and now a writer and filmmaker, had come out to Baku and Gabala to make.

When I then spoke to David, we talked detail – terms and conditions, salary, accommodation, flights for the family – and he sorted out a visa for me to fly out and meet the owner. Before that could happen, though, Ivan called me again, on a Friday when I had just finished with the Arsenal under-18s. Another club, this one a step up in the Chinese Super League, were interested in me.

They were Chongqing Lifan, lower to mid-table. A quick search revealed that it was a city in the middle of the country with 8.5 million inhabitants, double that figure with its suburbs taken into account, and around 30 million living in the district. That sounded astonishing in itself – a place I had not even heard of that had three times the population of London.

The owner was a guy called Lizhang 'John' Jiang, who had made his fortune through his sports marketing business called Desports and had sold it to a company called DDMC Culture for a reported 820 million yuan (around $120 million). He still ran the company, which also owned Granada in La Liga, and he was a basketball fan who had bought into the Minnesota Timberwolves in America's NBA.

Ivan said that John, as he liked to be called, was in Europe for Euro 2016 and was going to be in Bordeaux for the Italy v

Germany game on the Sunday. Would I meet him there? I agreed and a first-class plane ticket, there and back in a day, was emailed to me.

John, who was just 35, had only patchy English but we had a good translator. He was bright and humble and reminded me of Tale Heydarov. He wanted my help and my knowledge, he said. It was refreshing to hear, and flattering. After seven years of not being wanted in England, except for an under-18 job – even if it was with the Arsenal – it was, quite simply, nice to be wanted, as I had been by Gabala. I knew I was a good coach. I just needed other people, in positions of authority and power, to believe it. After the meeting, we had lunch with his wife and seven-year-old son. John shared a photo on his phone of his son wearing an Arsenal shirt. Nice touch.

The job in Chongqing, it turned out, was for a sporting director again but with a view to taking over as head coach sometime in the future. The team, John said, could get sucked into a relegation battle this current season, which was halfway through, and he did not want that for me. It was considerate of him and he clearly wanted me to do well.

I was willing to go out there to get my feet under the table and get to know the club, the culture and the league as sporting director until the end of the season in November. Chongqing Lifan had only been formed in 1995 and John seemed to be interested in me repeating what I had done at Gabala in building a club.

In relationships between owners and sporting directors, managers or head coaches, trust and loyalty are paramount and I sensed a connection with John, who had a great zest for life and passion for his business. After Portsmouth and some of the people there, I promised myself I would never again get involved with those who did not feel right to me. John was a serious, and cautious, man. We virtually agreed the deal there and then.

The money would be good but not outrageous, better than

I had earned at Portsmouth, but certainly not in the league of Sven-Goran Eriksson and the former Brazil and Chelsea manager Phil Scolari, who were also managing in the Chinese Super League, the former in Shanghai, the latter in Guangzhou. It was an attraction, yes, but not the motivation. Had the money at Arsenal been better I might have had second thoughts, but I was simply always of the opinion that my dad had instilled in me: a fair day's pay for a fair day's work.

I certainly never felt trapped by money or the need to earn it. As a family, we could have downsized if need be and still feed and educate the kids. My own self-worth had never come from money or status or work, even though I had to acknowledge my basic needs and those of the family.

Thus it was the challenge of what was an emerging competition that appealed most, a competition that was beginning to make waves in world football. The Brazilian Hulk joined Sven at Shanghai SIPG from Zenit St Petersburg for a fee of £45 million and a salary reported to be £320,000 a week. Soon the league's impact would be greater on England, for one, with Sky Sports signing a contract to show live matches – and some big players being targeted.

A week after meeting John, I boarded a train to Paris, where I changed to go to Munich to link up with the Arsenal under-18s, who were having a training camp and friendly there against Bayern. I got as far as Strasbourg when my phone went. It was Ivan to tell me the contract had been agreed. I got off the train, got another one back to Paris and headed home to Gloucestershire where I packed my bags to go to Chongqing.

I rang Kwame Ampadu to say I would not be joining up with him and the under-18s and emailed Andries Jonker, the academy head, on the way home to explain why I would not be seeing out my month's trial. I apologised, saying that a good opportunity had come up and I hoped he understood. Andries did. He thanked me for my honesty and my fortnight at London Colney and wished me well.

There were people who thought I was doing the wrong thing – Lee Dixon was one who gently told me so – and that I should have stayed at the Arsenal for that year, given the previous failed attempts to get back into the club and that my complicated relationship with Arsène was now a smoother one. Perhaps the manager's job would come up, they said, with Arsène going past 20 years at the club and into what looked like his final phase as manager.

Also, it would have been a simpler life, with more time to spend with the family. The job might, too, have brought me some recognition at home again – according to the arguments of some – and I would be in the country and available should a manager's job come up elsewhere.

It was not going to happen, though. It was made clear to me that the under-18s job was not a preparation for bigger things, even if I was inside the club when Arsène departed. Of course I wanted – still want one day – to come back as Arsenal manager, but I don't think at that time I was seen as management material by the hierarchy at the club, given my CV.

My love of the club, and my relationship with the fans, would always endure. 'Play for the name on the front of the shirt and people will remember the name on the back,' I once said and I meant it. That was not going to be a qualification for the job, however. Better, I thought at that time, to be a success in China – since no other English club seemed to want me – to enhance my reputation as a coach, as Arsène himself had done in Japan. I was simply not going to get a decent job in England without having succeeded in a big challenge abroad.

I also liked an adventure and for me the attractions of China were manifold. They wanted profile but they also wanted to build properly, certainly at Chongqing. In fact, the Super

League would divide into two: those willing to pay fortunes for immediate impact and those looking to improve their infrastructure and youth development. Being flash was never my way and not the way of most of the Chinese people, and their customs, I would encounter. When I went to a game in Shanghai early on, I didn't go through some VIP entrance; I went through with the crowd. It is, after all, still the People's Republic of China.

You can't be anything but humbled when you know that there are 1.4 billion people in the country. I'm not sure how many of them were watching my first press conference but I was told plenty were. I spoke for five minutes live on TV but didn't feel intimidated. Once, I would have been terrified but AA has taught me to speak from the heart. It seemed to go down well. I was complimented by club officials and that was gratifying.

And so I settled down into hotel life, dividing my time between the sprawling Chongqing and the now awe-inspiring skyscraper city of Shanghai, where the club also had offices, 1,000 miles and a two-hour flight away, though I still preferred to take the eight-hour train whenever I could. My brief was to analyse the club, observe the team, identify new signings and work in the background to improve it all, ready to challenge the bigger clubs of Beijing, Shanghai and Guangzhou the following season.

It was not quite that simple, though. Life became tough, indeed, as I endured what I can only describe as an emotional crisis. One that would bring me to my knees.

After about a month in China, I began to feel very lonely. There was some AA in Shanghai but none in Chongqing and, much as I spoke to people on the phone, read my literature and shared FaceTime with my therapist James, a sense of gloom began to overtake me. I was not sleeping or eating well and lost a stone in weight, which took me back to my prison weight of 25 years earlier.

I was nearing my 20th AA anniversary of stopping drinking and my 50th birthday and my vulnerability, my mortality, really hit home. It dawned on me now that I was nearer the end of my life than the beginning. I had endured the heart scare and began to think a lot about my great buddy Peter Kay's relapse and death. He was 52 and we had been sober the same amount of time. I began to get pains in my chest, real or perceived I could not be sure. Alone in a hotel room a long way from home is not a good place to be experiencing these things. At least in Azerbaijan I had around me people I'd appointed.

I sobbed like a baby at times and was beset by panic attacks and bouts of depression. I had never had them before and they came as a huge, overwhelming shock. It was terrifying. I felt paralysed, immobilised, demotivated. There was no pleasure in the small joys of life, like the taste of a meal or a Skype call home. I would sob during the call, wondering what I was doing to the family and ashamed that I couldn't snap out of it. Otherwise, I wouldn't want to talk to anyone.

Taking a shower or shaving became a real effort, as did going down from my room to the restaurant in the evening, and I wasn't even cooking the meal. Often I would have room service, which would mean even greater isolation. I cried a lot alone, dived into AA tapes and tried to cling on to what I had been taught: this too shall pass. But I knew what was happening wasn't right.

The only respite came on the occasions when I did drag myself to a running machine, when I could check my heart rate on a self-testing kit I had and be reassured the readings were normal. I would also take my blood pressure six times a day. But I couldn't live my life on a running machine. Poppy asked me on the phone if I felt suicidal or like drinking again. I said I felt neither. Later she would say that when she heard that, she knew then we had some breathing space, at least.

In Azerbaijan, I had knocked at the door of death and didn't like the experience. My tears came because I wanted to live, because I loved my family, had a good home and job, but still felt so low and didn't know why. And, after so long sober, drinking simply wasn't an option. Those with long-term sobriety will understand that, even if people who don't have a problem with alcohol might not comprehend why anyone wouldn't just have a drink or two now and then to make them feel better.

But I had learned how to tolerate emotional pain without booze, knew the madness that it brought up in me, knew that it was the first drink that did the damage by leading to more and more and more. I wanted none of that back but did want to be free of this darkness that was stopping me from functioning properly.

By now it was October and familiar echoes of the past were assaulting me too – of how I had left Wycombe and Gabala at this time of year too. They say in AA that FEAR can stand for 'Face Everything And Recover'. It can also stand for 'Fuck Everything And Run'. And so, convinced that I would have a heart attack if I stayed, and not able to distinguish between physical pain and emotional, I ran. One Sunday, in my desperation, I got on a plane back to England, thinking I would be safe there, free from panic attacks.

On the Monday, I went to see my cardiologist, Dr McCrea, who told me that my blood pressure and heart were fine. I was just stressed. I went to see my GP, Dr Borg, a lovely man and an Aston Villa fan.

'Welcome to 50,' he said. He told me that physically I was in reasonable shape but that I was not immune to a midlife crisis. He thought I might benefit from beta blockers and antidepressants.

I was very wary. In recovery, I had always been careful not to take anything that could be mood-altering and had often thought less of people who went on medication. I didn't want to swap one flavour of addiction – alcohol – for another, in the form of pills. I'd always believed that I should be feeling what I was supposed to be feeling. Dr Borg insisted that what I would be taking was not addictive, however, and that it was only for the short term to get through a crisis. In fact, the pills could be seen as relapse prevention.

I also checked it out with people I trusted in recovery and one piece of advice stuck with me: 'If you've been in a road accident and you're bleeding,' somebody said, 'you need medical help. You ask to be taken to a hospital, not an AA meeting.'

The benefits of the medication would take a while to kick in. Over the next couple of days, I went out for meals with Poppy and Amber but was still sweating and suffering panic attacks and pains in the chest, which the doctor had told me might be side effects of the pills. As this was still happening at home, with my family around me, it showed me that China was not the reason behind my state. It was simply about me. I needed to go back out there and get on with what I do.

A flight was booked for the Thursday but I just couldn't face it. Poppy said she would come out to China too and see it through with me, which got me to the airport. Once on the plane, I told the steward I was a nervous flyer and that I was having a panic attack. He said that since the doors were still open, if I really was in such distress, I could get off now but needed to make a decision quickly.

I turned and looked at Poppy.

'If you were going to get off, you would have done it by now, so let's go,' she said.

We did, but it was a scary, scary experience. Waves and waves of panic overcame me, my breathing felt short. I took beta blockers and sleeping pills but got no sleep. Every other hour of the 13-hour flight, I would check my heart and blood pressure readings.

For the first three or four days after we arrived, my condition stayed the same. One night I went out in Shanghai for a meal with Poppy and we had to leave after the starter. There were AA meetings there, with so many expats from America and the UK now working in Shanghai, and I went every day. Bit by bit, my anxiety eased as I met other kindred spirits. The antidepressants probably also began to kick in after about 10 days of taking them and I gradually came to accept that the chest pains worrying me were side effects of the tablets. I even went one whole day without a panic attack.

The time came for me to go up to Beijing for a match and for Poppy to go home. It was tricky but I managed it and was pleased with myself. The panic began to leave me. My head cleared, though I was still on edge, fearful that it could all return.

My son Oliver, now 24, flew out to be with me and we had a precious fortnight together. It was probably good for him to see his dad vulnerable, human, like this, no longer on any pedestal as I might once have been. I was still planning each day, what we would do and where we would go, as I didn't want to be taken out of a comfort zone I had created for myself. There's a saying in recovery that if we're not careful, we get ourselves into a rut and then furnish it.

Then one day, Ollie asked me what we would be doing that day. I answered that we were just going to go with the flow and see what happened. He was pleased. I was relieved. We just walked out of the hotel and found a restaurant instead of me booking one. Over the meal, he wanted to know more about my alcoholism. We spoke about my drinking and he just couldn't identify with it at all. I was grateful that he couldn't, especially as he manages bars for a living. He has turned out a pretty cool kid.

After Ollie went back, Poppy returned for a week around my 50th birthday, on 10 October, and we had a wonderful few days in Hong Kong. I had been there twice before, once on that drunken tour with Arsenal, then with England before Euro 96 when I didn't dare leave my hotel room for fear of getting drunk.

This time I went to an AA meeting and shared what was going on in my life, being grateful that I was coming through a breakdown of some sort without the need to have a drink. I told of the contrast between now and 20 years earlier. Instead of the dentist's chair, I was sitting in an AA chair.

By November, I felt more like myself and that I had come through the storm.

The sense of impending doom had left me. I started an AA meeting in Chongqing with another expat who was in the fellowship and we would meet once a week. A combination of working my AA programme and accepting that, yes, I did need help in the form of temporary medication had got me back on track, so that I could see what I was supposed to learn from my existential moment, in the process of accepting my mortality.

I had no concern that I would be unable to stop taking the antidepressants. At first, I began to look forward to taking them each evening. They became my security blanket as I knew that I had something that was going to make me feel safe. That feeling of looking forward to taking them left me, though.

I started doing transcendental meditation and I began to read again, now able to concentrate for more than a few seconds. I got into Alan Watts' *The Wisdom of Insecurity*, which advanced the idea that the more you try to make yourself secure, the more insecure you become. And the more you let go of things you can't control, the more spiritually content you become.

I'd known that through my AA programme but, having lost sight of it because of the depression, I was now reintroduced to the concept. Sometimes, you do simply have to concentrate on not taking one drink of alcohol one day at a time and then, once the storm has passed, you find out what you are supposed to learn from the experience.

I also got back to concentrating more fully on my work with Chongqing. My brief was to find ways of improving the infrastructure of the club – the 58,000-capacity stadium, pitches, offices, gym – as well as playing standards. That meant finding the best young players in the district beyond the under-17 and under-19 teams we had, as well as working with the head coach, Chang Woe-Ryong, to offer him my support and advice.

I observed and analysed, watched training, and wrote four reports for John on the club and the squad. I advised on recruitment, though Chang said he wanted to wait until the end of the season. Fair enough.

Watching games, I noted that they kept conceding from set plays and met with Chang and a translator. Fortunately, he was open to my input, even though the concept of a sporting director was new to him, and we talked about defensive options. He then implemented new training drills and they didn't concede again from set pieces for the last few games of the season.

As I worked in the background on budgets and contracts for the following season, which would begin with pre-season training in January ahead of the season starting in early March, the team rallied to finish a reasonable eighth in what was becoming an extremely competitive league. Indeed, the Chinese told me they were the England of Asian football – a wealthy and entertaining domestic league but a poor national team.

Just how wealthy would become clear when some of the teams began throwing silly money about ahead of the 2017 season. Even the second tier team Shenzhen got in on the act, recruiting Sven-Goran Eriksson after he had been sacked by Shanghai SIPG. They had finished third but that was apparently not good enough.

SIPG then recruited Oscar from Chelsea for £52 million and their city rivals Shanghai Shenhua signed Carlos Tevez for £71 million from Boca Juniors. They were both reported to be on around £600,000 a week, a sum that also turned the head of Chelsea's Diego Costa when an unnamed Chinese club reportedly came in for in.

It was all a bit crazy and not the way we were doing things at Chongqing. Our overseas starting players were more modest but solid. We had a Brazilian striker with a good attitude in Alan Kardec, whom the owner suggested and I vetted, another attacking Brazilian in Fernandinho and a Croatian defender who would keep you up in Goran Milovic.

The potential for boom and bust, a bit like the old North American Soccer League, along with the poor showing of the national team, may well have been one reason why the Chinese football authorities changed the rules for the 2017 season, with clubs now only able to field three overseas players in the starting line-up, rather than four.

Come the end of the 2016 season, John Jiang and everybody else at the club was happy enough and the coach got a new contract. I wasn't quite able to come home for Christmas yet, though. I had a five-hour meeting with John about all his football interests, at the end of which he asked me to go to Granada to prepare a report for him on why I thought his team in Spain was bottom of La Liga and what might be done about it.

On taking over the club, for which he and his group had paid €37 million, he had said something I liked: 'You can't change the direction of the wind but you can take control of the sail.' It seemed he wanted me to see which way the wind was blowing with a view perhaps to putting a firmer hand on the tiller.

I felt healthy again. In hindsight, the lesson of my emotional crisis had been not to worry about outcomes but just to play my part in things and see how they worked out. And so I agreed. I still wanted to be a coach, which remains for me the best part of the football business. One of the main reasons I had turned down chances to go on *Strictly Come Dancing*, despite the money on offer being good, was because I was concerned about not being taken seriously as a football coach after it.

Being seen as a sporting/technical director or adviser was OK for now, however. And so I took a flat in the beautiful city of Granada, home of the magnificent Alhambra palace, right next to the cathedral and began to attend training, observe and analyse again. The squad was deficient in certain areas and it became my job, certainly during the January transfer window, to use my contacts and advise on recruitment.

John and his group had bought the club from the Pozzo family, who also owned Watford and Udinese, and Granada's policy had been based on loans, with the rules on the number allowed at clubs far more relaxed in Spain. It was efficient in many ways, with a club not being lumbered with long contracts, but it meant that players felt like guns for hire and might have little affinity with the club. It was a policy I was charged with reviewing.

I had to strike a delicate balance. I did not want to interfere with the work of the coach Lucas Alcaraz or to foist players on him, but I had to represent the interests of my Chinese employers, particularly John, and ensure that any players coming in were going to be good enough to help avoid the relegation that would be a serious setback to the Chinese owners.

While relations were always civilised, there was naturally some friction as I suggested remedies for poor results or players at the right price and quality, but I had to do my job. For the rest of the season, I would just do what was being asked and see where it led, with the Chinese group also looking to purchase other clubs around the world where opportunities might arise.

By the early spring of 2017, it became clear that after a brief rally, Lucas Alcaraz was not bringing the results John wanted and expected. Indeed, after a home defeat by Valencia in early April that meant Granada had taken just one point from their previous six games, he rang me, including club vice-president Kangning Wang on the conference call.

I was back in Gloucestershire for a few days, mainly to take in Hector's birthday, but the trip would be curtailed. By this stage, nine months into the relationship, John trusted me enough to want to make me a vice-president with the DDMC football management company that owned Granada. Now he wanted me to take over the team for the rest of the season.

And so, early on a Tuesday morning, I found myself on a plane to Spain and by lunchtime was conducting a press conference. The media back home seemed to wonder where the appointment came from, and also had some fun with some of my beloved colourful suits, but it illustrated again the insularity of our game sometimes. I had been working in the game abroad for a long time now, almost going under the radar but building a reputation in the world game.

Keeping Granada in La Liga was always going to be a monumental task, given that they were seven points adrift of safety with just seven games left, but the idea was that it was just an interim appointment to liven things up at a club that was struggling, until such time as a new sporting director and coach could be recruited, a process I had been involved in. My report to John had been all about giving Granada a new identity, with players on contracts who would feel something for the club, rather than just recruiting guns for hire on loan.

I got some criticism for talking in my press conference about giving the team a kick up the arse, as if I was just some old English stereotype of a coach, but I knew what I was doing. I had observed the Granada training for months and knew how I could change things technically, blend players.

It would be good to get the grass under my feet again as a coach, if only for a few games, before taking up whatever challenge John and DDMC had in mind for me next.

I also liked John's reasoning for sending me to Spain. 'You are loyal and trustworthy, Mr Adams,' he said. 'That's why I got you and that's why I am going to keep you.' That would do for me. Sobriety had made me only too aware of my defects of character, but it had also got me in touch with the assets that I possessed as well.

20

What we are like now . . .

True ambition is not what we thought it was.
True ambition is the profound desire
to live usefully and walk humbly
under the grace of God.

As Bill Sees It

A friend of mine in Alcoholics Anonymous has a dry saying – literally and metaphorically. 'If I'd known I was going to stay sober this long,' he says, 'I wouldn't have worried so much.' The fact is, though, as I look back on my clean time, that worry – or, more accurately, self-doubt and vigilance in taking care of my sobriety – is what has kept me off alcohol and living a free life for these past 20 years.

It may look odd from the outside that this big guy Tony Adams of Arsenal and England suffers from self-doubt, but it is just a part of being human that has to be acknowledged for anyone in recovery from alcoholism. As was that anxiety and depression that beset me around the time of my 50th birthday in October 2016 when I was alone in China. Even those who don't have the disease of addiction suffer from self-doubt, and when I see seemingly super-confident people in football like Louis van Gaal or Jose Mourinho, I wonder what is going on underneath that. I wonder if, in private, they too endure periods of doubt and depression and who they share those moments with. I am sure they do.

I remember doing a 'chair' – that talk by a speaker to kick off an AA meeting – one night at Tetbury, near my home in Gloucestershire, and feeling a need to share my vulnerability. There were perhaps 12 people there, the usual mixed bag of men and women, from a famous actor to a refuse collector. As I found out early on, the illness is no respecter of gender, status or wealth.

Before the talk, I went into a toilet for a quiet moment to pray, to the God of my understanding, a Higher Power. I wanted to calm myself as I still get nervous before I give my talk, and I wanted to pray that I might be given the right words to help myself and somebody else in the room. At such times, I try to ask that, 'Thy will not mine be done.' It is amazing that sometimes the words that do come out of your mouth do not feel like your own, but that you are a channel for a message that needs to be delivered and heard that night.

I talked about the doubt, fear and anxiety that can overwhelm me, about how we are all the same, that no one is any better or worse than the next. There is a real power in surrendering, in exposing your flaws and weaknesses. I had been a guy that kept everything in and was trying to do things my way for so long. Actually, to let go of all this stuff and be under the new management of a Higher Power was and still is wonderful. There will always be things, some dark stuff, that I can only reveal to my closest confidant James West, but otherwise at meetings my motto is: mad, sad or glad – share it. Secrets, they say, keep you sick. Sometimes, I can think I am strange with what goes on in

311

my head but, once I share it, in my experience it loses its power over me.

The feedback from the meeting was amazing, as it so often is. The actor responded by saying that if someone like myself, who had been at the peak of his profession and so often looked assured in the public eye, could talk about that in a calm, courageous way and get through it, then so could everyone.

Another guy, who was head of a major corporation, said that he doubted whether he could do his job properly given his worries about hiring and firing. I had similar feelings when I set out in management at Wycombe.

One of those sometimes funny paradoxes of the AA programme is that you have to surrender to win. That can be difficult for a sportsman or woman to grasp. You are taught never to give in, to show no weakness. But that is your professional life, not your personal one. There is a difference between what I do and who I am. I had to find new attitudes that would not be so self-defeating and lead me back to a drink.

It can be confusing for everyone and it certainly was for me at first. What will you become if you let go of who you were? You become you, is the answer; what and who you were meant to be. There is a fear, though, of being a shell. You represent a certain type of character to people out there for so long – in my case the tough defender who prompted that chant of 'Ooh, Ooh Tony Adams' (along with the 'There's Only One Tony Adams') – that you end up believing that's who you are.

It goes back to what I told James: 'I get drunk and I play football but I don't know who I am.' Recovery has been a journey from the head to the heart for me, to quieten the voice in my brain that tells of insecurity and self-loathing and quell the thinking that got me drinking, then to learn to trust my intuition, instincts and feelings. Once you are free of all the mayhem around the drinking, the brain can become a powerful tool – a terrible master but a great servant.

People often ask me how I have stayed sober for these last 20 years. They find it hard to believe how it can be done and, when I look back, it has been remarkable. The answer is: 'By the grace of God' – but that is hard to explain to people, some of them struggling after quitting the drink. There are practical ways of doing it, too.

It has, I have to say, never been easy – though easier than my previous life – but it has always been simple. That is to say, the programme of Alcoholics Anonymous is a simple one. I stay around people in recovery by going to AA meetings, I read the AA literature and I live the AA life as outlined in the Twelve Steps. Gradually, over the years, that has brought a new mindset and different approach to life. Life is no longer the battleground I perceived it to be and which I made it, even if you can never escape bad times – only learn how to deal with them when they arrive.

It was James who took me through the Steps and, whenever we met, we would treat our sessions together differently. One would be designated for therapy and the next to work on a Step. Step One is about admitting your powerlessness over alcohol and that your life has become unmanageable. I had to get a dictionary out to go through words like powerlessness and unmanageable. And acceptance.

One thing I did know was that, during that summer of 1996, I was broken and had no sense of myself. James was practical about the remedy. He got me to write down three examples of my powerlessness over alcohol and the unmanageability it caused – in other words, that once I started drinking I didn't know where I would end up or the damage I would cause in my own life and to people around me.

Those examples came to me easily enough, as they do with

most alcoholics – in my case, episodes such as smashing up the car and going to prison, falling down steps and getting my head stitched up, and ending up in a urine-soaked bed somewhere. Then I would go back and discuss them with James. Talking them through, gradually my shame would lessen.

In the early days, I didn't even know what to wear as I stood there in front of a mirror with a wardrobe full of clothes, such was my lack of confidence as a person. Do black and yellow go? Yellow and red? I used to ring up Steve Jacobs at Arsenal, the guy who was helping Paul Merson with his recovery from gambling addiction and who I was also using for guidance then, and ask him for his advice. He said just to do heads and tails with a coin – and that was how I lived my life for the first six months after giving up drinking. Then I would wear something and think the alternative looked better.

I was told in meetings that AA was a programme of change, so I would do anything to change. I was that eager to stay off the booze. If I was going out for a walk, say, I would turn left out of my front door instead of right to do something different from the day before. And the more work I did on myself, the more I learned. And the more I kept going to meetings, the more I met great people who could help me.

There was Frank O, who went off to Tibet and lived as a Buddhist monk for months at a time. I admired him so much for his serenity and calmness. He taught me a lot about prayer and meditation and yoga and breathing. But I was impatient. Sometimes in those days, in fact, I would jump up and do something at home just because I had to. When the gardener came, I would feel guilty and go out and help him, even though I was a professional footballer who needed his rest. It's a guilt thing too, a bit like having to tidy up the house before the cleaners come so they won't think badly of you.

I shared some stuff with Frank about not working hard enough at the prayer and meditation, and said that I was agitated in my work. It was around the time that autumn of '96 when I came back from injury after quitting the drink and got sent off at Derby County as I was getting in touch with how angry I was.

'Tony, do your job,' Frank said. 'That's what you were put on God's earth to do. I go to Tibet and I'm in silence for three months. Of course I am going to be better at prayer and meditation than you. But I can't play football. In time you will get a balance and find your path. You just can't be totally serene in the job you do.'

There were so many other pearls of wisdom that I clung on to – and for those who have suggested that AA might be like brainwashing, I describe it more as brain-cleaning. I recall one occasion when I was in so much emotional pain that I was lying in the passage at the house in Putney crying. I rang Robert P, a doctor who was in AA and who was then my sponsor – that is, a person in the AA programme with longer sobriety time than you and who helps you out. 'Have you read page 449 about acceptance in the Big Book?' he suggested. And so I did.

'. . . Acceptance is the answer to *all* my problems today,' it said. 'When I am disturbed, it is because I find some person, place, thing or situation – some fact of my life – unacceptable to me, and I can find no serenity until I accept that person, place, thing or situation as being exactly the way it is supposed to be at this moment.'

I would never have believed that reading could fix anything. But it did – along with the open-mindedness and willingness to do something I wouldn't normally do – and it kept me sober for that day.

Those early days of sobriety were very special but it can't be denied that life does kick in. It's said that the good news is that you get your feelings back. And the bad news is that you get your feelings back.

Fortunately, in my job, I felt a drive and a passion come back as I recovered from injuries. It went hand in hand with the new determination I had in my recovery. As they say, 'You don't take a drink even if your arse falls off.' But there did come a time when the 'pink cloud' of relief I felt at giving up drinking disappeared and the realities of life hit home. It happens to all in recovery. And it is why you need the Steps to help you get over these things and take you to the next phase of recovery.

Step Two is about finding a Higher Power so that our sanity – that is, our health and balanced thinking – returns. I love the book *Came to Believe*, which AA has put together, containing 50 stories of people who have had spiritual experiences. I identified so much with people who had hit rock bottom – for me, it was that time in a Romford pub when I could drink no more and was too scared of living, too scared to kill myself – and found that moment of surrender and clarity when it all just clicked.

I had tried so hard to find a Higher Power in my life but, when I did, it was because I had given up trying – that surrendering to win. I don't know if it was a God I found – or who found me – but I do know there was a power stronger than me that appeared in my life. This was not about religion but spirituality. Religion, I was told, is for people who don't want to go to hell. Spirituality is for people who have been there.

Then Step Three, which talks of the need to turn our lives and our will over to the care of a Higher Power. It sounds difficult but all I had to do was make a decision to do it. I did know that under my own management, my life hadn't been working out too well, so I decided it couldn't be any worse with someone or something else having a go.

I have to admit that sometimes I can forget some of the intricacies of the AA programme when I am not feeling great or things are going badly – though never Step One: that I am an alcoholic who doesn't drink, one day at a time. It is usually when I am doing things my way instead of the way the God of my understanding has in mind for me. I can occasionally turn the title of the book *As Bill Sees It*, based on the writings of the organisation's co-founder, Bill W, into 'As Tony sees it'.

But even if I can feel disconnected and I go off path, AA has given me the tools to recognise when and to do something about it. When I stop trying to force events and let God – my Higher Power – take over, the help I need always materialises. He's never let me down to this day. I remember early on, the *Footprints in the Sand* poem by Mary Stevenson, given to me by Mandy Jacobs, having a deep effect on me. It tells of a doubting person looking at their life and seeing only one set of footprints at the darkest times. They are actually those of God, carrying the person.

This was all big stuff for someone who had decided at the age of 14 that God was not for me. I had prayed to him when I was desperate to get in the England age-group team and he hadn't answered my prayer. I couldn't have seen at that age that maybe he did and the answer was no, because he had other plans for me.

Steps Four and Five are the cleaning-house process. I was being asked to make 'a searching and fearless moral inventory' of myself and to admit to myself, God and another human being 'the exact nature' of my wrongs. That meant listing all the nasty incidents in which I had wronged myself and other people through my drinking, then sitting down with another person and telling them about it all. It was a vital part of the process. If you don't go within, I was told, you'll go without.

I did all my house-cleaning in sessions with James – and also very publicly in *Addicted*, my first book, published in 1998. You can really only do those Steps once you have found a Higher Power because they are emotionally painful and draining. You need a faith to believe that all will work out as it's meant to, to combat the fear of the self-revelation. In reality, I didn't experience a release from sharing all my painful memories with James, but I did get a lift from doing *Addicted*. Not only did I feel clean, but I was gratified that so many people got so much from it, some even recognising their own alcoholism and getting into recovery. To this day, people come up to me and say that it helped get them sober, or helped them understand someone close to them, and that was one of the main aims in doing it.

Steps Six and Seven are difficult to grasp as they are about asking your Higher Power to remove your defects of character, after you have been through the painful process of finding out what they were in Four and Five. They are often called the forgotten Steps for that reason. Well, I have had to go back to those over and again, to revisit and change my episodes of selfishness and arrogance, for example, should they resurface. Six and Seven never feel done with, in fact.

I found it simpler – though certainly not easier – to work Steps Eight and Nine, which talk of making a list of all persons we have harmed and making amends to them. The Steps are practical and achievable, though it takes some humility to go and see people who you may have damaged or embarrassed yourself in front of. You also have to be prepared for people to refuse any apologies, though you have to say sorry anyway for your own peace of mind.

First I had to make amends to myself, forgiving myself for some of the stuff I did. From that everything else flowed. I began saying my sorrys on a daily basis straight away when I got sober, but getting to Eight and Nine formally took me about three years, though I never made a written list. I knew who I needed to apologise to and I talked to most of them inside those three years. Step Nine talks about making amends 'except when to do so would injure them or others'. Sometimes, there were people with whom it was best just to let things lie.

I very quickly realised I needed to speak to my mum, dad and family, and my stepdaughter Clare. But Oliver had just one memory of me as a drunk and that was being in a bar when very young. Did I really need to stir that up? As for my ex-wife Jane, who would make her own attempts to get clean, I thought the best way of taking responsibility for my role in the past was in being sober and bringing up the kids as best I could.

And then there were Arsenal team-mates. Some of them may have had their own issues and I didn't want to intrude on them. They had their own paths to walk. Also, they probably had a lack of understanding about alcoholism – because I know I did when I was drinking. I wouldn't want a recovering alcoholic with whom I had drunk in the past coming up to me saying, 'I don't drink any more and sorry for all the pain I caused.' It would have been cruel and they would have run a mile.

It's simple really. I carried, and still carry, the message of recovery through actions as much as words and if people want this, I am there. If they don't, there is nothing I can do.

Mostly, the people I spoke to took it well. Martin Keown had trouble believing that I was an alcoholic. It is indeed difficult for those who haven't got the illness to understand when looking at it from the outside. I remember being at Ilford Palais with Martin when we were young players and all he had to drink was a shandy, so it is going to be hard for him. Besides, he had left the club, playing for Everton and Aston Villa, when a lot of my worst drinking was taking place.

Also, sometimes educated people just don't get it, believing alcoholism is simply a sign of self-inflicted weakness, though Arsène Wenger was very receptive and did things by understanding rather than confrontation. We had a great, grown-up relationship as manager and captain and that was fortuitous, for us both, at the time. We were both what the other needed. He needed a team leader who would help him adapt to the ways of the Premier League and I needed a manager who would show a benign tolerance when required. It was all meant to be, our trophies together the physical proof.

Having a sympathetic boss is not always the case for people who get into recovery. One girl at AA said she was having issues with hers and I said that sometimes it is best just to talk to them honestly, as we have things going on in our head that may not be accurate. She was unsure, and with reason. Not all bosses are like Arsène. They may be a raging alky themselves and look at you as if you're off your trolley.

Arsène had had experience of what alcohol can do when growing up in a pub with his mum near Strasbourg, and he knew how it changed people. So if I did have an issue at work, more often than previously I didn't bottle it up but instead went to him (though it was never the other way round if Arsène had an issue, I have to say – I'm not quite sure where he went or goes).

'Yes, yes, you were angry today, Tony,' he might say. He was very sweet and amiable.

I had a lovely six-year relationship with him, and today too in many respects, even through all that stuff when he just would not tell me what was going on when I was interested in jobs at Arsenal. It's always worse in your head, imagining what people are thinking and saying about you. It's futile and tiring and best simply to speak to them directly, I have found.

After I got sober, all my relationships improved, in fact. I was now attracted to a different type of person. I now liked conversation and the company of others, meeting new people and hearing their stories, particularly those in AA, who told of some hilarious exploits but without romanticising or glamorising them. We shared a common bond of knowing that there were more sick antics than amusing, after all. We were realistic and honest. Coming through it does produce a gallows humour, though.

You do Step Nine once, though I am a firm believer that if anyone comes back into my life to whom I still need to make amends I will do it. After that Step, I reached what are called the maintenance steps in AA. Ten, Eleven and Twelve are all about how I conduct myself today, having cleared up the wreckage of the past, and how I live well and to the best of my ability. It is called alcohol**IS**m, after all, not alcohol**WAS**m.

Today, I don't turn anyone over, don't nick anything, don't lie and don't smash up places as I once did through my drinking. It doesn't mean I don't do and say things I regret, however, which is where Step Ten comes in – continuing to take personal inventory and, when I'm wrong, promptly admit it.

I do have the ability to do that these days, unlike in the past, though my pride does try to stop me now and then. Admitting you're wrong is tough, especially when you've believed for a long time that it is a sign of weakness, not strength. When I do swallow my pride, it pretty much always turns out for the best and people respect you for it. In the past, I probably didn't think I needed to apologise, with the arrogance and even invincibility that active alcoholism produced in me.

That word invincibility always reminds me of an encounter with Ken Bates, the old Chelsea chairman, when I was just 20 and at the PFA Awards dinner back in 1987 having been voted Young Player of the Year. I was sitting next to Ken, with George Graham the other side of me. I remember the first words Ken ever said to me: 'I bet you think you are fucking invincible.'

I was intimidated and turned to George, wondering who this bloke was. George just smiled.

In those days, I was confident I could play football all right, but I didn't feel invincible as a person – and that is always the disparity within the alcoholic: big ego, low self-esteem. It can still affect me even now with that ability to think one day that I should be managing the biggest club in the world only to feel on another day that I'll never work again. The difference nowadays is the insight I've gained through years of not drinking, the ability to understand what is going on with me.

The booze made me flash and turned me into something else. I was never really that kind of character. I was a working-class boy and flash was knocked out of me. You didn't show it, even if you won the pools. You didn't flaunt fortune by buying a Ferrari or something.

Now I am sober, life is a balance. If you have worked hard and earned the money to buy a Ferrari and your motives are good, why not? Not that I would. I don't need one to prop up my ego. Anyway, it won't carry kids around.

Today, though, it is a simpler decision than in the past – just buy it or don't buy it. Once, early in recovery when I was thinking everything through, it would have been, 'Can I justify it? Am I buying it out of ego? What will people think?' No wonder I couldn't get dressed in the morning. The whole day seemed so long with all the decision-making. And no wonder people turn up at AA meetings so tired. There is a saying that recovering alcoholics get much more out of the day than other people.

I tried to simplify my life as much as possible and now I try to begin days with the prayer and meditation that Step Eleven tells of. It is about seeking to improve contact with your Higher Power and accepting that power's will for you that day, whatever it may be.

In the early days, I was told just to get through 24 hours without a drink and that seemed like such a long time, especially when you are waking up alert at 6am. I'm not religious but it was nice to go round to the little church near me in Putney to be there and at peace. I would then come back home and do some stretching and yoga.

After dropping the kids off at school, I would drive to work, train, eat well, come home, put my feet up, have a snooze, get up at 4pm and walk the dog over the park. Then it would be a bit of supper with the kids before getting the nanny in and taking myself off to an AA meeting. I would stretch before bed, take my personal inventory to see what I had done well and badly that day and to learn the lessons, before finally surrendering myself to sleep. A simple life but a great grounding for a lasting sobriety.

I also work to try to remember, and live by, the prayer of St Francis of Assisi which AA has adopted as the Step Eleven Prayer. I know I am going to fall short frequently, but it is a credo to aspire to:

> Lord, make me an instrument of thy peace, that where there is hatred, I may bring love. That where there is wrong, I may bring the spirit of forgiveness. That where there is discord, I may bring harmony. That where there is error, I may bring truth. That where there is doubt, I may bring faith. That where there is despair, I may bring hope. That where there are shadows, I may bring light. That where there is sadness, I may bring joy. Lord, grant that I may seek rather to comfort, than to be comforted. To understand, than to be understood. To love, than to be loved. For it is by self-forgetting that one finds. It is by forgiving that one is forgiven.

Finally to Step Twelve, which says that having had a spiritual awakening as a result of the Steps, we should try to carry the message to alcoholics who still suffer. That means helping others to discover and bring into their own lives what has freely been given to you.

Well, I can do that individually and have been on calls to talk to people when they have asked for help. I have also sponsored people – taken newcomers under my wing, if asked – though not always with success. One guy I took through the Steps kept relapsing and I had to let him go. It helped me, mind, by getting me back in touch with the Steps. On another occasion, I went to see a footballer who had relapsed and took him through Step One, as James did with me.

Given the travelling I have had to do and my lifestyle, I have done less in recent years. It is not being fair to people if I am not available to them. My way of using my attributes best to help others was to write *Addicted* and establish Sporting Chance. You've got to give it away to keep it, after all – which is another of those paradoxes of recovery.

Some respect you for this way of life and who and what you are, others find it confusing, even strange, in my experience and I know I get comments that judge me. I have done 20 years of therapy on this subject and it is very poignant to me. As James said to me in the very early days when I would worry what people were thinking about me: 'Tony, what people think and say about you has got nothing to do with you.'

It is indeed something I can have no control over, but at the start I wasn't as good as I am now at seeing that. We are human. We do care. These days, there are no outside opinions that are going to dictate the way I live my life. Often, too, those opinions are more about the other person, and what they might feel about themselves, than me.

I can still get echoes of my previous life, though. The drinking dreams may be less intense than they were but the football ones are still vivid. I have even woken Poppy up now and then having kicked her, believing I am clearing a cross.

And I can get flashbacks when I am in a hotel room and go to the door first thing in the morning expecting the *News of the World* to come under it with a picture of me on the front page, making me break into a cold sweat. It is odd for two reasons: one, that I don't do what I used to; and two, that paper is no more. It does show, though, the power of things that can trigger feelings.

One day, Atticus came home from school and said that one of the kids had told him that I crashed my car when I was drunk and went to prison. That was hard for him. I just said: 'Atty, tell your mate that, yes, your dad did do that once but he is a recovering alcoholic now and doesn't drink.' I sat down with Atty and explained more, and I hope it helped him with any embarrassment he might have felt.

You never quite get immune to criticism but I have got better at handling it. I find it harder coming from people I love and respect, actually, and this still comes up in my therapy sessions, which I have twice a week when I am in the UK. If I'm criticised by people who don't know me, I try to brush it off. I know I too can make judgements about people I don't know and haven't met and I am forever getting it wrong. If I am doing that, then others must be as well.

And people change, don't they? Glenn Hoddle is a case in point. We had our issues as manager and player at the 1998 World Cup, but I have met him in recent years and found him a very approachable man with a sense of humour. Something right a few years ago may not be right today. How I deal with it in practical terms is quite simply talking about it and processing it myself. James always said that he wanted me to become my own best therapist. He said that with all the work I would do, I'd be able to tell what was bollocks and what wasn't.

I recall when I was Harry Redknapp's assistant at Portsmouth and went to watch a game at Southampton, not just because they do a great sausage and mash for the scouts. Matt Le Tissier was there, as he generally is, and somebody had told me that he had once overheard Matt describing me as 'a weirdo'.

Well, how do you deal with that? Thoughts raced through my head . . . Did I need to say anything? I had played with him in the England set-up and maybe that was how he felt about me. Or maybe he never even said it. If he did, he may just have been having a bad day himself. Today, I am comfortable with myself and felt no need to do or say anything about it. It did show, however, how these things can be upsetting, and how my head can go, which is why I need a programme of recovery to tell me this is not a massive issue and I don't need to drink to subdue the anxiety.

For a moment, I had it in my head that Matt hated me and would maybe put in a bad word for me if I ever went for the Southampton job, but it was all just going on in my head. It was a perfect example of how I would drive myself nuts if I didn't have therapy to talk these things through. No wonder I drank. No wonder I wanted to stop the thoughts racing in my head.

I remember when I used to do media interviews as manager of Portsmouth and a reporter would tell me what another manager had said about me or my team and then ask me if I cared to respond. I would say, 'Well, to be honest, what he thinks has got nothing to do with me.'

At that point they would look at me as if to say: 'Well, that's not a fucking answer, is it? You've got to have a go back at him. Give me something to write.' I didn't care really. I had a job of work to do and was concerned only about myself and my own team.

I wonder occasionally if my sobriety, my attitudes and way of looking at life these days, has sometimes held me back in my career, stopped me from getting jobs. Maybe I raise too many issues for certain owners and chief executives, who might be uncomfortable around me as I hold up a mirror to their own problems, and they prefer to surround themselves with different types of people – drinkers maybe, certainly the dysfunctional. It was one reason I enjoyed Azerbaijan, it being a dry Muslim state – nominally anyway, as I am sure there is some drinking beneath the surface – with people who don't drink.

Maybe people do think I am different. It might be because I

am. In recovery, you are told that you are not special or different from other people – because you need to replace ego with humility – and alcoholics are not, by and large. We probably become so, though, and especially in football, which is a unique industry where there are not many of us – in recovery, at least.

It was one of the reasons I set up the charity. Football is rife still, despite higher standards of fitness, with addictive behaviour, be it drink, drugs, gambling, pornography or whatever. And depression within it, of managers and players, is growing. Very few are happy, joyous and free in the game.

I consider myself to be one of them. I feel proud of myself that these past 20 years I have shown a spirit of adventure and exploration that has taken me round the world. In fact, I recall sailing up the Yangtze river not long ago with the family and thinking that this was quite something for a kid who thought that getting over to the Railway Tavern in Stepney for a drink was a bit of a hike. Must have come from my parents, who wouldn't move a few miles in Essex, from Rainham to Harold Wood, as they thought it was too far.

I've had a wonderful life since putting down the drink and, though I realise that it may not be as compelling a story – at least for some people, who like the gory details – as my life with the drink, I do think it is one whose message of gratitude needs to be out there.

Some will criticise me for that, and some in AA have. They believe we should always protect our anonymity. Indeed, Tradition Twelve of AA does state: 'Anonymity is the spiritual foundation of all our Traditions, ever reminding us to place principles before personalities.'

It is worth remembering, though, that the AA message spread more quickly after a journalist called Jack Alexander wrote an article about it for an American publication called the *Saturday Evening Post*. The Traditions, including AA's belief in Tradition

Eleven that we should always maintain personal anonymity 'at the level of press, radio and films', were written before even TV, let alone the modern internet and explosion of social media, came along.

Also, I was outed by a newspaper as an alcoholic, so had no choice or control over that. Not that I resent it. I was relieved. It is just that, given the circumstances, I took the decision that the best way to use what had happened was to reach out to people.

Addicted was about helping people to stop drinking. I hope *Sober* will further that cause for those who want to stop, as well as help people stay stopped.

There are many players who have been through Sporting Chance, and three or four managers whose anonymity I will protect until they want to talk about it themselves, but none has been sober for as long as I have now. It is another reason why I wanted to do this book. I have experience, strength and hope. I do not boast about my length of sobriety. I cite it merely to show what is possible – and available to all.

What I really want to do is what Bill W asked us to do and everyone in Alcoholics Anonymous has repeated ever since: Pass it on.

THE TWELVE STEPS OF
ALCOHOLICS ANONYMOUS

1. We admitted we were powerless over alcohol – that our lives had become unmanageable.

2. Came to believe that a Power greater than ourselves could restore us to sanity.

3. Made a decision to turn our will and our lives over to the care of God as we understood Him.

4. Made a searching and fearless moral inventory of ourselves.

5. Admitted to God, to ourselves and to another human being the exact nature of our wrongs.

6. Were entirely ready to have God remove all these defects of character.

7. Humbly asked Him to remove our shortcomings.

8. Made a list of all persons we had harmed, and became willing to make amends to them all.

9. Made direct amends to such people wherever possible, except when to do so would injure them or others.

10. Continued to take personal inventory and when we were wrong promptly admitted it.

11. Sought through prayer and meditation to improve our conscious contact with God as we understood Him, praying only for knowledge of His will for us and the power to carry that out.

12. Having had a spiritual awakening as the result of these steps, we tried to carry this message to alcoholics and to practice these principles in all our affairs.

© *AA World Services Inc. Reprinted with permission.*

Anyone seeking help for a drinking problem can call the **Alcoholics Anonymous 24-hour National Helpline** free on 0800 9177 650 or email at help@aamail.org. www.alcoholics-anonymous.co.uk

Sporting Chance Clinic:
Physio for the Mind, Body and Soul
Get in touch by calling 0870 2200 714 or email at info@sportingchanceclinic.com
www.sportingchanceclinic.com

ACKNOWLEDGEMENTS

In *Addicted* I acknowledged all the people that had helped me get sober. A lot of these same people have also helped keep me sober.

Firstly, to my co-writer Ian Ridley. Ian I think you have done a remarkable job with this book and I have really enjoyed the last two years on this project. *Addicted* was a very different book with a very different message from a very different man. I think you have really encapsulated the change in me and got the balance right between sobriety and soccer! Thank you for making me see that I wasn't saved from the sea to be kicked to death on the beach.

Secondly, thank you Simon & Schuster and in particular, Ian Chapman. Thank you for your faith, patience and understanding. I love you Ian C and hope that we will remain friends forever.

Pops, you really are an exceptional woman, I thank God that I was sober so we could be together. I rarely make things easy for you, last September and the previous year when my heart nearly gave up on me especially. You were so brilliant and so strong that I truly don't know what I would have done without you. Thank you for your strength, love and constancy. Deep down it's all about you really ... Oh, and a P.S, thank you for finding Jay Lucy – without her, you know what a mess we'd be in. You may not be the original Jay, but you are by far the best.

Clare, Ollie, Ambs, Atty, Hec, Chick – at your moments you drive me mad (I'm sure the feeling's mutual). But what madness and what joy you bring to me. Each one of you a big, fat slice of love.

Sandra, as ever. Fifty years you've looked out for me. I'll never stop looking out for you.

The Teacher family, thank you for showing me what family love is.

James W, I said at our first meeting that I know how to play football and get drunk but I don't know who I am. Well James, thanks to our continuous therapy, it has taught me how to do football, how to stay sober and at last to know who I am.

Lastly, I would like to thank the thousands and thousands of AA members that I have shared with over the last twenty years. I believe my higher power works through people and there is no such thing as coincidences. Bill W couldn't have got sober without Doctor Bob and vice versa. I couldn't have stayed stopped without the help of other addicts, thank you HP for a life beyond my wildest dreams!

INDEX

(the initials TA refer to Tony Adams; SC to Sporting Chance)

p against Arsenal team-mate Dennis Bergkamp during Euro 96. Because of our mutual fear of flying, ve spent some time together on trains to away games.

aul Gascoigne played a key role in our great run to the semi-finals in Euro 96 under Terry Venables. aul Merson and I tried so hard to help him get fit and ready for the 1998 World Cup.

Ahead of our important World Cup qualifier in Rome in November 1997, I had an overwhelming sense of peace that all would be well. The goalless draw that night ensured we would go to France the following summer.

Celebrating with David Beckham after his goal against Colombia in the World Cup. He and I always got on well together, despite the Arsenal-Manchester United rivalry in the England camp.

Celebrating my goal in a friendly against Ukraine in May 2000. It was the last goal by an Englishman at the old Wembley, and meant I set a new record for the longest gap between international goals.

In training, we'd asked Kieron Dyer to play the Luis Figo role against us before we took on Portugal in the 2000 European Championships. Kieron destroyed us, and here we found the end result as I am just too late to stop Figo from scoring.

Leading England out against Germany in my last international, 7 October 2000. I knew my time was up – and so did Kevin Keegan, who resigned as England coach after our defeat.

Wednesday 15th December, 2004 – my wedding to Poppy. My finest match.

Atticus, February 2004. His sudden arrival meant a race from Wycombe at half time to make it to the hospital bedside

Hector, Baku 2010. An image captured mid-way through a happy and extraordinary six years in Azerbaijan.

Iris with our dog, Ladykevin, April 2016. Iris came up with his name, it was too good to change . . .

Above left: With Oliver on the Great Wall, almost twenty years to the day after going with England.

Above right: Amber on her 21st, 26 January 2016.

Left: With my big sister Sandra – a constant in my life through the many considerable downs and now ups.

Below: Working in Azerbaijan, China and now Spain, I have only had rare chances to be with all my children – and now grandchildren. This taken in August 2014 was a very happy day with my step-daughter Clare and her first child, Jedi. Clare has always been and is very much one of my children – I have cared for and parented her from four years old after all.

Fishing in Ireland – some of the best times after football have been low-key holidays with friends.

Sand surfing in Jordan – a welcome break for Pops and me.

We found this photo in my files and as Pops says, it's so good it's deserving of a wider audience – god knows what Martin Keown, Tim Sherwood and I were promoting, but if anyone's looking for a boy-band . . .

Caprice with Oliver at his football awards. I was supposed to give the awards out to Olly's team but when I turned up with Cap, I was quickly substituted! A clever businesswoman, a beautiful person inside and out, she was an integral part of my life outside football in the early days of my recovery.

With my dearest friend Peter Kay, who was godfather to Hector. Not the best singer, but one of the best men. I miss him daily.

Two of the greats. Lee Dixon, Ian Wright and I have shared so much – and long may we share more.

With Robin van Persie – a gentleman, an incredible player and a friend.

A proud day in 1999
when I picked up my MBE
at Buckingham Palace.

I was delighted that my
parents could join me on
that special occasion.

That goal against Everton in 1998 . . . Put me in Steve, I shouted, and Bouldy did.

Happy days! Celebrating the Double that season with Arsène Wenger at Islington Town Hall.

I go in for the tackle against Luis Figo of Barcelona during our game in October 1999. Afterwards, Jose Mourinho came into our dressing room and asked for my shirt from the laundry basket as a souvenir.

John Carew shields the ball from me during the quarter-final of the Champions League tie against Valencia. After the game, I had to hold up my hand and admit to a mistake that may have cost us a chance of winning the trophy.

The full monty . . . Lee, me, Steve and Nigel. The famous back four.

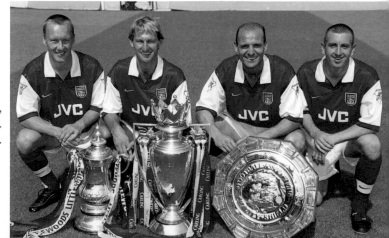

Chasing Diego . . . In action against Maradona at the inaugural Robbie Williams Soccer Aid match at Old Trafford in 2006.

was thrilled to line up alongside Olympic gold medallist, and huge Arsenal fan, Mo Farah in a charity match at Barnet in 2013. After the game, we became good friends.

I took the job at Wycombe Wanderers in November 2003 because I wanted an opportunity to practise my coaching, albeit at a very different level to the one I was used to.

It wasn't the easiest of tasks, as the club was run on a shoestring, but Ivor Beeks was a great chairman and the experience was a valuable one.

Celebrating with Harry Redknapp after Portsmouth had won the 2008 FA Cup – but the troubles would soon emerge.

My first training session with the Portsmouth squad after I had taken over as manager of the team just a few months after that Wembley triumph.

I point out the danger as Dirk Kuyt runs on for Liverpool during our game against them in February 2009. Sure enough, a 2-1 lead with five minutes remaining was transformed into a 3-2 defeat. It was time to go.

PA

With assistant Gary Stevens, technical analyst Fatih Kavlak and physio Faraz Sethi at Gabala.

My role there was not only to coach the team, but to help build a club – there was a lot of work to be done.

Gradually we got there, and this team photo showed just how much the facilities improved. We even managed to qualify for the Europa League – an immense step forward.

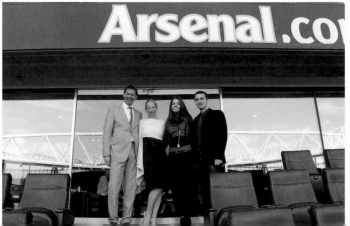

At the Arsenal with my Azerbaijan boss Tale and his wife Aylel. A singular man possessed of great sincerity, intelligence, dignity and kindness. His vision for football in Gabala and Azerbaijan remains unwavering.

With John Jiang, president of DDMC, in Granada, with the impressive backdrop of the Alhambra.

In Granada . . . My first game as interim coach of the La Liga club.

Well, I was described as a statuesque defender at times, mostly a compliment, I hope.